JUNIOR
A SON OF THE GULF CARTEL

MIKE CHAVARRIA

PARK AVENUE PRESS

Published by Park Avenue Press 2025
www.parkavenuepress.nyc

Copyright © Mike Chavarria 2025

All rights reserved. No part of this publication may be reproduced, stored in a retrieval system, or transmitted in any form or by any means, electronic, mechanical, photocopying, recording or otherwise, without the prior written permission from the publisher.

Cover design, typesetting and e-book formatting services by Victor Marcos

ISBN:
979-8-9937129-0-1 (Paperback)
979-8-9937129-1-8 (Hardcover)
979-8-9937129-2-5 (eBook)

For my wife, Trisha, and our beautiful, blended family, my heart has reason to beat;

For my brother, Carlos, your undying support and inspiration, the wind beneath my sail;

For my grandchildren, the future is yours.

"BROKER"

Per the "Urban Dictionary":

1: one who acts as a middleman in large quantity drug deals.

a: a person with lots of connections, both socially and business-related, whom both the buyer and the seller trust to facilitate the actual transfer of product and payment for a nominal fee or commission.

b: a person who negotiates the terms of a drug deal and guarantees a safe and smooth transaction.

CONTENTS

Acronyms ix
A Note on Names xi
Introduction xii
Chapter 1: A Rite of Passage 1
Chapter 2: We Met in 2005 9
Chapter 3: The Protege's Beginnings 32
Chapter 4: La Mona 53
Chapter 5: Guadalajara, Jalisco 2001 75
Chapter 6: Miami, Florida 2003 84
Chapter 7: Un Chingo de Perico 101
Chapter 8: It's Our Operation! 117
Chapter 9: Call me Bond… Junior Bond 132
Chapter 10: Smoke City 148
Chapter 11: The Big Apple 168
Chapter 12: Monkey Boy 182
Chapter 13: What Happens in Vegas 205
Chapter 14: Show me the Money! 221
Chapter 15: We've Been Hit Again! 238
Chapter 16: El Lobo 251
Chapter 17: The Call Never Made 257
Chapter 18: The Search for Junior 268
Chapter 19: What Now…? 276
Chapter 20: Compadre Beto 288
Chapter 21: Lucky Coin 295
Epilogue 301
Acknowledgements 305
About the Author 307
Photo Gallery 309

Acronyms

AFI—"Agencia Federal de Investigacion" ("Federal Investigative Agency")
ASAC—Assistant Special Agent in Charge
AUC—Autodefensas Unidas de Colombia ("United Self-defense Force of Colombia")
AUSA—Assistant United States Attorney
Cartel Milenio—Millennium Cartel
CI—Confidential Informant
CISEN—Centro de Inteligencia y Seguridad Nacional (Center for Intelligence & National Security)
CIA—Central Intelligence Agency
CPOT—Consolidated Priority Organizational Target
DEA—Drug Enforcement Administration
DFS—Direccion Federal de Seguridad (Federal Security Directorate)
DOJ—Department of Justice
DTO—Drug Trafficking Organization.
FEADS—Fiscalia Especializada para la Atencion de Delitos contra la Salud (Mexico's Office of the Attorney General Specialized Crimes Unit for Health/Drug Crimes)
SIEDO—Subprocuraduria Especializada en Investigacion de Delincuencia Organizada (Deputy Attorney General's Specialized Prosecution Unit for Organized Crime)

FARC—Fuerzas Armadas Revolucionarias de Colombia (Revolutionary Armed Forces of Colombia)
GAFES—Grupo Aeromovil de Fuerzas Especiales (Special Forces Airmobile Group)
GS—Group Supervisor
GUEROS—Blondies
MFJP—Mexican Federal Judicial Police (Mexico's "Policia Judicial Federal" or "PJF"); name changed to "AFI" in 2001.
CARTEL MILENIO—Millenium Cartel
NDDS—Narcotics & Dangerous Drugs Section (Dept of Justice)
OCDETF—Organized Crime Drug Enforcement Task Force
OGV—Official Government Vehicle
PGR—Procuraduria General de la Republica (Attorney General)
PFP—Policia Federal Preventiva (Federal Preventative Police).
PTJ—Policia Tecnica Judicial (Technical Judicial Police)
SA—Special Agent
SAC—Special Agent in Charge
SEDENA—Secretaria de la Defensa Nacional (Secretary for National Defense)
SEMAR—Secretaria de la Marina (Secretariat of the Navy)
UC—Undercover

A Note on Names

Spanish names typically comprise a first name (e.g., Armando) and two surnames (e.g., Valencia Cornelio). The first surname is the patronymic of the father (Valencia), and the second surname is the patronymic of the mother (Cornelio). Generally, to reduce repetition, writers use the patronymic to refer to the person in question. However, occasionally, with some common first surnames, both the first and second surnames are used (for instance, trafficker Caro Quintero). And, to add additional confusion, descriptive nicknames are richly used in Mexico, especially in the drug traffickers' world, where real names are mostly taboo; hence, Flaco (Skinny), Simio (Ape), Azul (Blue), and Lobo (Wolf) are a few examples found in this story.

Introduction

This isn't your typical drug trafficker's story of good guys versus bad guys, where good triumphs. It's far from a DEA fairytale. As a thirty-two-year veteran agent of the Drug Enforcement Administration, primarily focused on chasing Mexican drug lords, I believed I had everything figured out. It wasn't until I met Raul Valladares, aka "Junior," that I truly understood how things operate, especially within the upper echelon levels of the powerful drug cartels in the western hemisphere. Junior, the son of a high-ranking Gulf Cartel capo, did the unthinkable—he betrayed his father and broke his criminal oath by becoming a US Government informant. Junior faced a life-changing decision: continue his criminal ways or turn into a spy for the gringos. The deciding factor was his love for his wife and children, especially his youngest, an infant facing a life-threatening emergency caused by a congenital heart defect. Despite a lifetime of crime, he remained deeply faithful and loyal to his family.

By 2005, his drug trafficking career was thriving. Junior was trusted by many of Mexico's most powerful drug lords. He had street credibility as a broker, making a fortune for everyone around him. His commissions were in the multi-millions. Junior was believed to have shipped over forty-seven metric tons of cocaine to the US before his career abruptly ended. Junior was untouchable in the cartel's eyes.

Our fateful meeting occurred in Houston, Texas, in late August 2005. After transferring from the DEA's Guadalajara Resident Office, I gradually readjusted to being a US agent again. I wasn't ready for what was about to unfold. Running into Junior set me on a life-changing path, an experience that affected me both professionally and personally.

It was a fortunate meeting, and somewhat surreal how the timing of our alliance with Junior coincided with one of DEA's priority operations. Junior helped us infiltrate what were once considered impenetrable cartels. His involvement jump-started a special operation called "Band of Brothers" targeting command-and-control leaders of the "Sinaloa Federation," a group of Mexican drug trafficking capos regarded as a global threat.

What sets this book apart from others is its focus on the human side of the narcotraffickers' story and the toll it takes on those on the front lines of the drug war. It is primarily narrated from both Junior's perspective and mine. As an informant, he was officially called a "cooperating source," a role known by so many other street names: "snitch," "rat," "stool," "spy," and the classic "narc." Among criminal sources, Junior was especially unique. He managed to warm our hearts from the start. He eagerly accepted his new role as a government informant, determined to transform his life and support his troubled family during their crisis. Junior's karma desperately needed a change.

Once he joined the team, there was no hesitation. Junior's undercover (UC) efforts quickly amassed valuable evidence on some of the world's deadliest, most powerful drug lords operating between Colombia and Mexico. Unlike DEA UC agents, however, the "Juniors" of the world are primarily on their own. There is no cavalry standing by for the rescue. If compromised, survival is entirely dependent on one's balls and wits. Some informants disappear, leaving no trace, no hint of their fate. It is a hazardous occupation. Junior didn't hesitate.

Junior's story is one of irony and conflict. We met him as an antagonist, but he quickly became our main protagonist, while the so-called good guys unexpectedly turned antagonistic, nearly derailing our mission. I struggled with how to tell this story, given how much it affected me personally. I endeavored to portray individuals, depict their actions, and describe events with accuracy, respect, and compassion. It was a challenge, especially with the occasional rage I felt during the process. Then, I had an epiphany… I would tell it the way Junior would have wanted it told. I used notes from interviews and interrogations and relied on my own recollections and those of others involved. Many events are well-documented and verifiable through simple internet searches. I wrote this story with Junior's voice in my mind. Although it is non-fiction, dialogue has been artistically added to provide the reader with a vivid sense of realism and emotion as experienced by those of us involved.

CHAPTER 1
A RITE OF PASSAGE

The regional military commander caught wind of an incoming cocaine shipment hidden inside a container of coal. He directed his special unit to intercept the cargo as it was being unloaded at the seaport. The ship's manifest reflected the container's departure from Panama's free trade zone, notoriously used as a transshipment point for drugs entering Mexico. It was the summer of 1991.

The Army lieutenant arrived, secured the container, and detained the port inspector for questioning. Within minutes of contacting the port official, the young lieutenant was alerted to the incessant, unanswered calls to the inspector's bulky, brick-shaped cell phone. The nervous inspector avoided making eye contact with the lieutenant, who noticed beads of sweat forming along the inspector's forehead.

Despite his father's advice to be patient, Junior was overconfident and impatient, nervously bombarding the seaport official's phone with excessive calls while waiting at a nearby hotel.

"Give me your phone," the lieutenant ordered the seaport official. All the calls came from the same number. He called his second in command, whispered something in his ear, and sent him off with three other soldiers.

After searching the container and finding its illegal contents—1,250 kilo-bricks of cocaine—the inspector was handcuffed, grabbed by the neck, and shoved into one of the military sedans. The lieutenant jumped into the backseat and began his rough interrogation.

After a few elbow shots to the face, the port official relented and confirmed Junior's identity and that he was waiting at a nearby hotel. He also identified another associate, a police officer, who was on standby, waiting for clearance to enter the port in his patrol car. The local officer was to retrieve a sample of seventy kilos from the larger shipment and deliver it to Junior. A half hour later, the uniformed patrolman was found and taken into custody. The lieutenant's men also managed to track down Junior. It was Junior's first time being handcuffed. Within three hours, 1,250 kilos of cocaine, wrapped in cellophane and secured with beige-colored duct tape featuring images of a gray dolphin, were confiscated. The drugs and three prisoners were on their way to the Army's installation.

As Junior was pulled from the first vehicle, he looked back at his cohorts as they were being removed from their respective vehicles. With his deliberate head nod and laser-eyed warning gesture, he was certain they wouldn't cooperate. After catching Junior's stare, they diverted their eyes and lowered their heads while being escorted into the drab colored, dilapidated building. All three prisoners were blindfolded as they shuffled in. Junior could hear his two cohorts being shoved into separate holding cells, and then found himself lodged in a separate, rancid-smelling room. He was uncuffed, told to strip down, and was forced to sit in a cold, hard chair while being tied with rope from his shoulders to his ankles. The rope was so tight it was cutting into his skin, restricting his blood flow, and making it difficult to breathe. Until that moment, Junior had lived a charmed life as an emerging narco. Now, blindfolded, sitting naked and tied up in a holding cell, he realized the world might not be his oyster after all.

It was within the Army's 19th Zone of the 6th Regional Headquarters, located in Tuxpan, Veracruz. Unlike the "Posse Comitatus Act," which limits US military involvement in civilian police actions, Mexico's Army and Navy have had carte blanche in Mexico's so-called drug war. Military officers have been embedded with Mexico's Federal Judicial Police for years as an anti-corruption measure. Raul Sr. routinely warned his son, "Mexico's military is not to be fucked with."

With his body tightly confined to the rigid chair, only his mind was free to wander, focused on calming his nerves and gaining some sense of control. The door opened with the sound of boots echoing against the floor. Two men whispered unintelligibly. A brief silence sent shivers down Junior's spine. While he was focused and waiting for his interrogator's first question, the silence was shattered by a violent blow to the side of Junior's head, knocking him to the floor. *Was it a book or a thick telephone directory?* He was numb from the pain, and his ears were ringing.

"Pick him up," someone said. "Hmm, Raul Valladares… any relation to Raul Valladares del Angel?" Junior's mind raced… *how to answer?* "What… not talking, asshole?"

Wham! Another blow, this time to the other side of his head, sending him and his chair once again to the floor.

"Let's try it again…, fucker," the officer said tersely.

"Yes, my father," Junior acknowledged, moaning in pain.

"Hmmm, you think that's gonna help you now?"

"No, sir." Junior was paralyzed with fear for the first time in his life. *Had he chosen the right career path?* Thoughts of doubt entered his mind.

"I want to know everything about this shipment... everything. But not just yet... we need to loosen things up a bit and jar your memory." Two men jerked him back to his upright position, still tightly roped to the chair. The numbing began to dissipate, and his senses slowly returned to normal.

"He looks thirsty... bring him something to drink, some Tehuacan." It was one of Mexico's sparkling (carbonated) water varieties. Junior, although thirsty, knew it wasn't meant for his consumption. His moaning grew louder as he heard his captors chuckling.

The door opened again and shut. More footsteps echoed, along with a brief exchange among his captors. One of them held the bottle of fizzy water next to Junior's ear so he could hear it being shaken. Then he felt a hand reach around his forehead to force his head backward. What followed was excruciating pain as the bubbling liquid was shot up his nose. His brain felt like it was on fire. Junior wet himself from the shock and pain.

"They call you Junior, right?" The man asked calmly.

Yelling and gasping, Junior answered, "Yes."

"Address me as 'sir' or as 'Colonel,' son." There was a sharp backhand across Junior's face, designed to effect an attitude adjustment. The officer's class ring knocked Junior's tooth loose, leaving him tasting blood. His blindfold was damp with sweat and tears.

"You're in the wrong line of business," the colonel snickered. "You Gulf Cartel boys are fucking pussies." Junior felt the officer's breath against his ear, "I'm not sure you're gonna make it to jail, Junior." He felt a sudden thump to his chest from what felt like a military-issue boot. The chair flew backwards. Like a case of reverse-whiplash, his head shot forward and then backward, squarely smacking the concrete floor. Junior momentarily lost consciousness. The concussion left him with a metallic taste, mixed with the blood lingering in his mouth. He wanted to puke. It was the first time he experienced that kind of physical trauma. His mind curiously wandered to a boxer's twelve-round fight.

Still reeling, he was then yanked backward several feet. With his body tightly strapped to the chair, Junior wished the damn thing would break apart and free him from his bonds. Thoughts of dying raced through his mind.

"Give the fucker a bath... he stinks," the colonel barked.

"Pleeease...," Junior cried out. He suddenly felt his captors cutting him loose from his restraints. A non-religious Junior quickly began praying that the worst was behind him. He was pulled back up and forced to stand, his hands bound behind him, tied with rope. Still blindfolded, Junior was forced to move forward until bumping into what felt like a table. A second later, his head was driven downward into a large bucket of ice-cold water. Caught off guard, he took an unwanted gulp. Just as he was about to succumb, his head was yanked out of the bucket. Spitting water and gasping for air, he wanted to yell out for them to stop so he could confess and repent. Before he could utter any words, however, his head went back into the bucket, then out... back in... and out again. His blindfold was removed, and Junior stood in the middle of the room fighting to catch his breath, focus his eyes, and settle his brain. The men walked out, locking the door behind them, their laughter fading as they made their way down the hall. Junior was terrified.

Looking at the floor, he saw old bloodstains. As time went on, he heard screams coming from the next room. The windowless, dingy room was dull gray. Its walls were chipped and badly in need of paint. The foul odors were a mix of human sweat, blood, and urine. *Where is my father? Where is the rescue party? Would my family even know what happened to me?*

The door opened, and two men entered with the colonel, who was easily recognized by his commanding presence. He was bald, and though short, he was built like a bull. Junior estimated him to be in his fifties.

The soldiers placed a new blindfold on him, sat him down in the unbreakable chair, and left him alone again. He welcomed the brief break, but their mind games were messing with his sanity. After what felt like an eternity, he heard voices approaching. The door swung open, and Junior began to tremble nervously, fearing what they had planned for him. He jumped to his feet, mentally bracing for another waterboarding session.

Readying himself for the dunk, he was shocked by a sudden jolt of electricity shooting from his genitals to the rest of his body. It felt like nails running through his veins. He now realized the reason for the screams he had heard earlier from the next room. He knew immediately what it was… an electric fucking cattle prod. His father told him it was the preferred tool for both police and military interrogators. Junior was in so much pain that he just wanted it to end. He figured he was dead anyway. They shocked him again, this time on his back. He let out a second deafening scream.

Then, something miraculous occurred. His brain switch flipped to the off position, no longer caring whether he lived or died. Whatever his captors intended to achieve through tormenting him, Junior vowed they wouldn't get a fucking thing out of him. He was going to die with dignity and make his father proud.

"Fuck you!" Junior yelled. "Kill me, mother fuckers!" After a second jolt to his balls, which by now were on fire, he shouted, "I said kill me!" now crying from anger. After a few quiet moments, sudden laughter erupted in the room as the colonel and his officers chortled at his predicament.

The colonel sneered, "You're fucking pathetic! We're done, asshole… just having a little fun now." The men kept laughing. "We got everything we needed from the other worms." Junior was untied, his blindfold taken off, and was told to sit down and dry his cowardly tears. His interrogators were hungry and wanted to take a break. As they left, the colonel said, "We need to consider your fate."

Later that evening, Junior was handed over to the Mexican Federal Judicial Police (MFJP) officials and was officially charged. Besides the loose tooth from the colonel's ring, there were few signs of visible abuse. Despite Raul Sr.'s attempts to get the charges dropped, the military's involvement prevented any behind-the-scenes antics. It was Junior's first time behind bars, and he was wise enough to keep quiet and accept his punishment. Junior's romanticized view of the powerful Gulf Cartel was shattered. He realized that traffickers weren't always the ones calling the shots.

The MFJP was the investigative arm of the country's federal prosecutorial authority, known as the "Procuraduría General de la República (PGR)," equivalent to the US

Attorney General's office. Although Junior's father had strong ties within the PGR, the agency could not undo what had already been done with the military's involvement. Junior was forced to face the consequences of his actions and was sentenced to five years in prison in his home State of Tamaulipas.

While standing on death's doorstep, he experienced a spiritual epiphany that the whole ordeal was just a rite of passage. He not only survived the experience but also emerged from it with more resolve and conviction in his chosen path. Junior embraced his time in prison, made a valuable connection, and left prison a wiser outlaw. Despite his youth and inexperience, Junior managed to impress his mentoring father.

Raul Valladares ("Junior") became a world-class cocaine broker, generating billions of dollars in the world's most lucrative industry. He managed the distribution of cocaine in metric tons worldwide. Ironically, it was Junior's brief time in prison that helped propel his drug trafficking career. Being a successful trafficker was no accident; his career was planned from the start, as he was the son of a Gulf Cartel capo.

CHAPTER 2
WE MET IN 2005

Junior's wife, Sara (*) (* denotes use of pseudonym to protect identity), was frantically dealing with their second family crisis. Their infant daughter, Xochilt (*), was diagnosed with a life-threatening congenital defect—a small hole in her heart, which affected the blood flow to her vital organs. Emergency efforts were underway to get approval to fly Xochilt to Houston, Texas, where she could undergo life-saving surgery at the world-renowned Children's Hospital. Xochilt's pediatrician found a capable and willing surgeon to perform the delicate operation. Sara and Junior were still devastated from losing their first child— their toddler had died in an accidental choking incident. Murphy's Law was in full effect as Junior had to rush south to Panama's free trade zone to meet with his transportation contact, Ramiro (*), to discuss an urgent cocaine shipment. Junior needed the money to pay off a debt stemming from the loss of another load. "It'll be a quick trip, down and back," Junior assured Sara.

Junior was being pursued and harassed by a Colombian source over the loss of cocaine, which he and his partner, Beto Bravo (*), were accused of storing in Monterrey. Loads were occasionally lost, but that was part of the game, and Junior understood it. Profits from another shipment usually covered the loss; it was like borrowing from Peter to pay Paul. Junior was a cat who could land on his feet no matter how high he fell. Still, his nine lives were beginning to run out.

Awaiting receipt of "Humanitarian Visas," Junior assured Sara that the Panama trip would take no more than a day or two. He understood that time was critical and needed to return to his wife so they could get Xochilt to Houston. Sara was furious over Junior's sudden urgency to leave.

Junior wanted to contact his partner, Beto (*), but Beto was busy with their Colombian associate, La Mona (*). The two were in Guadalajara meeting with other investors about a separate cocaine shipment also waiting to be containerized in Panama, a project they were coordinating with Ramiro's partner.

While in Panama, Junior had a quick meeting with Ramiro and immediately hailed a cab to the airport. On his way to Tocumen Airport, Junior called his wife to let her know he was heading home. Seconds after pulling away from the curb, the cab's movement was blocked by a large suburban. Junior was pulled from the backseat at gunpoint, while the cab driver was released unharmed. Junior was then forced into the suburban and driven around town by his Colombian abductors.

"What is going on?" Junior asked, shocked and frightened.

"Where were you headed in such a hurry?" asked the man seated next to him.

"To the airport," Junior replied, still in shock and cringing at the thought he wouldn't be home for his wife and daughter. He said a quick prayer, "Oh lord, please don't let it end this way."

He felt the butt of a handgun strike the side of his face, near his eye. "Aaaaaah," he cried out, his head swirling from the pain. The Colombian in the backseat looked like a cage fighter, his face rugged and scarred with wrestler's cauliflower ears. Junior was no stranger to pain at this point in his career.

"You have two months to pay your debt, you worthless fucking Mexican," the man said. "You'll not be alive to see your kids grow up, you stupid fucker."

"What debt?" Junior demanded.

"The one you owe our boss, Tony," he replied. "La Mona has told you already… you're overdue, mother fucker. Now pay up or get a fucking bullet in your fat head."

They arrived at the airport. Junior was shoved out, his face puffed, swollen, and bloody. He couldn't see very well out of his right eye. He managed to check in at the counter and make it to the gate in time for his flight. The pain was excruciating, his face swelling by the minute. The little ice offered to him on the airplane was a slight relief, but it did nothing to cover the fact that he looked like he had been struck by a truck.

Several hours later, Junior entered his Monterrey home through the front door. It wasn't a mansion, but it was modest in size and tastefully decorated, reflecting Junior's desire to avoid drawing unwanted attention, something he also learned from his father. He found Sara sobbing in the living room, not bothering to stand up and greet him. He knew better than to try to talk to her. Instead, he sat down and draped his arm around her. She was too exhausted and depressed to be angry about his poorly timed trip. Suddenly, she wiped her eyes, looked at Junior, noticed the bruise around his eye, and asked,

"What in the hell happened to you?" Despite his vague and ridiculous story, Sara shook her head and headed to the kitchen to pour herself something to drink. Her mind was on Xochilt. The necessary travel authorization had been obtained, and there was no time to waste. They were scheduled to fly out early the next morning.

As night turned into morning, Junior and Sara sat quietly in their living room, saying nothing, simply reflecting, praying, and wondering why this was happening to them now that things were starting to look up. It was 4 a.m., and they hadn't slept at all. They sat there, lost in thought, staring at the floor and occasionally glancing at one another as they wiped away tears from a long night. From the moment they learned about Xochilt's diagnosis, they jumped into action, rushing around in a frenzy, calling family, and arranging for someone to care for their two boys (ages 5 and 7). The earliest available flights were on an Aeromexico plane leaving Monterrey's International Airport that morning at 7 a.m. Fortunately, the Houston-based surgeon was on standby, waiting for their arrival. They were scheduled to land at Houston Bush Intercontinental Airport at 11:50 a.m. after a quick layover in Mexico City.

The sudden chime of the doorbell woke them from their pensive state. They jumped to their feet and greeted the taxi driver at the door. He quickly collected their suitcases as Junior and Sara raced to grab Xochilt. They left the house at 5 a.m., worried that something unforeseen would interfere with their planned arrival in Houston—a car accident, a flat tire, or a mechanical issue with the plane. Although the airport was just a twenty-minute drive, it felt like an eternity in the backseat of the taxi. There was no talk from the moment they left the house until well after they arrived at the airport, checked their luggage, stood in line, and went through security. It wasn't until they boarded the flight that they started to breathe again, feeling a bit more relaxed about the possibility of experiencing a miracle for their daughter.

Junior stuffed their two carry-on bags in the compartment above their first-class seats as Sara made her way to her window seat, holding Xochilt in her arms. Junior took the aisle seat beside her. He reached over to secure her seatbelt, then his own, still without words.

"Thank you, Junior," were the first words she uttered since leaving the house. "I love you."

"I love you, too," he said, starting to well up again with tears.

"God couldn't do this to us twice... *could he?*" Sara asked, not wanting an answer.

Junior wiped his eyes and squeezed her hand. "We're going to do everything humanly possible to save our daughter." He paused. "Our boy's circumstances were completely different. It was an accident."

"Maybe God is punishing us, Junior," she quietly mused.

The mere fact that she uttered those words stirred feelings of guilt within him, prompting him to release her hand and look away. It was painful even to let his mind wander into that rarely visited realm. He knew where she was heading with her comment. He refused to believe in God's capacity for punishment in that way. Despite his Catholic upbringing, he lacked faith in the sanctity of the Catholic Church. He avoided confession like the plague, even though he had plenty to confess. "How ironic," he thought, "religiously attending mass on Sundays while living an outlaw's life."

Noticing his troubled mind drifting into darkness, she gently touched his hand and said, "Junior, it's gonna be okay… no matter what happens… it'll be okay." She paused as he looked up at her, and she added, "You're a good man, Junior. You've always provided for your family. We have two beautiful, healthy, and happy sons at home; let's not let this tear us apart. We'll get through this, my love."

By now, his eyes were filled with tears. People sitting across the aisle couldn't help but notice as they looked over at him, wiping his face and nodding in affirmation of her comments. He was unable to speak, fighting back an emotional release. The pilot's announcement came as the doors were secured, informing passengers of the plane's imminent departure. Junior and Sara held hands throughout the entire flight. They stopped in Mexico City and then continued onward to Houston. The lack of sleep was beginning to affect them. However, their adrenaline kept them going as they prayed for their trip to be blessed with a miracle.

They finally arrived at Bush Intercontinental in Houston, the fourth-largest city in the country, often called the "New York of the South" due to its international, cosmopolitan atmosphere. Luckily for the Valladares family, Houston also features the world's largest medical complex, providing the latest medical technologies and services.

"Were you nervous about clearing Immigration?" Sara asked, knowing that Junior had been arrested years ago in Denver, Colorado.

"No, I wasn't… that case was dismissed for lack of evidence, remember?"

"Well, maybe they could still be looking to get you on something else," she said, her voice laced with nervous concern.

"That was all about my father escaping from that jail in Edinburgh back in ninety-three... they tried to pin it on me, but they didn't have a case, so the charges were dropped. That's why I was able to travel, don't you see? Don't worry."

"I'm just worried that you might be arrested again, Junior."

"Sara, it didn't even come up when we were being asked questions by the Immigration inspector." He laughed, adding, "I guess the gringos are just as fucking dumb as we are." They both chuckled.

After forty-five minutes southbound on I-45, they reached downtown, pulling onto Fannin Street as the West Tower of Texas Children's Hospital came into view. Once their cab stopped at the entrance, Sara felt Junior's hand gently squeeze hers and interlock with it. They knew they were doing everything humanly possible. All necessary arrangements had been made with the Houston surgeon. It was August 2005.

While Junior's family was rushing Xochilt to the hospital, I was organizing my pens and pencils and walking around the office to introduce myself. Houston's DEA office was a six-story commercial building located in an area known as "Uptown," northwest of Houston's downtown, not far from the Galleria Mall – a touristy attraction famed for being one of the largest malls in the country.

My new supervisory role involved overseeing a team of twelve agents. I managed what was called an "Enforcement Group," like other domestic offices in large cities. In Houston, we were responsible for targeting drug trafficking networks affecting the region. Since it was Texas, most cases involved the Gulf Cartel and the drug flow through their corridor. Most of the cocaine passed through Houston on its way east to Atlanta, North Carolina, and further north to New York, Chicago, and other cities.

Texas was the last place on earth I thought I would be assigned. Born and raised in California, I assumed my career would keep me on the West Coast. However, anywhere else was better than going to DEA's headquarters in D.C. For street-oriented supervisors, heading to headquarters was like the kiss of death. Bureaucratic desk-jocks loved it, but most street agents described it as "getting one's lobotomy."

During my first week, I sought out Keith Bishop, a fellow supervisor, because I knew he had also been posted to Houston. Bishop was a headquarters-based "Staff Coordinator" at DEA's Special Operations Division (SOD), supporting investigations at the Guadalajara office. SOD served as a central hub for intelligence generated globally from the DEA's high-profile cases. Located in Chantilly, VA, it was a multi-agency unit led by the DEA. Its purpose was to connect investigations and facilitate communication among agents and their offices to coordinate efforts. The goal was to prevent conflicts and avoid duplicating work. SOD's main role involved collecting and analyzing suspect telecommunications data, stored in a specialized database. Links between cases were created and shared among those targeting the same high-value individuals. Most of the time, SOD's involvement promoted collaboration and contributed to many successful operations, ultimately helping dismantle criminal networks. The Cali Cartel's dismantling marked one of SOD's first major successes.

I learned Bishop was a supervisor assigned to Houston's Strike Force, located on the second floor. Although I had hoped to surprise my good friend, I ended up leaving him a note on his desk and then went to the sixth floor to see the Special Agent in Charge (SAC). The boss called me in for his usual "welcome aboard" briefing. SAC James Craig, a native Floridian, was an old-school, no-nonsense agent's kind of boss. He was focused on street operations and taking down the biggest, baddest criminals working for Mexican and Colombian cartels. He wasn't shy about going to headquarters and demanding operational funding and resources to support the mission. Having been involved in many complex investigations, he was no stranger to wiretap cases. Wiretaps also required a lot of manpower and often involved collaboration between different offices and agents. He emphasized the importance of his agents collaborating and sharing information with other agencies, including the FBI, DHS/ICE, local, and state law enforcement. It didn't matter—he was even open to sharing with "Spooks" (CIA). Mr. Craig believed, "We are all cops with a badge, and charged with keeping the streets safe from the outlaws." I was glad to be working under that kind of leadership.

"I like the fact that you're coming from Guadalajara, Mike," SAC Craig said, adding, "We need your institutional knowledge to help us stay focused on those traffickers that are impacting our area. "I want you to consider using wires whenever possible. I know there's some resistance to it in this division, but it doesn't matter...it's the way to go these days. We need to take the entire organization apart...not just a cell here or there, Mike."

"Yes, sir... understood."

"The agents don't like 'em... hell, they're a pain in the ass but it's how we wrap the bastards up these days."

"Will do, sir."

"Bishop tells me that he worked a lot of your Guadalajara cases when he was up at SOD."

"Yessir, we did a lotta good work together. I was hoping to see him this week," I added while noticing the boss's office was decorated with cool baseball memorabilia.

"You caught him on leave. I told him to take some time off. The guy never sleeps. He is a fuckin machine. Pair up with him if you can." He went on to explain how the Strike Force was created to focus the DEA's resources more on international priority targets. "Do you like baseball, Mike?"

"Yessir, I'm a San Diego Padres fan," to which he laughed and shook his head.

"Well, you're in the home of the Houston Astros now. Whenever you get a chance, take your group out to a ball game. It builds morale," he encouraged. I gestured with an agreeable nod.

He shook my hand as he welcomed me to the Houston Division and wished me luck. I started to walk out of his office when he said, "Hey Mike, why does Bishop call you 'Pinche?'"

I stopped, turned around, and with a quick chuckle, I explained, "The short story is Bishop called me one day and asked me what 'Pinche' meant? I gave him a five-minute, long-winded dictionary explanation, starting with the formal definition, describing a menial kitchen worker.

Then I explained its more common use in Mexico as an expletive noun, adjective, verb, and adverb version of the word, 'fuck."

"Huh!" Was the SAC's wide-eyed response. "And so why did he need to know that?"

"Beats me… after my lengthy explanation, Bishop simply replied, 'Thanks, Pinche!' and then he hung up the phone. I've been 'Pinche' ever since." The SAC laughed so hard I thought he was gonna pee himself. I could hear him as I made my way out of the office and down the hallway to the elevator.

It was Wednesday, August 24th, at around 10 a.m. when I finally tracked Bishop down. I arrived with coffee in hand.

"Pinche! Come on in!" Bishop's voice boomed. "Welcome to Houston, you're gonna love it here." He paused as I sat down and handed him his coffee.

"So, what are you working on these days?" I asked.

We're on command-and-control phones used by the Gulf and the Zetas. Do you remember when I asked you for intel on Osiel Cardenas operating in Guadalajara and the surrounding areas? These bastards are expanding into nearly every state in Mexico, even Guatemala.

Osiel was known as one of the country's most violent cartel leaders. In the late 1990s, he was credited with assembling a deadly ninja squad comprised of deserters from Mexico's Army Special Forces. Osiel lured them away from their military positions with promises of fame and wealth. Their modest salaries couldn't compare to the riches they gained as hired guns.

As Bishop started to detail his case and invite my group's participation, his desk phone rang. He answered it and passed the phone to me. "It's Diana, your assistant."

"Yes, ma'am," I answered.

"Mike, sorry for interrupting but an agent down in Guadalajara, I think he said Jimmy something… he's on the line and says it's important. I'm gonna transfer the call, okay?"

"Jimmy, what's up?"

"Hey, how's Houston… you guys getting used to the crazy heat?"

"Oh yeah, sweating my balls off here in August," I laughed.

"Anyway, bro," he said. "Our Colombian… you know who I mean… he's passed a very time-sensitive lead regarding an associate of his, a guy he's only recently talked about."

"Uh-huh…"

"He says this guy's dad was a serious player with the Gulf. They call him Junior. I'll email you the last name now. Anyway, he's up there somewhere at the Medical Center getting treatment for his little girl—no more details. You know how this Colombo hasn't done shit so far. Now that he's under a little pressure, I think he's throwing us a bone to get us off his back."

I asked, "What does he think we're gonna do if we can track this guy down?"

"He thinks you guys can follow him, take some photos, maybe ID some other assholes he might meet up with," Jimmy responded. "There's no paper on him, so it'll just be surveillance stuff, Mike."

"Okay, no arrest warrant, so we can't play that card," I said. "Send me everything you have on him. I'm with Bishop, but headed back up to my office now to see what you're sending." I left Bishop's office, made my way down the hall, and jumped on the elevator to get back to my fourth-floor office. Within minutes, I was reading Jimmy's email:

"Junior is Raul Valladares, Jr. His dad was big with the Gulf during the 90s. Our Colombian La Mona didn't provide me very much other than 'Junior' and a compadre, 'Beto Bravo', who were working together and moving loads for 'Los Gueros 'and other Sinaloans. He also identified a couple 'Cantu' brothers using a trucking business to move dope from their border town in McAllen to New York. La Mona said the main brother, Jerry, is Junior's guy, and he works exclusively for the 'Gueros.' Junior is of medium height and build, with dark hair and an olive complexion, and is typically clean-shaven. He wears nice clothes but not a bunch of flashy jewelry. La Mona says Junior is big and moves tons of coke. He says we need to follow him around to see who he meets and take photos. Junior has distributors in Houston, as well. Good luck, Mike!"

I sent a reply email thanking him for the information and then went to the group's bay area to pick up a couple of agents to join me at the Children's Hospital. I knew it was a long shot, but I thought I had enough knowledge about the Gueros (translated "blondies") to take a chance and try to turn Junior into an informant. The "CI" ("Confidential Informant") Jimmy mentioned was La Mona, a Colombian recruited in Miami, Florida, who was brought to Guadalajara several months earlier. He was assigned to reconnect with the Gueros brothers and their Sinaloa associates. He was our "Golden Goose," and the only informant we had at the time who had close access to the Sinaloa Cartel leaders—someone we relied on to help us get indictments against Sinaloa's top capos. He was our only hope at that moment.

I approached two partnered agents: Mickey Teague and Darren Butler. They were seated in the far corner of the group, busily planning their next search warrant execution. They were considered the office's experts on marijuana indoor grows and organized money-remitting operations being managed by Vietnamese organized crime members.

"Hey Mickey, Darren… can you guys spare an hour or two and accompany me downtown to the Children's Hospital?"

"Is everything okay?" Darren immediately jumped to his feet, thinking it was a family emergency.

"No, everything is fine… it's only a tip I just received from Guadalajara. I'll brief you guys on the way down. We're gonna look for a Mexican guy and approach him."

"Are we gonna arrest him?" Mickey asked, setting down his early morning jumbo-sized Whataburger iced tea, and then retrieved his DEA-issued Glock from his desk drawer.

"No arrest… we don't have any paper on him… just a quick chat."

"Oh…," Mickey said, still a bit confused. "Is he a witness or something?"

"Nope, he's a crook… we're gonna try to find him, then flip him as a snitch," I suggested.

"Oh, okay. I'm in! What happens if he tells us to fuck off?" Mickey asked.

"Let's just swing the bat and see if we can get on base," I said with a smile.

"Screw getting on base... let's hit a homerun," Darren said as we walked towards the elevators.

It was usually a 20-minute drive. Darren got us there in ten. I provided them with background information on the Gueros case, La Mona, and the details Jimmy shared about Junior. As we pulled up, I offered, "I think I have just enough to scare the shit out of this dude. He'll think we've had a tracker up his ass for months."

We parked in the reserved space usually used by the Houston Police Department and displayed our government placard on the dashboard. The agents called the placard a "get-out-of-tickets placard." We went to the Children's Hospital's information desk and asked to speak with the head of security.

"Certainly, can I see some ID?" I produced my credentials. "Thank you, you're looking for Lieutenant Leland (*)," the elderly female receptionist said. "I'll page him overhead... which agency?"

"Please, just indicate there are three law enforcement officers here to see him," I politely requested, praying that the letters "D-E-A" wouldn't be heard throughout the building as the security guy was being summoned.

As the announcement went out, the three of us stood there, looking around at passersby and wondering if our target was among them. The receptionist's desk phone rang. The head of security informed us that he would be down shortly.

Within minutes, we observed a large, portly man, clean-shaven, wearing an ill-fitting suit, exit the elevator and approach us. He had that retired detective swagger about him.

"How can I help you gents?"

"Lieutenant Leland, we're from the DEA here in town," I said as he handed me his business card. "I'm sorry, I'm new in town and don't have any cards yet." After identifying ourselves, I added, "We would like to get your help in quietly tracking down the father of one of your patients... at least, we believe he is here with his daughter and possibly with his wife."

"Do you have a warrant for him? Are you planning on hookin him?" he said with a thick Texas accent.

"No, sir, we don't. We want to talk to him."

"What's his name? We can have a little looksie to see if we can locate the patient... do you have the patient's name?"

"I do not, unfortunately... the father's name is Raul Valladares, though," I said, crossing my fingers.

"Alright, let's see here," he responded while walking over to where the receptionist was seated. He picked up the phone, dialed an extension, and said, "Charlie, look up a patient's family name... look for the last name 'VALADARUS,'" with a twang. There was about a two-minute, nervous pause before Lt. Leland answered, "Much obliged, Charlie... we'll be headed up."

I glanced over at Mickey and Darren, suddenly feeling a little bit of luck coming our way, when Lt. Leland confirmed, "Appears we have an infant by the name of 'Xochilt' who is currently in the Pediatric Intensive Care Unit. Dad's name is as you indicated, with a second last name of Hernandez. And the wife is Sara. Do you want to speak with Mom and Dad together?"

"Definitely not, sir. We were hoping to speak with Raul privately and without alarming his wife or even letting her know he's being contacted by law enforcement. If possible, we were hoping you could come up with an excuse to get him away from his wife and into a private room. Sorry, I know it's asking a lot." I could see the experienced cop's inquiring mind at work, so I added, "We don't have a warrant and no plans to arrest him. We're hoping that he'll cooperate with us."

"Got it, say no more. Should my folks be concerned? Is this gonna be a scene out of 'Scarface?'" Leland asked, half-joking.

"Let's hope not," I answered, cracking a smile. "We only have one gun between us," which, for a second, he thought me serious, and his mouth flew wide open. "No, there's nothing to worry about, but if you could give us about an hour with this guy without momma getting suspicious, we'd appreciate it," I politely requested as we stepped into the elevator.

I'll see if I can locate him. If he's here, I'll find him and arrange for you guys to have a private office on the fifth floor. As we got off the elevator, we accompanied the retired Houston Police Lieutenant into his office, where his Sergeant immediately informed him that "Raul" and "Sara" were both on the premises.

"Cannot thank you enough, Lt. Leland. What are you gonna tell him, by the way?"

"I'm gonna have one of the nurses send him down to the cafeteria to set up a special account for those patients and families that are here on lengthy stays. I'll be there to intercept him, and then I'll escort him up to you guys. Are you sure he's not gonna pull a goddamn Uzi on me?"

"Hehe, no... not likely," I replied, realizing he was genuinely worried. "But if he does, don't bring him to us!" I joked. After a brief pause, I asked, "By the way, what's the situation with his daughter?"

They are running a bunch of tests in preparation for her surgery. It appears she has a rare heart defect that must be surgically repaired for her to survive. Several surgeons are currently checking on her. The timing of your visit sucks, but I guess that's the way a cookie crumbles sometimes."

"I know it does… no real choice, though," I responded. He shook his head in acknowledgement. Lt. Leland was a seasoned cop whose vast experience involved a shit sandwich or two.

We were taken to the fifth floor and left in the office, waiting for the unsuspecting trafficker to arrive. It was arranged like a DEA interview room, with a table, a lamp, a phone, a pad and pen, and two chairs—one on each side. Darren and Mickey stood against the wall, partially out of view of where Raul would be sitting. About half an hour passed when sounds of conversation and footsteps grew closer. The door opened as Mickey and Darren prepared for a possible confrontation. I remained seated.

"These gentlemen are agents of the federal government, Señor Valadarus, and they would like a moment of your time. I apologize for using the cafeteria as cover, but these gentlemen thought it best that your wife is not aware of this meeting. I'll leave you gentlemen alone now," he said, closing the door behind him, motioning to me, and saying, "Just call my desk when you're ready."

There he stood, perplexed. Raul Valladares didn't have the stereotypical look of a high-rolling Mexican drug trafficker. He wasn't covered in gold, nor did he wear flashy necklaces, bracelets, diamond rings, or "Gucci" shoes. Instead, he appeared neat and well-groomed—a good-looking man with short, wavy black hair. His light olive complexion made it easy to mistake him for an Italian, a

Frenchman, or any other European. Despite his youthful appearance, which hid his actual age of 38, his puffy and bruised face caught our attention.

"What... what is this?" he asked nervously, expecting handcuffs to come out. He looked around the room, noticing that I was seated at the table, with Mickey and Darren standing behind him, ready and posted at opposite corners of the room. They could see from Junior's fitted shirt that he was not concealing anything around his waist.

"Raul, come in and have a seat... please stay calm. It is not our intention to arrest you," I said, motioning to him with a hand gesture. He sat down directly from me. Junior was still sporting his black, swollen eye and a fresh scar on the right side of his face. "Jesus, what happened to you, Señor Valladares?"

Without responding to that question, he instead asked, "Who are you guys... FBI?"

I let out a laugh and replied, "Naaaah, just look at how we're dressed, Raul. That should give it away. We're with the DEA. My name is Mike Chavarria, this is Darren Butler, and that's Mickey Teague. Haven't you seen FBI agents in the movies? FBI guys wear suits, ties, and shiny shoes." Darren and Mickey were dressed in jeans and polo shirts, while I wore Dockers and a long-sleeved, collared shirt. "You knew this day would come. Please tell us you're not surprised."

"Am I going to jail?"

"I told you we're not looking to arrest you, amigo." Junior looked relieved, but was visibly nervous, constantly looking behind to see what Mickey and Darren were up to. He was visibly shaking. "Raul, I need you to be calm so you can listen carefully to what I have to say."

He just sat there, a look of shock and disbelief on his face. He began to tear up, thinking the worst – being taken away at this critical moment during his family's crisis. It was clear his imminent tears were not for himself but rather for his wife and infant daughter. In that instant, I thought to myself, "It was true the eyes were the doorway to one's soul." It was obvious that Junior's crime-hardened exterior was suddenly softened by the love he had for his family. It was a telling sign that encouraged me to stay on track for what was about to unfold.

"First of all, Raul. We're sorry we have to do this while your daughter, Xochilt, is in Intensive Care."

"What, who... what are you talking about?" Raul was visibly shaken by it all.

"Raul, you have been under surveillance for a couple of years now. We know quite a bit about you, your friend Beto, and the Colombians you've been associated with... like La Mona, for example." Suddenly, I saw Junior's eyes widen and his demeanor change. He sat up and paid close attention. It was working. An innocent man would have jumped to his feet to deny everything forcefully. I knew we were reeling him in.

"But..., but what about this threat?"

"You know we cannot reveal our sources nor talk about our long-term investigations, Raul. What I *can* tell you, however, is the threat has nothing to do with Los Gueros." Hearing that, he became visibly nervous, adjusting his posture. He turned slightly pale and clasped his hands together, finally placing them on the table. He sat up straight and was more attentive than ever, leaning forward, trying to read my eyes.

"What do you know about the Gueros?" he asked. I didn't say a word but instead held the stare. After a distinct pause, he asked, "Okay, if you're not here to arrest me, what do you want with me?"

"Well, you should probably know that it was initially our prosecutor's opinion that we should arrest you and be done with it. We convinced him that you should be allowed to come clean and work with us. It took some convincing. I believe everyone deserves a second chance, my friend." I could see his head begin to nod, a subtle acknowledgment. I felt my Pinocchio nose growing.

Then, he suddenly objected, "Like an informant? I can't do that!" It was an instinctive reaction for a man who had spent a lifetime dedicated to crime. "Gringo informants don't last very long," he said emphatically. "No way, Señores!"

"Well, look, Raul. We prefer to call it an 'Agent of the Government.'" I said, lowering the tone of my voice while leaning in toward him. It was as if it were our little secret. I added, "Informant has a tone of betrayal to it... I get it. But what we're looking for here is someone who can be an undercover operative—someone with the skills to infiltrate the biggest drug trafficking organizations, you know, to gather intelligence." I paused as he pondered the idea. "We've studied you, Raul. You're perfect for this role... You have what it takes, my friend." I was counting on the ego boost to work, and he slowly nodded his head again.

"Sounds like an informant to me," he responded.

"I'm sorry if you want to see it like that, amigo. The bottom line is that we had to go to bat to keep you out of jail."

"What do you have on me?"

"A lot of cocaine for one thing. We know you are working with the Gueros brothers and using a transportation guy in McAllen, Texas." Raul's eyes widened, then squinted. I was tired of the charade and wanted to drive it home. "Let me put it this way... we're not here to sell you on a fucking job, okay? You're goddamn lucky to be alive, and with everything going on in your life right now, you have no fucking options here. We are doing you a goddamn favor. It looks like I am going to have to end our conversation and slap the cuffs on." Raul looked scared and about to shit himself. I added, "We hate to do that with your family crisis going on right now... but we will."

Okay, fuck!" He looked down, then back up, now with a look of conviction. "I'll fucking do it." He quickly glanced at Darren and Mickey to check if they were holding handcuffs. It was almost done... all that remained was the ribbon-cutting ceremony. He then looked down and muttered, "I'm fucked." Sitting quietly, head down, he finally looked up and asked me, "So, this threat... it's from Tony down in Colombia, right?"

"Who?" I asked, quickly catching myself. The last thing he needed was to sniff out a bluff.

"Possibly, Raul... we don't have everyone identified just yet," I answered.

"Yeah... it's Tony... Tony Baca. That motherfucker has had me followed and roughed up," he said, pointing to the side of his face. *Wow, what luck... we hit the jackpot!* I thought. He was now on team USA.

"So, now what?" He paused, looked at me, glanced over at Darren and Mickey, and said, "By the way, you guys should just call me Junior, especially since it looks like we'll be partnered up." As he said it, he cracked a boyish smile, and it broke the tension in the room. He then explained he would likely be staying in Houston while Xochilt was under the care of specialists there at the hospital.

I told him we would arrange an interview in the hotel where he and his family were staying, making it easier for him to slip away. This would allow us to be efficient with the limited time we had with him. The key was to thoroughly debrief him and get him started in an undercover role so he would stay committed to the cause. We developed scenarios using codes for our frequent communications to avoid compromise, especially with his wife.

"Are you guys going to tell the Mexicans what I'm doing?" He asked.

"Are you fucking kidding, Raul? I may not be Mexican, but I've worked there long enough to know we can't do that." He visibly looked relieved. He suddenly stood up, shook each of our hands, and reassured us he would be the best DEA undercover agent we've ever had.

"And please call me 'Junior.'"

CHAPTER 3
THE PROTEGE'S BEGINNINGS

Raul Valladares Sr. was born and raised in Ciudad Victoria, Tamaulipas. A child of the 1950s, he grew up in Mexico's gulf region, sharing a swath of the southern Texas border from Laredo to Brownsville. Raul Sr. knew he wasn't cut out for ranching or farming. He was adventurous and sought out opportunities to make a lot of money, even if it meant breaking laws and living on the edge. Although audacious and a scrapper, he also possessed natural magnetism, charisma, and the ability to charm. His gifts not only served him well with the ladies but also with law enforcement, a talent that frequently kept him out of jail. As a teenager, he learned to survive on his own on the streets. Not just survive but thrive. Raul Sr. knew he was destined for bigger and better things and was convinced he had the brains and the balls to make it happen.

Barely out of his teen years, he married and had his first child, a boy who became his namesake, preferring to call him "Junior." Junior's father was already maneuvering to become a drug lord at an early age, initially serving as an intermediary between drug sources and clients. The clients, of course, were his bosses – mid-level drug distributors moving around fifty kilos at a whack. Raul Sr. learned that most of his drug "sources" were often cops. It was one of Mexico's unfortunate realities for those becoming law enforcement officials, whether local, state, or federal, that police were forced to supplement their poverty-level wages. Their typical modus operandi involved ripping off independent traffickers operating without cartel authorization. They would then turn around and sell the stolen dope to cartel-sanctioned street dealers and pass a percentage of the profits up the chain to the local cartel boss. In the 1980s and early 1990s, it happened to be Juan Garcia Abrego, the Gulf's top capo. Although harsh, Mexico offered little to no reward for a man seeking a noble career in law enforcement. Cops were merely security guards for the rich. The only way to get ahead was to play the game, and the game and its rules were designed and governed by the wealthy few – corrupt businessmen and politicians.

"Junior..., don't trust the cops... they're damn thieves, and they'll sell you out in a heartbeat. Now take this money over to the Chief of Police and tell him we expect to get what we asked for from the major hotels in town." Junior knew his dad's star was rising within the organization. Raul Sr. was considered one of the Gulf's top lieutenants, in charge of making corrupt payments to the local, state, and federal police.

"Should I give them a deadline?"

"Tell them we want immediate access now or there will be consequences." The Gulf Cartel was demanding updated rosters of all guests staying at the major hotels in Monterrey, Mexico's third-largest city and a booming industrial and manufacturing hub. The cartel was meticulous, keeping track of visitors coming into town, especially if they posed a threat—whether from rival traffickers or law enforcement.

During the 1980s and 1990s, the Gulf Cartel's influence on local, state, and federal governments was substantial. Cartel boss Garcia Abrego was rumored to have had direct access to newly elected President Carlos Salinas de Gortari and his brother Raul, whose six-year term began in 1988. It was still an era when the Gulf and Sinaloa Cartels respected one another's territories and smuggling operations, but only if turf rules weren't violated. Traffickers were fiercely protective of their respective areas of control. The principal, lucrative corridors giving access to US markets were those regions of the country where most northbound commercial trucking crossed overland into the US: Tijuana, Baja California; Nogales, Sonora; Ciudad Juarez, Chihuahua; Nuevo Laredo, Tamaulipas; Reynosa, Tamaulipas; and Matamoros, Tamaulipas. Of course, there were upwards of 50 or more overland (Mexico-US) ports of entry used to cross bulk drug shipments.

Junior was a quick study and learned the intricacies of the drug trade. He knew every aspect of the business, from organizing large-scale imports originating in South America to coordinating the movement of loads into Mexico and across the border. Most critical to any smuggler was having reliable access to transporters who could successfully transport the drugs from the point of origin, through Central American transshipment points and staging areas, and then into Mexico, where the drugs could be moved overland or via air to other staging areas. Of course, the ultimate objective was to get the drugs safely to market, where they could generate billions for those daring to play the game. The principal markets were in the United States, with secondary markets in Europe and Asia. Junior wanted to learn it all. Junior's expertise and claim to fame would eventually become his ability to serve as a middleman, brokering major transactions between sources of supply and major wholesale buyers (investors) who sought large-scale supplies of the drug, namely cocaine.

Raul Sr. recognized Junior's talents and skills, but cautioned him throughout the process to be vigilant, avoiding being naively manipulated, whether by fellow trafficker associates or conniving government officials. Junior was reminded there were no friends in the dope business. If everyone were making money, associates would be friendly, but never friends.

Knowing that Junior's best friend, Beto Bravo, was also his closest business partner, his father was careful but deliberate to point out flaws in Beto's character, particularly his competitive nature, inflated ego, and overconfidence. He warned his son that Beto could not be trusted but stopped short of insisting the two men part ways. Beto's connections were powerful.

Junior admired and idolized his father and closely followed in his footsteps. He was well on his way as the golden boy prodigy until the summer of 1991, when his drug-dealing career took a sudden hiatus. Before going to prison, his metal was tested during a torture session at the hands of a military counter-narcotics commander. Once Junior's criminal case was adjudicated, he began serving time. Once in prison, Raul Sr. went to work to secure his son's early release. Of course, it was done only after greasing the palms of key corrupt officials, including that of an appellate judge.

During Junior's four-month stay in prison, he made the acquaintance of a very important fellow inmate, Jhon

Jairo Aispuro (*), a Medellin Colombian who was doing time for an unrelated drug charge. Aispuro told Junior to use his nickname, "La Mona." La Mona would be the most influential person Junior had ever expected to meet. When Junior inquired as to what landed his new friend in prison, La Mona replied, "I trusted a fucking Mexican." La Mona was soft-spoken, well-groomed, and well indoctrinated in the art of facilitating multi-million-dollar cocaine transactions. He was a broker of cocaine for both Colombia and Mexico's most powerful cartels.

The two men hit it off and became close friends after Junior appealed to his father to help his new Colombian friend get out of prison. Fortunately for Junior, in the early 1990s, the Gulf Cartel still wielded significant influence within the Mexican government. A few hundred thousand dollars was all it took for Raul Sr. to secure a dismissal of La Mona's criminal case, based on a technicality, of course. A few government officials made off with enough cash to buy new homes for themselves.

Within weeks of Junior's departure, La Mona walked out and immediately called Junior with an invitation to join him in Colombia. La Mona pledged his lifelong friendship and encouraged a criminal partnership. With this alliance, they would jointly broker large-scale cocaine deals arranged between Colombian sources and wholesale buyers in both Central America and Mexico. The two men traveled to Colombia so La Mona could personally introduce Junior to the key players in the Colombian drug world.

It was the early 1990s, and Mexican investors were eager to expand their country's role in the growing cocaine industry. Frustrated with their subordinate transshipment role throughout most of the 1980s, Mexicans became shrewd, choosing to receive their payment in coke and demanding half of every load that passed through the country. This was much more profitable than waiting months for cash payments, which were often delayed until the drugs were sold north of the border. Given Mexico's history with US immigration, an established infrastructure was already in place. They had a strong presence in major cities like Chicago, New York, New Jersey, Los Angeles, Houston, Denver, and others. Their numbers far exceeded those of their Colombian competitors. They also had a network of transportation routes and reliable distributors from the heroin boom years earlier. Meanwhile, the US user market for cocaine was growing. The Colombians now relied heavily on the Mexicans, as increased efforts in the Caribbean pushed cocaine transit through Mexico. The timing couldn't have been better for Junior, and he was eager to take advantage of the opportunity.

Junior went with La Mona to Colombia, eager to build the contacts he would need to become a cocaine trafficking superstar. Before heading out, they ate at the "Rincon de Argentina," a popular steakhouse in the fancy, upscale neighborhood of Polanco in Mexico City. La Mona explained his role as an intermediary (broker), convincing Junior that this was where the real money was to be made.

"Junior," he said, "The real money is made by acting as the middleman for as many services as possible. The most important thing is, of course, getting the coke smuggled into Mexico by any means necessary – containers, fishing vessels, aircraft, speedboats – it doesn't matter. And then there's overland transportation once the product arrives in Mexico. It doesn't stop there — you can also charge for facilitating the storage and importation of merchandise into the US. You bring people together and serve as a mouthpiece."

Junior pointed out that his partnership with Beto allowed them to cover most of the services that are usually sought. "We have transporters to move it into Mexico from Panama, then we can charge for moving it overland, paying corrupt cops along the way. We can charge for storage in Monterrey and then get it across the border into Texas from the Mexican State of Coahuila, east to Matamoros. We can work with your associates, La Mona," he added confidently.

"So, you can get the coke into Texas?"

"Beto has that handled. His father and uncles have strong connections to the Mexican authorities."

La Mona nodded his approval. "I like to stay away from handling the drugs… way too risky. I focus on getting money back to its investors. It pays well." As they paid the bill, La Mona said, "But don't be under the illusion it's easy. It has its dangers, Junior. You'll have to be careful with everyone you interact with. *Trust nobody*," he warned as he took a thick wad of cash out of his pocket and laid three hundred dollars on the table. "Someone can fuck you and leave you responsible for an entire load. And not everyone is forgiving."

"I understand," Junior acknowledged.

"Do you? You told me about your compadre, Beto. He is your partner, but can you trust him?" Junior's mind went to his father's words of caution.

"I can trust him. I want you to meet him… Beto is like a brother."

The following day, Junior and La Mona departed Mexico City for Bogota. La Mona had arranged for the two of them to be received as if they were foreign dignitaries. La Mona had a three-car escort to the center of town, where they arrived at a luxury hotel – "Tequendama" – in the upscale neighborhood of Santa Fe. Junior marveled at how different Colombia was from home. The streets were filled with suit-wearing businessmen carrying satchels and man-purses.

Upon arriving at the hotel, he noticed La Mona's armed entourage fan out and establish a security perimeter. Junior asked, "Are all these bodyguards for you?"

"You're our guest. We don't want anything to happen to you. Besides, we're at war right now, Junior." Without checking in at the desk, La Mona walked Junior to the elevator, accompanied by two gunmen wearing suits. Junior was taken to the Presidential Suite and was provided with unlimited access to room service, which included an open bar. He handed Junior a business card and said, "Dial this number and describe the type of woman you're interested in… no charge, my friend." La Mona excused himself to arrange important meetings he had promised Junior, leaving him alone in the grandiose suite. Junior figured La Mona's people owned the hotel.

He couldn't believe that at his young age, he was about to meet the powerful men who ran the world's cocaine trade. He walked to the window and looked out at the sprawling capital city. He heard faint gunshots out in the distance. Junior knew both the US authorities and their Colombian counterparts were partnered in their aggressive search for Pablo Escobar, acknowledged as the Medellín Cartel's top boss.

A few hours later, La Mona knocked at the door. "Come with me, please. It's time to meet some of my countrymen."

It was a violent time in Colombia as Escobar had been on a murderous rampage, killing thousands in response to the government's threat of extradition. Escobar was in hiding and left his trusted lieutenants to run the business.

Junior was taken to a modern skyscraper in the downtown area of Bogota and was escorted through the lobby and up the elevator to the top floor. Upon exiting the elevator, he was greeted by armed guards and asked to submit to a search. He was scanned with a wand to detect the presence of a recorder or other electronic devices and then invited into a large executive office where refreshments were available – an array of snacks, soft drinks, and premium liquor options, including Colombia's national drink, "Aguardiente" ("Firewater").

As Junior started to serve himself, a distinguished-looking gentleman appeared, escorted by two men in business suits. He suddenly tensed up and put his plate down. La Mona stepped forward and quickly introduced him, "This is the gentleman I told you about, Don Berna." Diego Murillo Bejarano, also known as "Berna," was one of Escobar's trusted associates. He was casually dressed but carried himself with a sophisticated air. Medellín's cartel was made up of sub-groups led by allied crime bosses, all working under Escobar's authority.

Junior, trying to hide his nervousness and excitement, extended his hand to Don Berna.

"Diego Murillo at your service. My friends call me Berna for short." He stood about 5'9", had a thick build, was well-groomed, with short-cropped dark hair. He was looking at his Mexican visitor over the top of his glasses as they shook hands. He was impressive yet intimidating. Junior knew he was meeting narco royalty.

"Don Berna," La Mona addressed his boss, "I would never have secured my release without the help of Junior and his father." Berna motioned to Junior to have a seat.

"We are very grateful to both you and your father. La Mona's incarceration was a huge mistake on the part of your paisanos, but we're not here to discuss that."

He quickly glanced over at La Mona and caught him smiling. It was obvious Junior was undergoing the job interview of a lifetime with one of the underworld's most powerful kingpins.

They sat there for a couple of hours having drinks while Junior was peppered with one question after another. Junior was asked about his partnership with Beto and contacts along the US border.

"It's a reality that we here in Colombia require a relationship with Mexico. It's no secret that our business is expanding in the US, Señor Junior. Your countrymen are the key these days to helping us maintain a healthy, steady supply." He paused, still assessing Junior. "As La Mona has told you, it's in our nature to distrust the Mexicans. I hope you understand. You, on the other hand, have received a very nice endorsement from La Mona."

Junior sat there, sipping his Aguardiente, a clear, distilled alcoholic drink made from sugar cane with a slight anise flavor. La Mona wasn't much for drinking; he just sat quietly eating fruit, watching Junior's content expression. La Mona knew his boss would rely on his advice to get Junior to help in Mexico. He was eager to introduce his new Mexican friend into his business plans.

"La Mona will introduce you to some very powerful people in Mexico. You're going to help us double our business capacity, Mister Junior. Can you handle that?"

"Yes, sir."

"One more question… will your father have problems with you working with the Sinaloans?"

"No, sir." Don Berna sat there peering at Junior momentarily as if uncertain.

"Your function will be an important one… it is what we call an 'office.' For now, you will be supporting La Mona's office." Don Berna then turned to La Mona and gestured that the meeting was over. As he stood up, Don Berna turned to Junior and suggested he stick around for a few more days to enjoy a bit of Colombia's hospitality, to which Junior eagerly nodded his acceptance.

The next day, he was helicoptered to a remote ranch outside the capital, where he enjoyed the red-carpet treatment. It was more like an all-inclusive resort with multiple pools, tennis courts, and stages for performers. Junior had never seen such extravagance. There was a constant stream of visitors – several easily fitting the trafficker profile, while others looked more like government officials or maybe even politicians. When Junior asked La Mona about them, he was told to enjoy the ambiance and not worry about the others. "They're friends."

It was two full days and nights of food, booze, and entertainment. What started as a party graduated to drunken debauchery. Several scantily clad women stripped and skinny-dipped in the pools, enticing Junior and other guests to do the same. Junior didn't want to leave. He became the center of attraction once it was learned he was from Mexico. Expensive bottles of Tequila were brought out, and he was pressured to get up and accompany a Mariachi band playing songs from his homeland. He did so despite lacking the talent.

Junior made it back to Mexico, anxious to share the adventure with his father. Raul Sr. congratulated his son and told him, "It's all on you, now, Junior. Be careful with the Colombians. We need them. They need us… But I don't trust them." Those were the exact words La Mona uttered to Junior about his compatriots' distrust of Mexicans.

Junior knew he was stepping away from his father's world and embarking on a separate path… working with the powerful Sinaloa Cartel. Although not at war, the Gulf and Sinaloa traffickers were not bedfellows, either. They were tolerant adversaries.

"Last piece of advice I'll share with you, Junior," his father said. "I know you and Beto are close friends and business associates, that's fine. Beto's got a lot to offer. But you and he are very different. You are honest and trusting. He doesn't possess your character traits or your integrity. He paused as he looked his son square in the eyes, "It's money and ego that drives him… not his loyalty to friends." He paused and said, "Keep your head on a swivel, Junior." Junior nodded and hugged his father, his mentor and best friend.

Raul Sr. told his son the most powerful Sinaloan trafficker at the time was Amado Carrillo, aka "Lord of the Skies," whose nickname was earned after he amassed a fleet of commercial aircraft, effectively quadrupling Mexico's imports of cocaine. Although based in Juarez, Chihuahua, Amado commanded the respect of his fellow Sinaloa Federation associates and became the de facto leader of the Federation. Amado's 1990s era ushered in what would eventually become a slow but progressive displacement of Colombian control over coke's movement through Mexico.

Junior's newfound path took him further away from things at home. In December 1992, Raul Sr. uncharacteristically violated his own rule and crossed the border into Texas to personally oversee a cocaine transaction. Shortly after arriving in the US border town of McAllen, he found himself on DEA's radar. An anonymous tip was received regarding a parked Chevrolet Astro minivan, purportedly loaded with narcotics. Agents responded by surveilling the vehicle. Frustrated after several hours of no movement, agents decided to call in the McAllen Police Department's canine ("K-9") unit. "Gunner" was sent out along with his two-legged uniformed partner, and the two performed a cursory walkabout. Gunner's highly trained sniffer came alive and alerted to the presence of drugs. Using the alert as "Probable Cause," the DEA obtained a search warrant and seized 462 kilo-sized bricks of cocaine concealed underneath the van's floorboard. A query of the van's "VIN" (Vehicle Identification Number) revealed it was tied to a residential address in town.

The DEA quickly set up another surveillance operation at that address, suspecting it might be used as a stash house. Once they had eyes on the location, three cars arrived, dropped off bags, and left together. Agents dressed in raid gear approached, knocked, announced themselves, and then entered, using a battering ram to break down the door. They found Raul Sr. sitting calmly in the living room. After securing the residence, they obtained another search warrant and discovered additional cocaine bricks marked with the same "scorpion" symbol as those seized from the minivan. Also confiscated was a hidden stash of $194,336, bundled in $100 and $20 denominations, wrapped with rubber bands. Raul Sr. was placed in handcuffs and faced federal charges in a system he couldn't easily manipulate. While awaiting trial, he was jailed at the Hidalgo County Jail in nearby Edinburg, Texas.

Word got back to Junior while he was meeting with La Mona and Beto at a street-side Mexico City café in Polanco. "*What...?*" Junior said incredulously. He set his coffee down and sat up, intently focused on the startling news of his father's arrest.

"What time did it happen? What the hell was he doing in McAllen?" Junior knew it was not customary for his father to cross the border to supervise a delivery. Everyone in the business knew things were different across the border. With some exceptions, it was understood the gringos were not tempted by either threats or money. There was a rule of law, and it was typically enforced. There was a modicum of respect for US law enforcement and the justice system. Judges weren't as quick to succumb to either threats or payoffs, and although neighbors, the US and Mexico were worlds apart in terms of law and order.

Junior looked as white as a ghost when given the news. He quickly explained the situation to La Mona and Beto and then proceeded to Benito Juarez International Airport in a taxi to catch the first flight back to Monterrey. He was perspiring uncontrollably. His heart was pounding, his head was swirling, and he was feeling nauseous and helpless. Junior was confident the cartel would assign one of their local (McAllen-based) attorneys. Raul Sr. was considered one of the Gulf's top lieutenants. Both he and his partner, Oscar Malherbe, were in line to take the place of their boss, Juan Garcia Abrego, if called upon. Junior walked through the door and was immediately greeted by Sara, who threw her arms around him, giving a sympathetic hug.

Tearfully, she said, "Junior, I received a call shortly after we got off the phone and was told there's an attorney already assigned to your father's case."

"What's his name?" Junior asked.

"They wouldn't tell me. They instructed us not to get involved."

Two days later, Junior answered his front door and was greeted by a well-dressed gentleman, who said he was there on La Mona's behalf. He handed Junior a cell phone to be used exclusively to discuss matters concerning Raul Sr.'s situation. The man said, "We understand your hands are tied and there's not much you can do at this time. Please allow us to return a favor." The Colombian stranger never identified himself and departed after passing the phone to Junior.

It was the first time the letters "DEA" held any significance for Junior. DEA was usually called "las tres letras" ("three letters") in Mexico. The last time he heard those letters was in 1985, pursuant to the abduction and murder of DEA agent Enrique Camarena. Junior recalled frequent news reports of the DEA seeking Mexico's cooperation in locating the agent's body. Junior also knew it had triggered a massive response from DEA and the US government to bring those responsible to justice. It did, in fact, trigger the Guadalajara Cartel's downfall as the cartel's founders were being rounded up one by one. First, Rafael Caro Quintero was caught after fleeing to Costa Rica; then, Ernesto Fonseca Carrillo; and finally, the top boss, Miguel Angel Felix Gallardo. By 1989, the three main leaders were behind bars. As is typical in the world of Mexican drug traffickers, family members continue the business: Ernesto Fonseca's nephew, Amado Carrillo, stepped into a leadership role and would soon lead Mexico's most powerful cartel. The Guadalajara Cartel's death gave rise to the Sinaloa Federation.

It was a waiting game for Junior and his mother as they were reliant on the Gulf Cartel's attorneys for information. Tired of waiting, and in defiance of the Gulf Cartel, they hired their own private attorney (Alberto Arredondo) (*). By late February 1993, Junior received another knock at the door. It was the same Colombian stranger. He strongly advised Junior not to visit his father, that arrangements were being made to secure his release, but provided no additional details. He related, "The less you know... the better." He paused and reiterated, "Compliments of La Mona."

Junior closed the door and walked back inside, wondering what his Colombian friend had planned. Junior made several calls to La Mona, but La Mona acted clueless, as if he didn't know what Junior was talking about. "No favors here, Junior... have no idea what you are talking about." Junior was confused. Beto was also questioned by Junior, but he knew nothing.

There were no more calls until mid-April 1993. Junior was instructed by the same Colombian to avoid crossing the border to visit his father, that "efforts were underway to secure his release." *What does that mean?* Neither he nor his mother had any clue about what was happening. Their family attorney had no such information regarding an early release. Mr. Arredondo, as well, was puzzled, but continued to work to keep the family updated on motions hearings and the anticipated trial date.

It was early evening on Sunday, April 18, 1993, when Mr. Arredondo arrived at the jail for his scheduled visit. Visitors at the Hidalgo County facility were required to enter the building and check in at the reception window. They were greeted by an armed deputy standing behind bulletproof glass in a control room. After showing proper ID, visitors were asked to sit in the waiting area. Once authorized, they were searched and permitted to enter a meeting room to see an inmate. The guard in the control room pressed a button to open a slow-moving, reinforced door, granting access to the meeting room. Inside, the visitor and inmate chose any available cubicle to talk. During their visit, Mr. Arredondo and Raul Sr. discussed the need to liquidate assets to cover trial-related expenses.

When the meeting ended, Raul Sr. stood up and signaled to the guard that he was ready to leave the room. As the door slowly opened, allowing the attorney to exit, another man appeared in the lobby area. He was dressed like an attorney as well and did not arouse suspicion. He seemed to be waiting as if checking in with the control-room guard. The new visitor caught Raul Sr.'s attention, gesturing for him to head in his direction. It was at a moment when both doors—separating the meeting and waiting rooms—were open. Raul Sr., thinking quickly, responded to the stranger's gesture and headed toward freedom. When the inside guard reacted and ordered Raul Sr. to stop, the stranger withdrew a hidden Beretta 9mm pistol from his waistband and ordered the guard to the ground. The control-room guard was unable to do anything but sound the alarm. By that time, Raul Sr. was safely out of the building. As the front entrance door was closing, county deputies rushed in but faced a second armed accomplice who appeared, throwing a gas grenade. It triggered a forced evacuation of the entire building. It was like a scene from "Mission Impossible."

In the ensuing chaos, Raul Sr. was whisked away into a nearby van outfitted with ladders and the name of a local plumbing business. The driver took a pre-planned route to a building down the street with a covered parking garage, where Raul Sr. was transferred to a false compartment in the bed of an SUV. It wasn't more than half an hour before Raul Sr. found himself back in Mexico, headed to a "safe house." Once there, Raul Sr. would be transferred to another safe house managed by the Gulf Cartel.

Within a day of his father's escape, Junior received his last call from the Colombian stranger. "Your father is now back in Mexico. Neither you nor any of the family are to have contact with your lawyer, Mr. Arredondo. You are no longer in need of his services." The man ended the call without providing any further details.

The next day, Junior's mother reported that she received information from Raul Sr.'s partner, Oscar Malherbe, who said that "Raul Sr. was okay and would reach out when it was safe to do so." At least the family knew that Raul Sr. was now under the protection of Juan Garcia Abrego, the leader of the Gulf Cartel. Nothing happens without his approval. Junior understood that his father was now a fugitive, and it was only a matter of time before Mexico was pressured to hunt him down. Junior still felt puzzled about what seemed to be cooperation between La Mona's people and the Gulf Cartel.

The Gulf offered Raul Sr. refuge and kept him out of sight for several weeks before letting him see his family. Junior figured the Colombians had planned his escape with the help of the Gulf Cartel. He knew there was indebtedness attached to that favor. There were no free rides in Junior's world.

A Texas Ranger-led investigation later concluded that the visiting attorney, Mr. Arredondo, was not involved in the orchestrated escape. The investigation also led to accessory charges against Junior, which were later dropped due to a lack of evidence. Several weeks after the jailbreak, Junior and his mother resumed meetings with Raul Sr. They arranged meetings at hotels and safe houses with the help of Oscar Malherbe, Raul Sr.'s close friend and partner.

Junior's next meeting with La Mona occurred at the same café in the upscale Colonia Polanco. Junior asked again about La Mona's participation in arranging for his father's escape, to which La Mona responded, "My compatriots and Mr. Garcia Abrego agreed to work together to get your father released. Some good things happened, Junior. You ask too many questions, Junior."

A month later, Mexico was shocked by the fatal shooting of one of its most prominent Catholic leaders. The incident happened in the parking lot of Guadalajara International Airport on May 24, 1993. According to news reports, Archbishop Juan Jesus Posadas Ocampo was killed after "being caught in a crossfire melee between gunmen of warring cartels." Posadas's murder stunned the country and the world, as he was only one of two individuals in the country with the prestigious title of "Cardinal." It temporarily disrupted the activities of Junior, La Mona, and Beto, as the Mexican government went on high alert, with police and military forces sweeping the entire country to search for those responsible. Mexican politicians were aware that the world was watching. These were difficult times in Mexico during President Salinas's administration, amid numerous shocking government scandals and widespread public outrage over human rights abuses.

The following year (1994), Mexico's new President, Ernesto Zedillo, announced another major crackdown on those responsible for the country's drug trafficking ills. Typical of Mexico's politicians, Zedillo blamed his predecessor for Mexico's woes and pledged to correct wrongdoings. As part of his promise to the country, he announced a full-scale war on Mexico's cartels. Zedillo asserted that the Gulf Cartel's leader, Garcia Abrego, was under the personal protection of President Salinas and his brother, Raul. His campaign to eradicate corruption from the country began and concluded with the Gulf Cartel's upper echelon leadership.

Unfortunately for Junior's father, he was caught up in Zedillo's intense crackdown. Despite Raul Sr.'s efforts to avoid attention, both he and his partner, Oscar Malherbe, were arrested. They were detained in a Mexican prison for several months before being released due to lack of evidence.

"That's just a bullshit show for the gringos," Beto told Junior, and Junior knew Beto's information came from reliable sources. Beto's father and two uncles were Mexican Federal comandantes with other extended family members having strong political connections within the country's leading political party, the Institutional Revolutionary Party (PRI). The PRI had been in power since its founding in 1929 – the party of the revolution.

During the years (1994-1996), Junior, Beto, and La Mona were slinging more cocaine than they could keep track of. It was a new dawn in Mexico, given Amado Carrillo's arrangements with Colombia's sources of supply. Commercial-sized plane loads were arriving in Mexico virtually unhindered. Given Mexico's apparent reluctance to target Sinaloa traffickers, Junior and his associates were getting rich from successive coke shipments they brokered on behalf of the Federation drug lords. Most of the cocaine was sourced by two influential Colombian organizations: the AUC and the North Valley Cartel. Although the Federation and the Gulf Cartel weren't one happy family, the 1990s were a peaceful era for them. Everyone, from traffickers to politicians, was an investor. Despite the peace, however, President Zedillo was still under pressure to throw a bone to the US government. And that bone turned out to be the Gulf's leader, Garcia Abrego. He was captured by Mexican authorities on January 14, 1996, and extradited to the United States shortly thereafter.

His arrest left a void and power vacuum within the Gulf's ranks. It gave way to an internal struggle for control. Top lieutenants Raul Sr. and Oscar Malherbe briefly took control over the cartel. They began to re-establish their dominance over the region, but those efforts were short-lived, given the growing, dominant influence the Sinaloa Federation had on the government.

Junior was fortunate to have been paired with powerful Colombians who worked almost exclusively with the strongest Mexican kingpins in the country. And he owed it all to his friend, La Mona. Junior and Beto were finally making their move. Although he missed his father, Junior was reassured that Raul Sr. would survive and eventually be set free. After all, it *was* Mexico. Money and time could fix anything.

CHAPTER 4
LA MONA

In the 1980s, Pablo Escobar's Medellín Cartel controlled the cocaine market in the US. La Mona got his start working as an accountant for Escobar and trusted underboss allies, Luis Gomez, also known as "Rasguno," and "Don Berna." Medellin was making money hand over fist and desperately needed the expertise of a "money man." La Mona was the perfect choice. He was formally educated and trusted by Escobar and his subordinate bosses.

Before entering the drug trade, La Mona attempted to make an honest living. As with many ambitious but impatient young men, the money didn't come fast enough. La Mona couldn't wait to enjoy the fruits of his labor. He recognized his genius and put it to work. He looked around and saw his professional peers wearing ties, going to work every day, punching a clock, and making what La Mona considered meager wages. It wasn't for him. La Mona was a thrill seeker and couldn't see spending twenty years behind a desk. The Medellin Cartel offered him the opportunity he sought. He had the balls and used his smarts to step out and take some significant risks. It was a matter of risk and reward. He thrived on the risk and craved the reward. He even looked like an accountant. He was skinny and wore prescription glasses. But he wasn't just another nerd. Despite his appearance, he had "Herculean" courage. His mother described him as frail but intrepid.

Once he found a home with the Medellín Cartel, he wasted no time in building his reputation as a loyal disciple. Despite his education and skills, he started, like many in the business, as a mule. La Mona wanted to experience the thrill of smuggling firsthand. He carried bulk cash from the US to Colombia in suitcases with false compartments that could hold up to a million dollars in large bills. He avoided detection by taking circuitous routes on various commercial airlines originating from multiple cities across the US. His routes took him through several countries, including Mexico and Central America, before returning to Colombia. His time as a mule was short, as he was destined for bigger things. His genius was soon recognized, and he was quickly promoted to a position that befitted his skills.

With his accounting degree, he was able to enroll in an MA program at New York University (NYU) and was granted a student visa. The objective wasn't to get another degree, but to remain in the US. It transitioned from a student visa to a work permit, allowing him to engage in business while still enrolled in school. La Mona was hired as an accountant for a New York-based brokerage house specializing in commercial imports and exports. The company was just another storefront established by the cartel to give Medellín a legitimate means to operate in the US. Its purpose was to facilitate drug imports and launder the cartel's money. The legit business – on paper only – served solely to camouflage the cartel's massive shipments of cocaine secreted in maritime containers. La Mona collected the drug proceeds from various distribution cells throughout New York, New Jersey, and Philadelphia. He also went south to Miami, Florida to retrieve additional bulk cash when the need arose.

He arranged for monies to be deposited in various business accounts representing multiple companies engaged in importing and exporting various products between South America and the US. La Mona ensured that the deposits remained under $10,000 to avoid the reporting requirements established by the Bank Secrecy Act. La Mona knew the reports would trigger a "CTR" (Currency Transaction Report), which would alert federal law enforcement. This method of keeping small deposits in many accounts was known as "smurfing." By smurfing the money, La Mona ensured his activities remained off DEA's and Treasury's radars. By his mid-twenties, La Mona was handling millions.

La Mona was eventually rewarded with more responsibility. He began arranging meetings with cocaine distributors in both Miami and New York. At that time, US-based drug traffickers were killing one another to maintain a dominant foothold in the lucrative cocaine industry. The Cubans and Jamaicans were violent and wouldn't hesitate to challenge their Colombian competitors over a mere kilo. La Mona knew he represented the largest drug trafficking organization in the world and wasn't about to get killed over a couple of measly kilos of cocaine. He started out negotiating hundreds, then thousands of kilos at a time without blinking an eye. What he had going for him was his trustworthiness and loyalty to the bosses. These were qualities that were in high demand and ones richly rewarded.

With the arrival of the 1990s, the writing was on the wall for the violent drug barons of Medellín. Their days were numbered. Pablo Escobar and his cohorts were marked men and hunted like dogs by Colombian authorities, the US government, and even rival cartels. La Mona, being a good soldier, continued to follow orders and serve his Medellín masters, although he was savvy enough to see the tides shifting. He secured new relationships with those he knew would be coming in behind the Medellín regime. He was careful not to get caught in the middle of the transition and burn bridges. La Mona surreptitiously built alliances with those replacing Medellín's leadership. He made sure to avoid members of the Cali Cartel, however, since they were vicious adversaries of his current cartel employers. Besides, he saw their days were numbered as well. Cali leaders were rumored to have initiated surrender negotiations with the Colombian government in exchange for immunity from US extradition.

As the Medellin's dominance ended, La Mona's boss and mentor – "Don Berna" – saw his opportunity to switch teams and jump to an emerging organization: "United Self-Defense Force of Colombia" known by its local acronym "AUC," a far-right-wing paramilitary organization that served as an armed adversary to other political rebel groups such as the "FARC" (Revolutionary Armed Forces of Colombia) and the "ELN" (National Liberation Army). The AUC's leaders turned to cocaine to fund their political agenda.

Don Berna became an AUC commander and convinced La Mona to join him. It was then that La Mona met and became aligned with AUC commanders, known as "Los Mellizos" ("The Twins"). The twins, named

Miguel Angel and Victor Manuel Mejia Munera, were powerful and violent and preferred to operate in remote areas, managing their cocaine labs. The Mellizos helped catapult La Mona's career by expanding their operations, sending record quantities of coke to Mexico. La Mona developed an exclusive relationship with the Mellizos and became their sole broker. Junior became La Mona's subordinate partner to help him double his capacity. It was the perfect partnership, having both a Colombian and a Mexican intermediary in Mexico. It was cocaine's heyday for both countries' cocaine investors.

In 1997, La Mona acquired special authorization from the Mellizos to introduce Junior to Amado Carrillo. Having Amado's approval was like being knighted by the king of cocaine. Conservative estimates placed yearly cocaine imports at around 600 metric tons as of the mid-to-late 1990s, generating annual profits in the vicinity of ten billion dollars. The "Lord of the Skies" (Amado) and his Sinaloa Federated allies were responsible for most of it.

It was early February 1997 when La Mona arranged a surprise meeting for Junior with Amado. They arrived at a private residence in Mexico City. Junior was told only that he would be meeting a few influential individuals, with no further details. Sensing their meeting was important, Beto was frustrated and angry when La Mona excluded him. When Beto asked La Mona about it, La Mona placed the blame on Junior.

It was a vast, custom-designed ranch-style home situated in the upscale Mexico City Colonia of Condesa. The house overlooked Parque Mexico, located on an avenue lined with sculpted trees and Art Deco-style buildings. The community possessed a quaint, European vibe with small boutiques and outdoor cafés all facing the large park. La Mona and Junior arrived via taxi and were greeted by two armed guards with Uzi submachine guns slung over their shoulders. They stood just inside a black colored wrought-iron gate, which offered access to an expansive property. La Mona and Junior were greeted and promptly escorted down a long winding pathway. As they made their way along a winding walkway, Junior recognized an array of colorful plants and flowers that were among his mother's favorites. An older woman was watering the garden. She nodded and smiled as they walked the winding path.

"Just go to the door. There'll be someone waiting," the guard said as he bid them farewell, returning to join his partner at the gate.

Junior knew this was not just another typical get-together and guessed he would meet someone with significant influence. A man dressed in traditional butler attire opened the front door before they could knock. La Mona and Junior entered through a large, ornately designed double door made of mahogany. They followed the unfriendly butler into the foyer, leading to an open, sunken living room. Junior's eyes darted from one scantily clad woman to another. At least six women served appetizers and drinks to six or seven men seated around a plush leather circular sofa. Each man had either a drink, a cigar, or both. Most women looked ready to jump into a pool, with a few seated on the laps of the guests. Junior and La Mona were asked for their drink orders. Junior figured the others were members of the Sinaloa Federation and noticed they all acknowledged La Mona's presence with a nod or by raising a glass. Everyone ignored Junior except one young woman. She approached and asked if he would be staying long, inquiring about his interest in "a little female company." Junior knew there was no time for such distractions and politely declined her offer.

A few sips into his drink, and the butler reappeared to escort La Mona and Junior to another room where their host was waiting. As Junior left the room, he noticed the looks he was getting from the other guests. A few of them, dressed mostly in western-style attire, with collared, buttoned-up shirts, form-fitting jeans, fancy belt buckles, and exotic-looking cowboy boots, gave Junior a suspicious leer as he left the room. Junior and La Mona walked down a long hallway that opened into a larger living room. Junior couldn't help but notice the plush white carpet and teak furniture. There were collectibles and antiques from all around the world, with opulent landscape paintings hanging in hand-carved wooden frames. The home featured a country-style architectural design, complete with handmade terracotta floor tiles, which created a rustic yet elegant ambiance. Junior and La Mona were immediately offered drinks by the servant and asked to take a seat. "Don Amado will attend you shortly," the assistant said. Junior realized it was the Lord of the Skies he was about to meet.

While waiting, Junior also noticed a couple of stuffed exotic safari animals on display. Then their host appeared and called La Mona, motioning for the two of them to follow him into his office. La Mona was greeted with a warm hug, while Junior was greeted with a cordial handshake. Amado then took a seat behind an ornately carved mahogany desk. He gestured for his guests to make themselves comfortable in leather chairs that faced his desk. He pushed a wooden humidor in their direction, inviting them to choose from the selection of Cuban cigars. Junior couldn't believe he was in the legend's presence.

"Don Amado, this is the gentleman I told you about. We've been partners now for quite some time, and my associates and I trust his business sense and loyalty," La Mona told Amado.

As Amado sat quietly assessing the newcomer, Junior's eyelid twitched nervously.

"They call you Junior, correct? Your father's namesake? Yes, it is imperative for the firstborn son to take his father's name. I haven't had the pleasure of meeting your father. Still, I imagine he must be a man of integrity, given his position working for "Don Juan," Amado said, referring to the Gulf's godfather, Garcia Abrego.

After La Mona's brief introduction and a bit of Junior's background, he paused and deferred to Amado.

"Junior, what are you looking for today?"

"Don Amado, as La Mona indicated, I have been working hard and building a reputation. I need your endorsement for additional credit. I want to offer my services to your colleagues from the Federation. I have access to La Mona's associates, who will furnish me with 2,000 units on credit. With your endorsement, I would like to expand my influence here in Mexico."

"And what's in it for me?" he asked while lighting his cigar.

Junior was momentarily stumped by the question but rebounded nicely. "Well, sir, I know that my success would lead to profit for you. I would never think of arranging a sizable load without first offering you the chance to invest," to which Amado smiled approvingly.

"What I need is reliable transportation, Junior."

"Yes, sir, fortunately, I am in a position to offer the services of two men who own and manage front companies in Panama and elsewhere in Central America," Junior replied, feeling a rush of confidence. I can also broker transportation across the border and to US distribution cities.

"If I grant you my endorsement, you'll be working solely with our federated associates... no more independents, understood?" After a momentary pause, Amado added, "I am aware of your partner, Beto Bravo. He worked briefly with one of our colleagues, Mr. Arturo Beltran. That relationship didn't fare well," Amado said. It startled Junior and left him nervously awaiting Amado's conditions.

"I'm aware, Don Amado," Junior said.

"My endorsement is explicitly for you, Junior, and does not include anyone else, particularly your compadre, Beto," he said. La Mona sat quietly, occasionally glancing at Junior. Amado added, "For anything I invest in, it will not involve Mr. Beto Bravo... understood?"

"Understood," Junior responded.

Junior knew Beto to be a risk taker, occasionally careless and greedy, but Beto was not just a business associate; he was Junior's compadre – more like a brother. Junior reflected on his father's prophetic warnings.

"Okay, Mr. Junior, it's time you start working directly with my associates. As La Mona knows, there is so much product coming up from Colombia that we are always looking at expanding operations to satisfy the gringos' insatiable appetite. And now, I'm aware we have doors opening for us in Europe. You have come to me at the right time, Junior." He then picked up his desk phone and called for one of his close associates to join the meeting. "Junior, your world is about to triple in size."

There was a loud knock at the door. Amado called out, "Nacho! Come in, Compadre!" In walked a bearded gentleman of medium height and stature. Junior recognized him as one of the men wearing the fancy western attire. Although in his forties, the man had a baby face. He entered, smiled, and addressed Amado cordially.

"Take a seat, Nachito."

Ignacio "Nacho" Coronel greeted La Mona with a handshake and hug, and to Junior, he simply nodded his greeting.

"Nachito, it looks like Junior is someone we can put to work. La Mona thinks it's time our new friend spread his wings. I was hoping you and Los Gueritos could offer him an opportunity or two."

"Sure, Compa, whatever you think... there is no shortage of work," Nacho said. "What are we talking?" Nacho asked, looking at La Mona.

"Los Mellizos are currently sending two to three thousand per shipment but have indicated an interest in tripling that number now. With Junior as an independent operator, I think we can properly supply you and your associates with as much as you can handle," La Mona said.

"Okay, let's start with four to five tons, Compadre," Nacho related. He then looked at Junior and said, "You will have to join me in Puerto Vallarta to meet my associate, Esteban. He'll be very interested in what you have to offer. He and his brother work for me, but they have the capital for moving significant product right now." He paused, laughing, "We call them 'Los Gueros,' because they could pass for gringos." Junior was familiar with the Gueros from La Mona but was unaware of their actual names. As with most Colombians, Junior learned that La Mona was extremely distrustful and secretive about identifying other associates in the business.

La Mona instinctively knew when to end a business meeting and leave. It was never a good policy to become too familiar with Mexico's cartel barons. Despite an invitation to stay for dinner and drinks, Junior followed La Mona's lead and got up, shook Amado's and Nacho's hands, and left the room. Junior left the meeting more impressed than ever with La Mona's reputation among Mexico's most powerful drug lords. Junior's career was taking off.

While leaving the mansion, La Mona identified the more important capos seated in the living room as Amado's younger brother, Vicente, Ismael Zambada, Juan Jose "El Azul" Esparragoza, and Arturo Beltran. "These are the top dogs who run things in this country, Junior." The prodigy son of the Gulf Cartel was now an honorary member of the most powerful drug trafficking syndicate in Mexico. "They call themselves the Sinaloa Federation," La Mona said as they left the house.

La Mona made it clear that Junior's meeting with Nacho and Esteban would be without him. Like Raul Sr., La Mona was relinquishing control and wanted Junior to work more independently.

Two months later, Junior caught an early morning flight to Puerto Vallarta at Nacho's invitation. He arrived around noon at the small resort city's airport and was greeted by men dressed in dark suits. He was transported in an armored Suburban to a large condominium near the border between Jalisco and Nayarit. The condo sat on the beach, overlooking the Pacific Ocean, nestled within a gated community that contained several other furnished condos available for Nacho's visitors. It was a vast complex filled with tropical plants and trees like Bougainvillea and Coconut Palm, resembling a botanical garden.

Junior asked the driver, "Are all these owned by your boss?" The expressionless man didn't respond. Junior was dropped at the front entrance and instructed to follow a winding sidewalk to the front door. The path, like Amado's mansion in Mexico City, was lined with beautiful, tropical flowers native to the area.

A servant answered the door and guided Junior into the living room – another spacious, sunken room, with a zebra hide for a rug. There were drinks, cigars, bowls of tropical fruit, and lines of coke on the table. The stereo was blasting with music from the eighties.

"Come on in, asshole! Grab a drink, a cigar, take a hit of sweet powder, and join us out on the patio!" Nacho yelled out to Junior, motioning for him to follow as he walked through the kitchen to access the pool area. Junior grabbed a couple of lime wedges, squeezed them in a glass, poured some rum and coke, and made his way out to the patio. As he emerged from the huge kitchen area, he saw another man sitting poolside with drinks and a cigar in hand. They were wearing Speedos and Hawaiian shirts and were enjoying their view of at least five young women sunbathing topless, with one swimming nude in the pool.

As he took a seat, Nacho motioned to his friend and said, "This is the guy that Amado told me would make us some money... what do you think, 'Pelos'?" The nickname, "Pelos" ("hairs"), was a reference to his thick head of hair.

The man just looked up at Junior, studying him closely, and slowly took off his sunglasses. Pelos, grinning, said, "I think he takes it in the ass!" Pelos then glanced at Nacho, and they both shrugged and started to laugh.

"What do *you* think?" Nacho asked, waiting for Junior's reaction.

Without hesitation, Junior replied, "I wasn't in jail long enough to try it…," to which Nacho and Pelos burst into laughter, nodding their approval.

"You're alright, mother fucker!" Nacho exclaimed.

"Junior, this is my guy, Esteban. He and his brother, Luis, make a shit-ton of money for us. "He also goes by the nickname, 'Peligros'… I don't know why," Nacho said with a mile, adding, "cause he's a big pussy." Nacho slapped Esteban's arm as he joked.

Junior looked Esteban over nervously, wondering why his other nickname was "*danger.*"

"My pleasure, Señores," Junior said, extending his hand to Esteban, hoping the conversation would take a business turn.

"I understand you live in Monterrey," Esteban said.

"Originally from Ciudad Victoria, but now Monterrey is home."

"I have a home in Monterrey, as well. Maybe we can have a couple of beers sometime?"

"Of course," Junior said, smiling. "I like him, Nachito," he said. "Let's put him to work."

The three men sat there for at least an hour before any business was discussed. They sat and talked about everything from soccer to women. Junior had La Mona's voice in his head, along with his poignant advice. "Be all eyes and ears but reserved about giving too much information about yourself." It was the same advice he'd received from his father.

The discussion then turned from superfluous to relevant. Junior was asked about what he could bring to the table in terms of finance. Given the number of successful loads already moved with Beto and La Mona, Junior was ready to risk more of his own money, a sign of his willingness to share in the risk. It was common practice to split large loads up among multiple investors, even if the investors represented different cartels. It was especially important for the "broker" to own a portion of the load, as well. It was called "having skin in the game" and ensured everyone involved had something to lose. Unlike the other investors, however, Junior knew that as a broker, more was expected of him. Not only did he need to share the risk by investing in the load, but it was a general rule that he would make good in the event something went wrong. It meant everything from having a load seized by law enforcement or military, or getting ripped off by other traffickers. In any event, a thorough investigation by investors would ensue determining the percentage of responsibility heaped on the broker. It was a game of high risk, high reward.

What caught Esteban's attention was Junior's access to transportation, especially for cocaine that crossed into Texas and moved to northern US cities. Junior knew his Texas-based associate, Cantu, would be of great value to the Gueros brothers. Cantu owned his own trucking business in McAllen, Texas, and made regular trips to New York, New Jersey, Philadelphia, and Chicago, generally carting fresh produce from the valley. Esteban ran distribution for the Gueros organization and was elated at the prospect of having Cantu on the payroll. Reliable transporters were golden for drug smugglers.

"That's exactly what I'm looking for right now, my friend," he said, adding, "You'll be pleased you met me, Junior."

Junior knew his access to Cantu was valuable and was highly protective of it. Fortunately, La Mona wanted nothing to do with transporting cocaine north of the border, as it exposed him to more risk from the long arm of the US Justice system. La Mona watched and learned how gringo federal conspiracy laws entangled his many compatriots of the Medellin and Cali Cartels. La Mona preferred to handle the repatriation of drug proceeds... it was safer.

Junior stayed the night. The three men hung out, watching satellite TV and listening to music. It was almost surreal how Junior was now becoming part of Sinaloa's family, despite being a protégé of the Gulf Cartel. Junior declined an invitation for a midnight visit from a local teenage beauty contestant—one of many in Nacho's harem. It was one of the guilty pleasures shared by the narcos—a craving for and easy access to beautiful young women. There was always a steady stream of imported beauties from Russia and other Baltic countries. It was a simple business exchange—prostitutes and drugs—between organized crime colleagues from around the world, making money with and for one another. The criminal element had surrounded Junior since he was a child.

"Why marry *one* when you can just fuck 'em all?" Nacho said when the subject of marriage came up. Junior was newly married at the time and although he loved his wife dearly, he was a typical Latin male. Nacho pulled out a photograph of one of his recent conquests. "That's

Sandra Avila... she's beautiful, isn't she... yep, Felix Gallardo's niece... I fucked her, too." Felix Gallardo was the last of the Guadalajara Cartel leaders to fall. His lovely niece, Sandra Avila, was known as Mexico's "Queen of the Pacific." Sandra and her beautiful sisters were eye candy during festive get-togethers. The "Queen of the Pacific" was also on her way to becoming a respected Sinaloa trafficker, as well.

Junior was ecstatic and optimistic over his bright future, having first met the "Lord of the Skies" and then Nacho and Esteban – all considered crime bosses and associates of the Federation. He sensed the Gueros were going to be his golden ticket to fame and fortune.

Timing was everything, however. Just a few months after meeting the "Lord of the Skies" with magical doors swinging open for him, Mexican news headlines announced Amado Carrillo's death while he was undergoing plastic surgery in Mexico City. He died on July 4, 1997. La Mona told Junior that it was a botched surgery as Amado tried to change his appearance and leave the country. La Mona's information indicated that Amado's influence on Zedillo's administration was waning, and he was trying to preempt what he feared would be his betrayal. According to La Mona, Amado didn't want to share a US prison cell with the Gulf's capo, Juan Garcia Abrego. Junior remembered many conversations with Raul Sr., where he warned Junior about Mexico's corrupt and fickle politicians. Raul Sr. would tell his son, "Despite making millions for doing some favors, they will turn on you in an instant if it suits them."

Junior's introduction to La Mona was fortunate and timely. While he served La Mona's needs, he also enhanced his own chances for success. Junior now had access to both

Colombia's and Mexico's most powerful traffickers in the world. He would ride La Mona's lucrative coattails.

"Junior, it's time you come back to Colombia and meet directly with the Mellizos. They are interested in a face-to-face with you if we're going to start moving more weight." Although knowing Mellizos's rumored propensity for violence, Junior was confident in La Mona's ability to protect him.

Several months after Amado's death, Junior traveled to Colombia on board a private jet at the invitation of the Mellizos. The meeting didn't take place in a hotel, business office, or even a large Hacienda, venues to which Junior was accustomed. This one took Junior to the country's remote jungles. It was a dense region known as the "Valle de Cauca," an area notorious for its clandestine cocaine labs. It was Colombia's treacherous, snake-infested jungle and well-suited for cocaine's illicit production. The Mellizos and their parent organization, AUC, operated their massive drug business under the auspices and authority of the larger "North Valley Cartel."

Twin brother Miguel Angel, also known as "Comandante Pablo," extended a rare invitation to Junior, flying him in a private jet directly to Santiago de Cali, the capital of Valle de Cauca. From there, Junior boarded a Cessna 210 Centurion and arrived at a remote, hidden airstrip carved out of the jungle. Junior decided to invite his closest friend and business partner, Beto. The Colombian escorts ordered Beto to stay at the airstrip while Junior was taken in a battered Toyota Land Cruiser several miles into the dense jungle. At a riverbank, they boarded a speedboat and traveled miles down a winding river to a military base camp. There, Junior was told to swap his polo shirt, dockers, and Gucci shoes for camouflage fatigues and size nine and a half jungle boots. He left his clothes and jewelry in a thatched hut and was escorted through the camp. He arrived at a large, enclosed tent with two armed guards standing outside.

Junior was told to "go in and see the comandante." Comandante Pablo, a slenderer looking version of "Fidel Castro," sat there in his jungle fatigues, with a plate of food that looked as though it had been prepared by a renowned chef.

"Sit down, Junior. They're bringing another plate for you."

They sat and ate their late lunch, a local Cauca dish, "Aborrajado" (a plantain filled with cheese and guava, deep-fried to create a flavor contrast of both sweet and salty). Accompanying it was a typical Colombian "Arepa" (fried dough, filled with egg and corn) and a bowl of "Mondongo" (well-seasoned soup containing soft pork and a variety of vegetables). They didn't speak for at least half an hour while eating. The Colombian sat there, studying Junior. It was unnerving to Junior, typically the life of the party, rarely short on words.

"That right there… it's called 'Aborrajado' and people come from all over the world to that city you flew into, Cali. They come just to try that dish," Comandante Pablo said, proudly.

"It's delicious, Comandante," Junior said, his mouth still full.

"My men will escort you to one of our labs so you can see our capacity. Then, you can return and have dinner with me. If you'd like femail companionship, that can be arranged my friend. We just got a new batch of talent flown in from the capital. After all, this is the first time I've had to welcome you to my country properly." There was a pause as they looked at one another. "Junior, I want to double up on our shipments. La Mona says you can handle it. I hope he's right."

Junior swallowed hard, trying to wrap his head around the quantities being discussed — loads of ten tons or more! He suddenly thought of Beto back at the airstrip. "Comandante, would it be possible for my associate to be brought to the camp to wait for me here as opposed to the airstrip?" Junior knew Beto wasn't happy taking a backseat.

"Hmm, about your friend… I'm not sure why you invited him. You're the only Mexican I trust. Not sure if La Mona made that clear, but I don't like Mexicans. You can't trust them, sorry if it offends you. Junior, you are an exception, now my business partner. I don't care to know your friend."

"Understood, Comandante." Junior stood up, smiled, and excused himself as he exited the tent. Three gunmen escorted him as they made their way back to the river's edge. Boarding the speedboat, Junior realized Beto was going to be furious about being left behind. Junior wasn't about to argue with one of AUC's most powerful and ruthless leaders, however.

Two hours later, Junior could see the sun setting atop the canopy's foliage. He closed his eyes, taking in the pungent odors emanating from the decaying vegetation, while listening to the singing of birds and deep-throated howler monkeys. Soon, they arrived at another sandy clearing along the winding river. His escorts secured the boat and handed Junior off to two other gunmen who accompanied Junior for a pre-arranged tour of the facility. It was the first time he had ever laid eyes on a clandestine cocaine lab, hidden deep in the jungle. He couldn't believe his eyes. It was a sophisticated complex comprising numerous buildings, two of which were large, covered patios with drying tables. As Junior walked through the complex, he observed stacks of freshly wrapped cocaine bricks bearing various markings – used to identify both source and client. There were massive, commercial-sized ovens at one end of the covered patio. There must have been two to three hundred kilos stacked and ready to go. He was taken to another makeshift warehouse containing an assortment of 200-liter barrels (labeled with German markings), each with precursors and essential chemicals used in the refining process.

Junior learned from La Mona that cocaine hydrochloride was produced from cocaine base, which, as the coke lab's foreman explained, was being flown in from Peru. Junior knew that it took approximately 500 kilos of fresh coca leaves to create one kilo of base, with the ratio from base to hydrochloride being approximately one to one. Junior was offered a sample of the finished product, which he declined, recalling his father's adamant policy: "Coke is for sale... not for consumption. Let the Americans poison themselves!"

Junior's field trip was suddenly halted when he was told that a small patrol of FARC soldiers had been seen nearby. Junior was hurried to the river's embankment to get on the speedboat. The guards had portable radios and stayed in constant contact with their commander, Comandante Pablo. The armed escorts carried Russian-made AK-47s (Kalashnikovs) and US military M-16s, along with both smoke and thermite grenades, all obtained on the black market.

Within minutes of heading back upriver to rejoin Comandante Pablo, the boat came under attack from FARC rebels hidden along the riverbank. One of Pablo's men began to scan the jungle in the direction from which the greenish colored tracers were flying and took a round to the head, knocking him overboard, with a spattering of blood hitting Junior's face. The boat driver took evasive action by wheeling the small vessel around and headed downriver towards the lab, knowing there was an armed cavalry standing by to provide cover fire. Meanwhile, Comandante Pablo's remaining gunman quickly unloaded blindly towards the riverbank, in the snipers' direction, emptying his magazine, hoping to silence the enemy's gunfire, which it did. The speedboat took several hits as it turned and got up to full speed, but miraculously, nobody else was injured during the narrow escape. Junior hadn't even noticed the blood stains and brain matter on his face and clothing while fixated on the greenish tracer rounds whizzing past as they darted out from the thick foliage. The boat sped past the lab's location and continued for another hour. The remaining gunman in the boat radioed ahead and coordinated a helicopter extraction at a pre-designated clearing in the jungle. Junior's heart was pumping so hard it felt like it was about to explode. Although Junior couldn't distinguish between the cracking sounds of the M-16s and the popping sounds of the AK-47s, Junior's boat crewmen were aware their camouflaged adversaries had both in their arsenal. The deadly exchange of gunfire was over in a matter of seconds.

Forty-five minutes later, they reached the extraction point. Before the boat was even secured, Junior was ordered to jump ashore and sprint towards the awaiting the H-1

(Huey) helicopter, also acquired on the black market. The boat sped off and headed back to the lab to safeguard whatever finished kilos remained at the lab site. FARC soldiers were way too close for comfort.

After a short flight, Junior arrived and rejoined his compadre at the remote airstrip. No time for conversation, the visiting Mexicans were asked to board the Cessna 210 and were promptly flown back to Cali, where they boarded the private jet headed for the capital city, Bogota. Junior and Beto spent a night in their hotel room in Bogota, where they were directed to stay pending their return flight the next day.

That night, before their return to Mexico, Beto verbally attacked Junior, complaining about being left back at the remote airstrip without so much as a taco. Beto hadn't even noticed or remarked on Junior's blood-spattered attire, nor the small pieces of brain matter stuck to his clothes. Once Beto aired his complaints, Junior detailed his traumatic ordeal, leaving Beto quiet for the remainder of the evening. During their return flight to Mexico, however, it was as if Junior's brush with death hadn't occurred. Beto tore into his compadre, Junior, and resumed his interrogation regarding the business matters discussed with the AUC leader.

CHAPTER 5
GUADALAJARA, JALISCO 2001

I was the youngest son of a Costa Rican-born commercial fisherman. By his late twenties, my father immigrated to the US and became a naturalized citizen. My father and my British Canadian mother raised me and my older brother, Carlos, in San Diego, California. Both parents were uneducated, but they were passionate patriots who encouraged us to pursue careers in government service. Seeking an adventurous life, I began with a brief stint in the military, followed by a career in federal law enforcement, starting with the Naval Criminal Investigative Service (NCIS) and later with the Drug Enforcement Administration.

Graduating from Quantico, Virginia, in April 1986, I was sent to Calexico, a small border town in California located in Imperial County. The Calexico Resident Office was a short drive from Baja California's capital, Mexicali. It was during that first assignment that I developed a fascination with Mexico. It was shortly after the horrific abduction and torturous murder of Guadalajara-based DEA Special Agent Enrique Camarena in February 1985. I was mystified by how little the Mexican government seemed interested in solving the murder and bringing those responsible to justice. It didn't take long to realize that some of Mexico's high-level government officials were involved. Early on, I decided I wanted to have the opportunity to work at the DEA's Guadalajara office so I could do my part in keeping Camarena's legacy alive. I wanted a significant role in our war on drugs.

That opportunity came in 2001 when I received a promotion and became the Resident Agent in Charge (RAC) at the Guadalajara office. I transferred from another foreign office in San Jose, Costa Rica. I transitioned from working in an embassy, where I wore a suit and tie, to a more relaxed environment at the consulate assignment, where everyday attire included a Guayabera and slacks. I managed a group of four Special Agents and one Intelligence Analyst. The transition from Costa Rica to Mexico was an adjustment, reminiscent of my days in Mexicali. Costa Rican cops were like dealing with US law enforcement – trustworthy and transparent – while working in Mexico was akin to playing poker with adversaries, where the consequences were potentially lethal. US agents in Mexico were always on guard, with Camarena's tragedy fresh in every agent's mind.

Although Guadalajara is the second most populous city in Mexico, it feels more like the countryside. There are no skyscrapers or dirty industries. It resembles Mexico's "Silicon Valley," with new high-tech companies like NEC, Motorola, Intel, Sony, and Hewlett-Packard, among others. The city sits at an elevation similar to that of Denver, Colorado. The air is fresh and clean, often carrying a pine-scented breeze. It has a temperate, Mediterranean climate and reminds me of San Diego.

Most travelers visiting Mexico would describe Jalisco's capital as the "most Mexican of Mexico's cities." Besides its beauty, the city is known for its amazing aromas of some of the best Mexican cuisine in the country. The smell of warm, fresh, handmade corn tortillas drifts everywhere, whether in the city center or out in the countryside. The region is also famous as the birthplace of Mariachi music and for its many popular varieties of Tequila made from agave plants native to Jalisco.

Guadalajara's attractions have drawn not only tourists and retired Americans but also Mexico's most powerful drug traffickers. The Guadalajara Cartel, founded by natives of Sinaloa, was established in the late 1970s after a mass migration of Sinaloa-based traffickers left mountainous strongholds with suitcases full of US dollars. They aimed to invest and hide their ill-gotten gains from drug sales. They formed their powerful cartel and expanded their criminal empire. The sudden arrival of gun-toting, gold-adorned outlaws disturbed the traditional, conservative residents of Guadalajara, a city known as the country's Catholic headquarters.

The influx of Sinaloa traffickers sparked what felt like an overnight economic boom, with massive cash investments in luxury homes, hotels, dealerships, shopping malls, restaurants, nightclubs, and banks. Although initially resistant, Guadalajara's traditionalists gradually accepted the newcomers and the economic growth they brought without questioning their suspicious income source. Today, Guadalajara stands as one of Mexico's leading centers for money laundering.

Guadalajara is also geographically advantageous for traffickers as it serves as a central hub for commerce, with routes leading in all directions, including cities bordering US ports of entry such as Tijuana, Juarez, and Nuevo Laredo. The timing was perfect for Junior, given the cocaine boom of the 1980s and 1990s. He was in the right place, with the right people, at the right time.

DEA acknowledged Guadalajara as a target-rich environment. Equating it to Safari's big-game hunting, it was frequently referred to as "Elephant Country." The elephants were more like lions, however, and were just as lethal. They were everywhere, even living amongst us and our families, sharing upscale gated neighborhoods like Puerta de Hierro and Valle Real. Of course, their children attended the best schools so they would have a leg up on getting acceptance letters to America's universities. One of those "best schools" happened to be the American Cooperative School, where we sent our kids.

Early into the assignment, we learned the top gangster in charge of the "Guadalajara Plaza" was Nacho Coronel. A "plaza" is a term used by both law enforcement and criminals to refer to a geographic area of control, typically a town and its surrounding region. Guadalajara's Plaza encompasses the metropolitan area of Guadalajara and its three adjacent cities: Zapopan, Tonala, and Tlaquepaque. Nacho also controlled the neighboring States of Zacatecas, Aguascalientes, Guanajuato, Colima, and Nayarit. More importantly, he had exclusive access to the busiest seaport on Mexico's Pacific Coast: Manzanillo, Colima. Nacho was Guadalajara's Federation representative. Federated allies were permitted to use the plaza with Nacho's blessing, but only after paying a tax which the Mexicans called "piso" (tribute). The Gueros were considered Nacho's subordinate partners and shared the plaza without paying a requisite tax.

The "Gueros" evolved into a significant threat without calling attention to themselves. They escaped DEA's radar. Although much was known about Nacho Coronel, little was known about the Gueros brothers. Nacho was one of several Sinaloa leaders who inherited the remnants of the Guadalajara Cartel's infrastructure. Guadalajara's predecessor kingpin, Miguel Angel Felix Gallardo, intended for his emerging lieutenants to grow the cartel's empire by having the underbosses control the country's most essential plazas – particularly those which fed key corridors for drugs smuggled north. Felix Gallardo sought to control the consortium and pool resources which could then be utilized to leverage power over the Mexican government. Felix Gallardo's 1989 arrest marked the dismantlement of the Guadalajara Cartel. The remnant leaders of the organization continued to thrive and ultimately became known as the "Sinaloa Federation." The term "Alliance" was also used interchangeably by DEA agents when referring to the Federation.

Mexico's drug trafficking syndicates were virtually impenetrable. We were in desperate need of informants who could gain direct access to the kingpins to collect basic intelligence. Our attempts to penetrate these allied, capo-led organizations were met with frustration, with efforts dismissed as futile. Finding an informant who was both willing and capable of meeting face-to-face with drug barons like Nacho was virtually impossible. To many potential informants, compromise equated a death sentence. The real question was how to find someone who could even get close to one of these powerful men. Drug lords at that level were generally surrounded by relatives and close friends – fellow drug traffickers – who were entrusted with the family business. The little information we had from reliable police sources was that Nacho, Los Gueros, and another cartel leader, Armando Valencia (leader of the Millennium Cartel) were working together using the Guadalajara Plaza as an operational base to coordinate large-scale smuggling ventures.

I assigned one of the new agents, SA Jimmy Martinez, to investigate both Gueros and Valencia. Although we had limited information at the time, I believed that something would eventually fall into place and help us realize progress. Jimmy transferred from Phoenix, Arizona, about a month after I arrived. He was awarded his first choice of offices in Mexico for his efforts leading to the capture of Augustin Vasquez Mendoza, the mastermind behind the murder of Phoenix-based DEA SA Richard Fass. On June 30, 1994, SA Fass went to a mechanic shop in Glendale, AZ, to meet undercover with three members of Vasquez's crew to purchase methamphetamine they had previously negotiated. Fass, along with two informants, met with Vasquez to complete the deal. Unbeknownst to them, Vasquez led a rip-off crew intending to steal the money Fass was expected to bring. Early in the meeting, Fass realized it was a trap and reached for his ankle-holstered weapon when he was tragically shot and killed. One of the informants was seriously injured, while his brother, also an informant, miraculously escaped unscathed because the shooter's handgun jammed. The DEA launched a priority manhunt for Vasquez, assigning Jimmy and others to work on the case full-time. Vasquez was eventually captured in Mexico and sentenced to seventy-one years in prison. Jimmy received his first choice of available offices and was sent to Guadalajara.

Jimmy began his law enforcement career with the US Marshal's Service in 1990 and joined the DEA the following year. He grew up in Riverside County, CA, and was raised in Parker, AZ, a small farming town situated along the Colorado River. His father had farmed the land for over 35 years after leaving Sonora, Mexico, at a young age. Jimmy inherited his dad's work ethic and earned a reputation as a tenacious investigator. Being a small office, we didn't have the luxury of ample manpower. Although I was a supervisor, I couldn't just sit in the office and sign reports all day, so I paired up with Jimmy and went to work on finding our window of opportunity to infiltrate the Gueros brothers. Other than us being sons of immigrants, we had much in common, especially our perceived roles while working in Mexico.

One morning, shortly after arriving at the office, something finally fell from the sky and gave us the break we needed.

"Yes, Chavarria speaking..."

"This is your boss, Mike. Don't you know you're supposed to pick up on the first ring when I call?" he joked.

"I'm sorry, Rick, I thought you wanted all your crime fighters out on the street!"

"Is that what you are now... a crime fighter?" He paused with a chuckle and said, "Okay, crime fighter, grab a pen and paper and write a number down. It's an agent up in Miami by the name of Mark Chapman (*). He has a Colombian in custody. The guy is hooked into some heavy players here and in Colombia. He has already mentioned two of your main targets, "Nacho and the Gueros."

"Holy shit! You're kidding! I guess things are starting to turn around for us, after all," I said, ecstatic at the news. I called Jimmy into my office so that he could join the call.

"Special Agent Chapman, please..."

"Yes, speaking."

"I'm Chavarria, the RAC here in Guadalajara. My boss in Mexico City passed me your info so we could discuss your cooperator."

"Oh, thanks for calling. I had our analyst contact Mexico City to find the best office for discussing your local targets. This guy isn't officially on board yet, but he's mentioning some interesting players in your area and from his own country, which interests us here in Miami." We spoke on a secure line, making it easier to discuss the players of interest. We were using our "STU" (a secure telephone line), which the NSA created to facilitate secure US government communications. Although it looked like a regular phone, it had a special ability, using an internal modem, to encrypt transmissions for each party, requiring both parties to be using the STU.

"Can you or an agent from your office attend an in-depth debriefing of this guy here in Miami? We have a lot of interest from the intelligence unit at headquarters. They are sending some analysts, along with a 959 agent, to assess this individual's information. But, since they're talking Nacho and the Gueros, you guys are in the best position to weigh in on his overall value as a cooperator."

"When?"

"As quickly as you guys can get up here."

"No problem, Jimmy Martinez will head up tomorrow."

"Hi Mark, this is Jimmy. Yes, I'll send my travel information your way once I confirm reservations. Please provide me with a nice hotel close to the office."

"Can we get just a little background on how you got this guy?" I asked.

"Sure, we scooped him as part of a wire we're working with the New York office. They've been targeting a distribution network tied to the Mellizos, and we discovered that money was arriving in Miami. The New York guys seized a couple hundred kilos at their end, and they asked us to take off the money."

"So how did your defendant get wrapped up?" I asked.

"New York got him on the phone, and we knew he'd be on a particular flight, so we pulled surveillance and followed him to his hotel."

"Did you guys catch him with the money?" Jimmy asked.

"No, it worked out perfectly. He was nowhere near the money when it was seized, so there was no way he could have been burnt. But he believes we tied him to the two hundred kilos. He still doesn't know about our wiretaps. Our long-term case still has legs." Chapman sounded eager and cooperative.

"Ah, nice. So, he's still cool if he wants to cooperate," Jimmy commented.

"He says he does… we'll see. That's why we want you guys up here." Chapman thanked us and the call ended.

CHAPTER 6
MIAMI, FLORIDA 2003

Jimmy arrived in Miami the next morning and looked for the two case agents, Mark Chapman (*) and Dave Williams (*). Jimmy's presence was crucial for the US Attorney's decision to let the DEA use the Colombian defendant (La Mona) as an informant. He was indictable for the 200 kilograms seized in New York. Jimmy was allowed to observe La Mona's formal proffer, where the agents could evaluate the Colombian's willingness and potential as an undercover asset. Proffers are simply the official term for interview assessments and a tentative agreement between a potential cooperator and the government. A defendant cooperating with authorities would provide information in exchange for some benefit, usually a reduced sentence, and sometimes, no jail time at all. That was what the Colombian was hoping for.

The defendant's name was Jhon Jairo Aispuro (*), but the wire intercepts revealed he used the nickname, La Mona. He was arrested after being linked to two related seizures: 200 kilos of coke and a confiscation of $1,000,000 in various denominations. Jimmy knew that if La Mona were half as connected as the Miami agents suspected, he would be a challenge to flip as a cooperator. Colombians were shrewd, savvy and scheming. Within the trafficker world, Colombians were the masters of manipulation.

There was no time to waste. Jimmy needed to pull Chapman and Williams aside and privately strategize an approach before sitting down with the street-smart Colombian. Jimmy was too late, however. By the time he got to Miami's office, La Mona's proffer was underway. Jimmy was taken to the conference room to join the meeting. He dropped his suitcase outside the door and walked into the room. Eight individuals were sitting around an oblong-shaped mahogany table. They paused and acknowledged Jimmy's entrance into the room. Chapman introduced Jimmy as the agent from Guadalajara. The Colombian, seated at the head of the table, turned his head and gave Jimmy a thorough eyeballing, silently questioning his purpose for being there. Jimmy gestured a salutation and took his seat, quietly thinking, *"What the fuck is going on here?"* It looked like a circus event with the Colombian as the ringleader, addressing an audience of star-struck fans. Jimmy was sure the Colombian had total command of the room. Everyone had a notepad out, jotting down every word coming out of the lying motherfucker's mouth. Jimmy sat there and watched the spectacle unfold.

His legs crossed, his hands resting on his lap, La Mona was completely relaxed and confident. His mannerisms were effeminate. He was tall, light-skinned, clean-shaven, immaculately dressed, and manicured from his eyebrows to his fingernails. He was dressed in a white, short-sleeved, button-down silk shirt, dark slacks, and wore shiny brown Oxfords. Normally, he would have worn an orange jumpsuit; however, he was never processed into the system as a defendant. The US Attorney's office authorized his house arrest while being evaluated as an informant for the government. Although La Mona was facing charges, he was kept out of jail to avoid the possibility of compromising the case. Colombian cartel attorneys were always on alert for cartel members being arrested and processed in the system, as it flagged them as potential government informers.

Jimmy sat quietly, watching the Colombian gracefully tap-dance his way around the room, rolling from one vague answer to another, giving the crowd just enough information (mostly about Colombian cartel history) to keep them in awe. Besides Chapman and Williams, there were two agents and two analysts from headquarters, as well as another analyst from Miami, assigned to work with the Miami agents. Also present were the attorneys – the Colombian's federal defender and an Assistant US Attorney (AUSA). Jimmy noticed that between comments, the Colombian would glance over at him. His eyes noticeably darted around the room, avoiding direct eye contact with Jimmy's. Other nervous tics included his incessant floor tapping with his right foot and a constant licking of his dry lips. He became increasingly unnerved by Jimmy's expressionless glare. La Mona's speech turned nervously choppy, and he began to repeat himself.

Jimmy spent three years as a DEA polygrapher, sharpening his interview skills. His lie-detecting instincts caught the defendant's nervous, deceptive body language. It was so apparent that even the others in the room noticed it. They also looked at Jimmy, waiting for him to ask a question, but he remained quiet.

The line of questioning shifted to specific drug trafficking cartel leaders and their respective methodologies. La Mona spoke in generalities and utilized traffickers' nicknames except in cases where the targets were either in jail or dead, like Pablo Escobar, who was silenced in December 1993 as he raced to evade capture.

"Jimmy, don't you wanna ask any questions regarding targets in Mexico?" Williams asked.

"No, I'm fine for now. I think I'll listen to his stories for a while." The quizzical expressions from those in the room were priceless. Although still in control of the room, La Mona's poise and confidence began to waver, his face grimacing.

"Is there something wrong, Agent Martinez?" asked La Mona's defense attorney.

"Yes, sir." By now, everyone's eyes were on Jimmy.

"Well, would you like to share?" The lawyer asked.

"Maybe at the break," Jimmy responded.

Chapman, the senior partner, said, "I think it's a good time for a break. Let's all take fifteen minutes."

Once out of the room, Williams looked at Jimmy and asked, "So what's going on, Jimmy? I thought you'd be all over this guy."

"He's got control of the room. You can't see that?" Williams looked surprised. Most of the others were walking to the restroom or the snack bar. Chapman was standing a few feet away, talking to the AUSA. The Colombian and his defense attorney stayed in the conference room.

Chapman broke away from the AUSA and joined his partner, Williams. "Hey Jimmy, so how's Guadalajara?"

"It's good, I like it... a nice change of pace from working domestic cases," Jimmy said. He then asked, "So whose idea was it to fill the room with so many people? They're all sitting there taking notes as if everything this fucker says is the gospel. He's not even committed to the team yet, and we're turning him into a goddamn Rockstar," Jimmy said. The Miami agents looked a bit stunned by his comments. Williams turned a shade of red, likely due to a combination of embarrassment, frustration, and irritation. Chapman nodded as if to acknowledge Jimmy's observations.

"Yeah," Chapman admitted, "there are a lot of folks in the room. The problem is that the out-of-towners are on a tight schedule, wanting to get as much done as possible before heading back to D.C."

"I get it," Jimmy replied, cutting the tension a bit.

"What would you suggest?" the younger Miami agent asked.

"Ideally, the fewer the better. Let's let everyone else fill their notepads with all the cartel history bullshit, and let them take off," Jimmy suggested, adding, "Then we can hit this asshole with the actionable stuff. You guys said he mentioned several traffickers in our area. I wanna know about that and where he fits."

"Yeah," Chapman responded. "We have no idea who's who down there... some guys named Nacho, Mayo, Guero. That's your stuff. We know he's super connected with 'Los Mellizos,' 'Don Berna,' and 'Diego Montoya.' He appears well-connected in Colombia and Mexico."

"Okay," Jimmy said, "let's push him to shit or get off the pot, then."

"Our bosses want this guy to get us a nice seizure," Williams explained. "We need to ask him about that." Reacting to the pressure coming down from Miami's bosses, Williams was more interested in putting dope on the table than looking at long-term prospects. It was a common theme throughout the agency – the unspoken reality regarding the "stat game." And young agents loved any opportunity to get a trophy shot standing next to a stack of cocaine or seized cash. Some hard-hitting agents were driven by action and quick results to please their stat-driven bosses.

"Oh yeah? Well, tell your bosses that if this guy is who we think he is... then the snitch can probably serve up 1,000 kilos and not even blink. If we use him to grab another 200 ki's, we'll be wasting our time and pissing away his value."

"Okay, Jimmy. Our AUSA is cool. He'll fight for us if we tell him we've got a serious opportunity here," Chapman explained, reassuringly.

"You guys need to consider shopping this all to NDDS up in D.C. They'll back a long-term case," Jimmy suggested.

The Miami AUSA walked up and introduced himself, asking, "Are we ready to go back in?" Chapman explained the concerns and related the new tactic of waiting for the D.C.-based agents and analysts to finish their line of questioning and then leave. "Sounds fine by me. Better yet, I have complete faith in Chapman and Williams to assess this individual. I have an appointment in an hour. I'll go with whatever you guys want, and I'll tell the defense attorney that if this guy jacks us around, he's going to the can." Chapman, Williams, and Jimmy nodded their heads in agreement, shook hands, and bid the AUSA farewell.

The meeting reconvened shortly afterward. The Colombian seemed a bit more relaxed and prepared for Jimmy's questions. As planned, the D.C. crew finished their questioning and departed the office, seemingly content with their information.

Jimmy and the Miami agents re-entered the room. Jimmy sat quietly for a couple of minutes, skimming over DEA's Form 202, looking at the defendant's bio. "So, what's up with the nickname, 'La Mona'"? Jimmy asked, catching the Colombian by surprise. The Colombian raised his eyebrow and explained it was his country's descriptive nickname for someone light-skinned, comparing it to Mexico's use of "Guero."

Jimmy looked back at the Colombian and said, "Hmm, 'Guero.' Now that's a name I'm curious about." La Mona glared back at Jimmy. "Now, let's talk a little about Mexico, 'La Mona.'" La Mona smiled, finally realizing the purpose of Jimmy's visit. "Now tell me about your role in Mexico," Jimmy said.

La Mona, after taking a noticeable breath, said, "My job is to represent sources of supply like the Mellizos, Don Berna, and Diego Montoya. I am their spokesperson in Mexico."

"What exactly does that entail?" The Colombian licked his drying lips, sensing Jimmy's impatience.

"You mean in Colombia or Mexico?"

"Well, I'm from Guadalajara. Let's pretend I'm interested in what's going on in Mexico."

"I'm a middleman... I essentially serve as a liaison between Colombian sources and Mexican investors. I help *broker* the loads."

"What was the last load you helped broker?"

"The 200 kilograms which these people already know about," he answered, motioning to the Miami agents. "It was part of a bigger load that arrived in Mexico from Buenaventura, Colombia."

"How big was the load, and who was it going to in Mexico?"

"It was a couple thousand kilos, and it belonged to Nacho. He runs things in Guadalajara. As Agents Chapman and Williams may have already told you, some of the load made its way up to New York and was seized. I was responsible for bringing the money back to Mexico."

"Through Miami?"

"Since most of the coke is moving through California, Arizona, and Texas, with bulk cash coming south through the same corridors, Miami doesn't draw too much attention. Besides, Nacho and his associates have their contacts at the airports in Mexico."

"Does Guero work with or for Nacho?"

"He works with Nacho... he's pretty big now."

"Okay, you had mentioned another load of a thousand kilos to Agents Chapman and Williams. You told them that it went to Mexico, if not mistaken, to Nacho and Mayo, correct? I want the details. Give me their full names. Jimmy sat up in his chair, tiring of the game he perceived being played.

"Nobody uses full names in this business," the Colombian replied. He crossed his arms in a defensive posture and began to test Jimmy's patience.

"Okay," Jimmy paused. "Tell me exactly what you did and give me names of the people you met with, and also your associates in Mexico who helped out."

"I'm just a go-between... you know... I pass messages," he replied, poker-faced.

Jimmy stood up and explained that he didn't have time to waste with a Colombian who was connected enough to represent sources like the "Mellizos" and "Don Berna," but lacked the details a man in his position should clearly have. *"Fuck this… I'm done."* He walked out of the room, pursued by the Miami agents and the attorney. Jimmy played the odds that it would trigger the Colombian to be more forthcoming. La Mona needed DEA more than the other way around.

"Agent Martinez…, my client is very nervous."

"That's BS," Jimmy responded. "He's playing the minimization game here. He'll give us as much as we can pull out of him. I don't have the time or the energy to play his fucking game." The Miami agents stood quietly, deferring to Jimmy.

"Okay, give me a few minutes with my client," he said as he walked back into the conference room.

"Hmm, my client is nervous…," Jimmy sarcastically muttered under his breath. "La Mona is one clever asshole," he said once the defense attorney stepped away to rejoin his client.

Two minutes later, the defense attorney walked back out of the room. "Okay, he's ready."

As they re-entered the room and sat down, La Mona said, "Okay, Nacho Coronel and Mayo Zambada are the big players on the Sinaloa side. They split most of their large coke loads coming into seaports in containers. Or they bring even larger loads onboard tuna or shark boats. There are others like El Azul, Arturo Beltran, and the Valencias. I can get to most of them."

"Okay, what about the Gueros?" Jimmy asked.

"I just know them as the Gueros brothers. There are four or five siblings, but I deal with the two main brothers, 'Guero' and 'Pelos.' 'Guero' is in charge, though."

"Where are they based?"

"Guadalajara," La Mona replied.

"Do you meet directly with any of them?"

"Yes, I've met with them." He paused, "I can still meet with them and others, if you want, all except El Azul and the Beltran brothers. The Beltran brothers are having problems with their cousin right now."

"Who's that?" Jimmy asked.

"Chapo Guzman… Arturo Beltran took over Chapo's business while Chapo was in prison. Something happened once Chapo got out of jail. It might be the Beltran brothers are getting stronger and have more connections with the government," La Mona mused. "But I don't know for sure." La Mona continued to provide Jimmy with information regarding Nacho and the Gueros brothers, enough so that Jimmy felt more confident about La Mona's cooperative prospects.

La Mona's attorney asked, "Are you guys satisfied?" He sat back in his chair, looking smug and proud of himself. He was about 6'0' tall, roughly 250 pounds, with flab hanging over his belt. He sat there in his chair, hands clasped, resting on his protruding stomach, fingers tapping in a contented rhythm. Being a court-appointed defense attorney, he didn't have the narco dollars his dope attorney peers had. They would wear $2,000 suits while he shopped at JCPenney for his ill-fitting, discounted, two-piece outfits.

"Well, if he does what he says he can do…, yes," Jimmy said, looking around the table and noticing a look of tempered euphoria on Williams's and Chapman's faces. This guy, if managed correctly, could make an agent's career, Jimmy thought to himself. After the meeting, La Mona was taken to a safe house where he was placed under twenty-four-hour surveillance. Jimmy followed Williams and Chapman back to their group and used the office phone to call me with the update.

"Mike, in my opinion, this is our guy for the Gueros case. It's worth the risk to get him down to Mexico," Jimmy said.

"We need to get with Miami and start the process of getting our friend to Mexico. It sounds like it'll take at least a few months to get the committee to review and approve it as a sensitive operation," I said. "Great job, Jimmy!" It was the break we were waiting for.

Jimmy stayed an extra day to hang out with Williams and Chapman, mulling over some ideas for tasking the Colombian while in Mexico. Everyone agreed his potential for laying "golden eggs" was limitless.

The formal process took months before La Mona was cleared to come down to Mexico at the DEA's request. He didn't set foot in the country until the fall of 2003. By that time, the DEA headquarters committee on sensitive undercover activities had already approved his role as part of a larger operation. La Mona's undercover activities in Mexico had to be approved at various levels and entailed some finessing with Mexican authorities.

Mexico's Attorney General's office had to approve the use of a source before any operational activities could proceed. Sources were considered operatives and thus required the approval of the "Sub-Procurador" (Deputy Attorney General). Mexico's Deputy AG was Luis Santiago Vasconcelos, the official responsible for the government's Specialized Organized Crime Unit, a prosecutorial division of the PGR. His reputation with the DEA and other US federal agencies working in Mexico was stellar. Obtaining such approval in Mexico was typically like walking on rice paper, however. Mexico was very cautious in monitoring the DEA's activities in the country, especially after the Camarena tragedy. The investigation into Camarena revealed Mexico's complex network of narco-political ties. Additionally, Mexico has always maintained a strong stance on sovereignty when dealing with its northern neighbors.

Thankfully for the DEA, the timing was perfect. Deputy AG Vasconcelos was riding high on our country's shared successes in the fight against drug trafficking. Both nations were closely collaborating in their relentless pursuit of the Gulf Cartel leader, Osiel Cardenas Guillen, who had threatened two US agents in Matamoros in 1999. Osiel and his Zetas faction brought so much unwanted attention to Mexico that it began hurting international trade and tourism in the Gulf region.

When we presented our operational plan (with La Mona), Deputy AG Vasconcelos wanted to know who our targets would be. Our response: "The same priority targets we are currently working on." He was fine with that reply and gave us the green light we needed. Except for the Gueros, the Mexican counterparts were aware of all our targets of interest.

When La Mona finally arrived in Mexico, he was subjected to another intensive questioning session. He was reminded of his directive – to provide operational intelligence on Nacho, the Gueros, and any other significant member of the Sinaloa Federation. We instructed him to acquire addresses, telephone numbers, businesses, and the names of key associates working for the Federation. We needed details on well-documented seizures so that we could build historical conspiracy cases. His marching orders were clear.

Being the crafty Colombian, we knew he needed to be reined in and kept on a short leash. We needed to hold him accountable for his assigned taskings. We brought him to Mexico in 2003 and set him loose. We were confident we had sufficient leverage over him as he knew he was not only working for himself but for his brother, as well, in prison, serving time on a separate drug case. La Mona knew his efforts would benefit both him and his brother.

We had him check in with us once a week for in-person debriefings. He was equipped with undercover recording devices but was hesitant to use them, saying it would put him in too much danger and could potentially compromise the DEA's operation. We didn't press him because we were genuinely concerned about his safety. He spent several months traveling around Mexico, meeting with various persons of interest, including the Gueros brothers, but was unsuccessful in his efforts to obtain their full names. We only managed to capture their photographs during a couple of his UC meetings in Guadalajara.

The arrangements we made with the Miami agents involved one or both routinely traveling to Guadalajara to participate in La Mona's debriefings. They were happy to do so since Guadalajara was such a pleasant place to visit – frequently referred to as "The Pearl of the West."

Although initially frustrated about what we were not obtaining regarding the Gueros and La Mona, our Chantilly, Virginia-based SOD Staff Coordinators, Keith Bishop and John McCabe, managed to link the Gueros brothers to documented seizures in ongoing investigations in Lima, Peru, and Los Angeles. The case in Peru was the first opportunity where we began to establish connections between the Gueros organization and other major Federated affiliates. We first linked Peruvian cocaine exports to Ismael "Mayo" Zambada. DEA Peru identified Mayo's brother-in-law, Manuel Rivera Niebla, meeting with Peru's cocaine sources. Local authorities determined he was there to arrange a large cocaine shipment to Mexico via maritime vessels. Peru's undercover investigation not only connected Rivera to Mayo but also to the Gueros. DEA Lima agents contacted us in Guadalajara and shared the phone numbers dialed during Rivera's visit.

The calling details were carefully analyzed, leading us to begin a series of surveillances in Guadalajara. We focused on businesses and residential areas in town, including a luxurious mansion on the outskirts of Guadalajara near the neighboring city, Zapopan. It was a Spanish-style home equipped with modern, sophisticated security cameras strategically placed around its perimeter. The place looked like the perfect kingpin mansion. It was grand in both size and opulence. Bishop worked the numbers to connect various US cases involving Nacho, Mayo, and other Federation allies. Our investigation gained momentum, and since the Gueros were our main target, Bishop came up with a clever operation name ("Band of Brothers"), inspired by the popular WWII mini-series airing on TV. Of course, like many of SOD's operational names, it was done tongue in cheek.

We enlisted the help of the other agents in the office to assist us in surveilling the identified suspects' residences. Jimmy and I started surveillance at the mansion where most cars were coming and going. One evening, while we were set up, we noticed unusual vehicle traffic late at night and early in the morning. Many of the vehicles were armored. We decided to follow one of the vehicles, a newer black Chevrolet Suburban with tinted windows. We tracked it into the neighboring town of Zapopan, where we had a close relationship with the Zapopan Police Chief. He approved one of his motorcycle cops to pull the Suburban over and identify the lone driver. The traffic stop happened as the Suburban was waiting to enter the gated community called "Puerta de Hierro." "Holy shit!" I thought. That's where I live. The driver was identified as Luis Rodriguez Olivera. He was described as light-skinned and could easily have been mistaken for a gringo. Surprisingly and thankfully for us, the motorcycle cop had no idea he had pulled over a key member of the Sinaloa Federation.

It was the gift we had been waiting for. The name Rodriguez Olivera was then run through all of DEA's databases, and voila... Luis Rodriguez Olivera, aka "El Guero," appeared in a case from Los Angeles, California, connected to a separate cocaine seizure. There was also a drug-related homicide linked to the Gueros brothers; however, there was not enough evidence to charge anyone in either the drug case or the related homicide.

"Fuckin A!" Jimmy quipped excitedly, adding, "Mike, Guero is your fucking neighbor!"

We spent time searching various other databases, checking both the paternal name "Rodriguez" and the maternal name "Olivera" to see if they were connected to other investigations, and indeed they were! Christmas came early. There were references to criminal associates with first names: Luis, Esteban, Daniel, and Miguel, all sharing variations of the last names "Rodriguez Olivera" and "Olivera Rodriguez." In a case from Los Angeles, it was revealed that three individuals listed as brothers—Luis, Esteban, and Miguel—were all born in Tecalitlán, Jalisco, Mexico. The phone numbers in those cases were combined with numbers from Peru and forwarded to Bishop at SOD. Within 24 hours, Bishop called the Guadalajara office with incredible news: "Several numbers are linking to other cases in Los Angeles, CA, and New York City." They connected to another major DEA operation called "Trifecta," managed by SOD Agent, John McCabe, targeting Mayo Zambada and his top lieutenants. Now, the DEA had established strong ties between the Gueros brothers and other leaders of the Sinaloa Federation. Things were finally starting to click for us. Bishop, for his efforts at SOD, was rewarded with his choice of domestic offices. He chose the highly sought-after Houston Division office and reported there in late 2003.

Despite our frustration with what we considered La Mona's half-hearted efforts, we were riding high, having fully identified the once-mysterious Gueros brothers. Jimmy and I wondered if La Mona was taking his sweet time in delivering the evidence we had requested from him. Of anyone, La Mona should have already collected dozens of evidentiary recordings. We wondered if he might be back in the game using us as his "stay-out-of-jail-card." We had no proof of it, but we wanted to discuss it with our Miami colleagues. We had reason for concern and wondered if we should send him back to Miami to let him serve some time. Miami's response was immediate and definitive: "Leave La Mona in Mexico… let's not rush things. Let him move at the pace he thinks is appropriate."

We knew he needed to proceed cautiously, but Jimmy and I were also aware of his nature as a lifelong criminal. We heeded their requests to give him a bit more time in Mexico while gently tugging on his leash.

About a year and a half later, it was my turn to rotate out. I left Guadalajara and joined Bishop in Houston. It was the summer of 2005 when I reported to the office, leaving Jimmy as La Mona's sole handler. La Mona managed to provide enough intelligence on other traffickers, both in Mexico and Colombia, to justify his continued presence in Mexico. Jimmy, however, on his own, found it increasingly difficult to keep track of La Mona's activities. The office was short-staffed, and Jimmy was managing multiple cases and sources. La Mona began directing more of his communications to the Miami agents.

CHAPTER 7
UN CHINGO DE PERICO

It was the day after our first meeting with Junior, on August 25, 2005. I called his hotel room at 9:30 a.m., and Junior quickly answered. We had a pretend conversation, which led Junior's wife to believe it was with an old friend. This was his signal to meet us in the lobby. He knew to follow us down the hall on the first floor to a suite we had reserved for our meetings. Although conflicted about his baby girl dealing with her life-threatening diagnosis, Junior understood he had to cleverly balance things so he could work with us without revealing anything to his wife. There was a very short window for him to show his willingness to cooperate. He needed to avoid jail at all costs. He also saw it as a life-changing opportunity. Maybe it wasn't too late for Xochilt's life-saving miracle, he thought. Junior told his wife he had to meet with one of his Houston-based contacts and would be unavailable most of the day but promised to check in with her at the hospital.

Once we made eye contact, he took the cue and followed me to a room at the end of the hallway. It was a suite large enough to accommodate all of us. The door was left slightly ajar so he could walk in. Agents were waiting, their weapons ready in case Junior had a sudden change of heart and wanted to go out in style. As he entered the room, Junior's obvious nervousness quickly assuaged the agents' concerns.

His boyish smile put everyone at ease. I began with the introductions: "Junior, you've met Mickey and Darren already. This is Mike Bostick and Trish Skidmore. This is the team you'll be working with. I call it the 'A' team," to which Junior smiled, catching Trish rolling her eyes. Everyone shook hands. As he shook Trish's hand, he said, "Wow, Miss Trish... that's a man-style handshake!" Trish, of Italian descent, stood about 5'1", with shoulder-length, reddish-auburn colored hair. Raised as an Army brat, she was recruited by the DEA while working as a civilian with the Department of the Army. Per Bishop, she was a little "Pitbull" when it came to putting a case together. Starting her career in Washington, D.C., her first assignment in 1990 was at DEA Headquarters, where she was assigned to work on the "South American Desk." Afterwards, a natural segue had her working on Mexico's growing nexus with Colombia.

Junior took an immediate liking to her, instantly disarmed by her feistiness and endearing personality. Trish's firm handshake reflected her philosophy, particularly in a male-dominated profession where men were quick to dismiss their female colleagues as the weaker sex. Trish wouldn't have any of that. She just looked at Junior with a smile and said, "Let's get started."

"Raul, there's no way around it. These first couple of days aren't gonna be fun. We are going to ask you some questions to account for every single kilo you've moved, my friend," I said. The idea was to extract all his narco history and get him started proactively. We also wanted to assess him as a potential "testifier." The exercise would leave him feeling like an exhausted Catholic parishioner after a lengthy session in the confessional. "Don't worry, Junior… you'll feel better after it's all over," I lied.

"Ohhh, God," he said, looking around at everyone. "How long will this take?"

"Depends on how many kilos, Junior," Mickey quipped stoically.

"Well, I'm starving. Haven't had breakfast yet. It's my understanding that the gringo police like their doughnuts. By chance, did you guys bring some with you?" Junior asked, smiling. He was beginning to relax.

"There's a Shipley's Donut place right around the corner," Darren offered. "I'll grab a dozen."

"Help yourself to some coffee, Junior," Trish offered, pointing to the freshly brewed pot in the kitchen. "Let's get started," she repeated, pulling out her notepad. "I'm sure you want to get back to your wife," she said.

"I may not be able to remember everything," he cautioned.

"Do your best to recall details," I urged. "We'll need to relate your cooperation to the AUSA," I emphasized. "We need to document your story, including all the kilos you sent here to the US. Don't worry, it's not a trick. We're not going to charge you with this, but we need to know, okay?" He shook his head nervously.

He sat there, with a shocked look on his face, mentally tabulating the numbers over the years, and started to massage his temples. From the look on his face, he wondered if it was all just a bad dream. But it wasn't. The bill came due, and it was now time for him to pay up and turn his life around. Junior knew he had to come clean and give us everything we wanted. His life as a drug trafficker was over.

"What happens if, after everything, your prosecutor decides I'm not worthy of being a friend of the DEA any longer?" Junior asked, holding his coffee.

"I've already spoken to our prosecutor, James Sturgis, and he has promised me he will commit to giving you 'immunity' but insisted you *must*… and I mean *must* come clean with absolutely everything you've done. I'll put him on the phone with you later today, but only after I see how much progress we've made," I explained.

"Okay," Trish said, "tell me everything…"

Junior started out by speaking admiringly of his father, as if to convince all in the room that his career choice was inevitable given his father's character and integrity. "Raul Sr. was a devoted father," Junior recalled. *Of course, my father wouldn't have intentionally steered his firstborn son down a self-destructive path,* Junior assured himself. His internal conflict was painfully obvious. It was an agonizing obstacle he had to overcome to put his life on the right course. Once he accepted its inevitability, Junior related Raul Sr.'s history with the Gulf Cartel and how he climbed through the ranks during the 1980s through the '90s.

Junior discussed his early experiences in the drug world, starting with his time escorting his father as he examined marijuana, heroin, and cocaine stored in various stash houses. Junior learned how to properly test cocaine to ensure it hadn't been intentionally diluted or tampered with. As he grew older, he delivered messages between trafficker lieutenants, counted cash, and paid off corrupt officials. He spent many hours learning the "dos and don'ts." It was a dangerous business, filled with pitfalls and booby traps around every corner—some even deadly. Mistakes and carelessness often led to ugly consequences. Junior knew that people could appear one day and vanish the next, simply because they lost a load of cocaine or money. And then there were those suspected of being "snitches," where sometimes, mere suspicion was enough to cause one's demise.

Aside from the basic ropes he learned from his mentoring father, Junior's star as a successful drug trafficker didn't rise without the help of the Colombians. He went into detail regarding his partnership with La Mona and Beto. He discussed his first taste of prison life, recounting his arrest by the Mexican military, detailing his savage beatings, and then briefly described his time behind bars. Then, to my amazement, he mentioned our Colombian informant, La Mona. I fought to control my reaction, worried my face was giving it away. He referred to meeting La Mona as a fortuitous acquaintance and spoke of La Mona's invitation to Colombia to meet some of his country's most powerful cocaine sources. I could feel myself leaning in towards him to make sure I wasn't missing a word. I thought about our good fortune in having two informants reporting on one another. It was a unique and rare opportunity for us.

"And once he introduced me to the 'Lord of the Skies,' the sky was the limit," Junior boasted. "Yeah, I met Amado Carrillo right before he died." Junior went on to describe how that one meeting opened so many doors for him in Mexico. Amado's endorsement boosted Junior's "street cred" with the leaders of the Sinaloa Federation.

"Where is La Mona now?" I asked.

"I left him with my compadre, Beto. They're probably in Guadalajara negotiating with Oscar Nava to run another load out of Panama. Either that or trying to resolve issues arising from a recent coke seizure we had organized." I was wondering if Jimmy and the Miami guys were aware of La Mona's whereabouts. I was particularly bothered by the fact that La Mona never mentioned either Junior or Beto when we initially brought him down to Mexico. "Fucking Colombian," I said under my breath.

"What?" Junior asked, hearing me mumble unintelligibly.

"Oh, nothing…, I'm interested in all you have on the Colombians you've been working with," I said. "Please continue…"

"Oscar Nava is the nephew of Armando Valencia. Nava took over his organization after Armando's arrest in 2003. Nava is a guy we can make a run at," Junior said. "Okay, if you guys want me to have success, you're going to have to leave La Mona and my partner, Beto, alone." He paused, adding, "Aside from being my partner, Beto is my compadre, my best friend. We grew up together. He can help us." He continued, "We were both born into the business." In Mexico, the term "compadre" holds different meanings. Formally, it defines the relationship between a child's father and godfather. Given its root importance in the catholic faith (predominant religion in Mexico), it implies an obligation to take care of one another's families in the event of an untimely death or incapacitation. More commonly, it is used as a term of reverence and endearment among the closest of friends. Junior's use of the word for Beto was meant purely as an endearment.

We spent the next hour discussing his compadre. Unlike Junior, Beto was raised with a proverbial silver spoon. Uncles and aunts surrounded him, all exclusive members of the "haves." His father, Salvador (*), nicknamed "Chava," was a respected MFJP Comandante with strong ties to the old-guard politicians of Mexico's PRI. While Junior brought Colombian cocaine sources to the table, Beto supplied corrupt law enforcement and intelligence officials within the government. Through his uncles' contacts, Beto also brought transporters to the partnership. Junior explained how, without Beto, he wouldn't have achieved all his success. Beto's partnership was essential to his business. Junior mentioned how his father had reservations about Beto.

"What were your father's concerns about Beto?" I asked.

"He didn't like Beto's privileged upbringing, calling him a spoiled rich kid, but mostly he had issues with him being careless and undisciplined." He paused and added, "But after many conversations, I convinced him to trust my judgment." From Junior's descriptive details about his friend, it was clear that Beto had a natural jealous streak and was competitive in everything, from sports to female attention. He couldn't stand to take a backseat to Junior.

"I'm telling you guys," Junior insisted. "You have to leave Beto alone while we work our undercover DEA thing."

"Okay, Junior. We'll do what we can to ensure he doesn't get handcuffed, but we'll need to coordinate carefully with you." The reality was that Beto would likely end up in jail after it was all said and done. At the very minimum, Beto would become another testifier.

I excused myself and left the hotel room to return to the office. I needed to sit down with Bishop and bring him up to speed on everything we had accomplished up to that point. "You're in good hands, Junior. I'll be back and bring my partner. He's a little guy, so don't stare when I introduce him to you." Junior nodded with a confused look on his face.

"Okay, Junior," Trish interrupted. "Let's get through with your history so we can get you out of here and back to your wife and child." The first debriefing was grueling as it continued into the evening. Trish was asking the questions, while Mickey, Darren, and Bostick took turns as notetakers. They also alternated between dozing off on the sofa.

Hours later, I brought Bishop back to the room with me. We knocked on the door and entered the room. Junior was now the one lying on the sofa with a cold, wet compress on his forehead. Next to his head was a glass of water and a bottle of Tylenol. Junior was quietly moaning in pain, rubbing his eyes and head. As we walked in, Trish and the others looked up, giving an exasperated expression.

"By the time Junior got to forty tons, he was completely devastated, certain he was headed to hell or prison," Darren said.

"He just wouldn't believe a narco-sinner of his magnitude could be forgiven," Mickey added with a grin. "Frankly, I find it hard to believe myself." Everyone laughed while Junior groaned. With his eyes still closed and the wet washcloth on his forehead, he could be heard repeatedly mumbling, *Un Chingo de Perico…*"

"Yes, he's covered a total of forty-seven metric tons," Trish related.

"What the hell is he saying? Bishop asked.

I approached the sofa and bent down to make out the words. I realized he was saying, "That's a fuck-load of coke." It must have shocked his conscience.

"Yeah, he kinda fell apart as we crossed the forty-ton mark," Darren said.

"Holy shit!" Bishop blurted, "Forty fucking tons?"

"Forty-seven to be exact," exclaimed Bishop's agent, Bostick.

"He's been popping Tylenol like they're Skittles," Darren commented.

Just then, Junior removed the washcloth and slowly sat up to see who else was in the room. His eyes fixated on Bishop, who stood there towering over everyone else.

"This is the little partner I told you about... and I asked you not to stare, remember? It makes him uncomfortable, Junior," which prompted a chuckle from everyone but Junior. As he slowly extended his hand to greet Bishop, a former offensive lineman with the Denver Broncos, Junior stood there, his mouth agape, staring at Bishop, standing 6'3", 260 pounds of muscle. Junior's hand quickly disappeared in the bear's paw.

Bishop let out a laugh and said, "Jesus, Junior... *forty-seven fuckin tons!*" Junior turned red and began sweating profusely, thinking the worst. "Don't worry, buddy... we're good Baptists here in Houston... all about forgiveness. And the important thing is that now you're on the good guys' team!" Bishop was naturally funny, although he rarely laughed himself.

Junior smiled and caught his breath. "Well, I am certainly warming up to the idea of being a good guy for a change," prompting another chuckle from everyone. Bishop slapped Junior on the back and welcomed him to the DEA family.

"We've pretty much covered his life story, and I believe we've accounted for all of his drug trafficking transgressions," Trish said, sitting at the dining room table, looking exhausted from it all. She sat there reviewing her notes, tapping her pen against the table. "I've got to get home to the kids now," she said.

"Junior, get some rest. Check on your family. We'll pick it up tomorrow," I said.

Before he left the room, he turned towards the group and said, "I would like to think that besides being work colleagues, we can become friends, as well. I know I must prove myself, but I assure you, I am a man of my word."

The following day, Bishop and I, together with our team, were summoned to the SAC's conference room on the sixth floor. SAC Craig wanted an update on the newly recruited informant and the direction we intended to take. I began the meeting by reviewing the history of how Junior came to DEA's attention, relating Jimmy's phone call, and the tip passed on by the Colombian informant, La Mona. I also reviewed Junior's unique access to the various cartel bosses of the allied organizations making up the Sinaloa Federation. "Junior has had face-to-face meetings with many of these kingpins," I explained, having to pinch myself to reassure it wasn't all a dream. "We finally have someone able to get inside these organizations, right up next to the cartel leaders themselves." Craig was incredulously smiling, knowing we had our hands around the tiger, on the precipice of something big.

"Is this part of an ongoing SOD Operation?" he asked.

"It's part of 'Band of Brothers,' which we started when I was still at SOD," Bishop replied.

Afterwards, Bishop discussed the origin of Band of Brothers and how he and I established the operation, based on the Gueros brothers. "Chavarria's guys discovered they were becoming as big as Nacho and the other federated assholes... completely off our radar."

"Trish, why don't you take it from here since you spent hours debriefing Junior," Bishop suggested.

Trish, having substantial experience working with cartels operating in both Colombia and Mexico, was well-versed on how things evolved from the 1980s forward. She knew the players, their respective alliances, and how they morphed and merged over the years. She began, "Guadalajara's informant La Mona is connected in Colombia. He works directly for Los Mellizos and was brought up under Escobar's Medellin regime."

"Catch me up on the Mellizos," SAC Craig instructed.

She explained, "They have been one of Colombia's biggest coke sources, their roots date back to the Cali and Medellin Cartels. They became part of the infamous right-wing, AUC paramilitary organization."

"Okay, yeah, I know about the AUC and how they got in bed with cocaine traffickers to fund their political agenda," the SAC replied.

"Yes, and as of late, they've worked under the umbrella of the North Valley Cartel and are heavily sourcing Mexico right now. Junior and La Mona, by virtue of their connections, are tied to major players in both Colombia and Mexico," she added excitedly.

"We are golden," I said. "Two informants infiltrated at the highest levels in both Colombia and Mexico... we can wreak some serious havoc if we can effectively direct both these cooperators."

"Jesus," the SAC said, nodding with enthusiasm as he stuffed chewing tobacco between his lower lip and gums.

SAC Craig asked, "How did we recruit La Mona?"

I explained, "He was picked up on a 200-kilo seizure there in Miami. He's been working off a beef in exchange for sentencing consideration for himself as well as his brother, who has been serving a sentence in an unrelated case." I added how La Mona was brought to Mexico in late 2003 to infiltrate the Sinaloa leaders, specifically Nacho and the Gueros.

"Where are you guys with La Mona on evidence collection, like recordings?"

"It's been a slow process with him. Part of the issue is that both the Miami and Guadalajara offices are directing him. We think he's been taking advantage of us a bit," I explained. "Jimmy Martinez is now the agent handling him from Guadalajara, while two other agents also oversee his activities from Miami. We believe he's fully capable of doing the job we've tasked him with, but he appears to be dragging his feet."

"Well, he turned you guys on to Junior, right?"

"Yessir, he did," I replied.

Bishop interjected, "Yes, sir, he did, but Pinche doesn't believe he has a clue Junior was approached to cooperate," to which SAC Craig let out a chortle – likely from Bishop's use of my nickname, "Pinche."

"That's correct, sir. La Mona passed the tip on, I believe, to alleviate some of the pressure we had placed on him in Guadalajara. Jimmy has been on him to get us recordings, but it's been a challenge."

"So, now we have two snitches we can use for this operation," the SAC said.

"God Almighty, I love it," Bishop liked to say.

Trish continued to summarize Junior's trafficking history, mentioning how Junior put his name to an astounding 47 metric tons, which he personally had a hand in negotiating. The SAC let out a gasp. Still looking at her notes, she smiled and said, "As you all know I live for these 'intel kilos.' And this guy has *plenty* of them. Yes... *forty-seven metric tons*. Of those forty-seven," she added, "approximately nine tons, give or take, were seized along the way, once we started doing the math, Junior began to develop a severe migraine," which prompted another round of laughter.

"Yeah, I witnessed the guy proned out on the sofa with a washcloth on his head," Bishop recounted.

"Can we track those seizures down?" The SAC asked inquisitively, looking to establish Junior's credibility while exploring the potential for charging co-conspirators with historical conspiracies.

"We're tracking it all down so we can establish some venue," Trish explained.

Bishop added, "We're working with both the DOJ's Narcotics and Dangerous Drugs attorneys as well as our AUSAs here in Texas. AUSA Sturgis from McAllen has been on board from the beginning. Sturgis has already initiated a prosecutorial case on one of Junior's transportation associates, Jerry Cantu. He and his brother Heriberto own a trucking company, which they use to shuttle coke concealed in produce from the valley."

"According to Junior, the Cantu brothers work exclusively for the Gueros," I added.

"Okay, sounds like you guys are sitting on a lot of potential here... so what's the game plan?" The SAC was nodding his head, delighted at what he was hearing.

"Bishop and I have developed a plan to combine resources from both groups. He will assign an agent, Mike

Bostick, and I will have Mickey and Darren work from my side. Trish will support both 'Band of Brothers' and Bishop's Gulf operation, 'Dos Equis.' We will focus on two areas – domestic and international." I felt exhilarated at what we were about to embark on.

"I sense you'll be up on phones pretty quickly," the SAC said, smiling.

"Yes, sir… it's an ambitious project, but with both groups working, we can handle it," I assured.

Bishop interjected, "As you know, Boss, we're up on multiple wires on Osiel's guys, and I can only spare Bostick working with Pinche's guys, full-time. The good news is, I think both operations will share some common ground." He paused, then added, "Junior's partner has a lot of contact with Gulf traffickers, and maybe even the Zetas who monitor dope crossing the border. Junior says his partner takes care of getting Gulf and Zeta approval for coke crossing into Texas."

"Trish, are you done with his debriefings?" SAC Craig asked.

"We've still got a long way to go, sir," she said. "But, we have enough to get him started with making consensual phone calls for recording purposes. We're gonna be busy," she concluded.

"Besides Miami, what other offices are involved?"

"The McAllen case ties directly to one of Guero's main distribution cells in New York. Then, we have leads in Philadelphia, Chicago, and Los Angeles. GS Chavarria says NDDS is already looking at 959 charges on coke shipments the Gueros received from Peru," Trisha explained.

"Who is handling the Peruvian connection?" The SAC asked.

"Jimmy Martinez is working with NDDS," she replied.

"New York's case is on a Dominican cell head named Vladimir. He receives coke from Cantu on behalf of the Gueros brothers. Mickey and Darren are in contact with their agent," I said.

"Good stuff," SAC Craig said, rocking back in his chair, spitting his dip into an old coffee cup. "Get to it, then," he concluded as he slowly stood up and prepared to head back into his office. "Trish, when time permits, send me a good list of the viable targets we have currently. I'm gonna need it to ask headquarters for resources to get this thing rolling. For now, get our boy Junior to work before he changes his mind."

After the SAC left the meeting, Bishop and I asked everyone to stay to break down the division of labor before embarking on what we all knew would be a manpower-intensive operation. There was much to do in a short time, and it all had to work around Junior's horrible family crisis. His wife felt abandoned, and, according to Junior, she believed he lacked compassion for her and their child. We could see how wrenching it was for Junior. It was the bitter and distasteful side of our profession, having to break cooperators down and twist them like pretzels. Despite the heart tug, we knew we had to keep pushing him.

Later that day, we issued Junior a burner phone to be utilized exclusively for his undercover activities. He began making recorded calls with subjects of interest, including Beto, Cantu, and La Mona. Much of the conversation involved the use of coded language, which Junior translated for us, and centered mainly on anticipated loads and those from the recent past. With La Mona, it was mostly his haranguing Junior over a debt of $750,000, which La

Mona was attempting to collect on behalf of Tony Baca (*). It made us wonder what La Mona was up to.

"We need to get Junior completely committed to Team USA," I told everyone. "The more incriminating conversations we can document, the more insurance we'll have that he won't change his mind and ghost us." Junior needed to feel there was no way he could back out, and we couldn't afford to lose him as a cooperator. The initial stages of his cooperation would be crucial.

"How can we be certain he won't come to his senses and change his mind?" Mickey asked. "After all, we didn't have shit on him in the first place."

"Well, Mick…, that's a good question, but I already took care of that," I said. "I kinda implied that if he disappeared, word would make its way back down to Mexico that he was working with us anyway."

"Oh, wow," Mickey replied.

As much as it hurt me to do that, I had to… we can't afford to lose him. It was a one-time shot that we had. I reasoned that it would all pay off for Junior and his family in the end.

"How did he respond?"

"Let's put it this way… from the look on his face, I don't think it'll ever be a problem."

Despite my not-so-subtle threat, I knew deep down his goal was to change his life's karma, wishing it might just reward him with a miracle for Xochilt.

CHAPTER 8
IT'S OUR OPERATION!

Junior came out of the gate swinging hard, burning up the phone with one recorded call after another. We had a hard time keeping up with him. Every conversation needed to be transcribed, translated, and reviewed. Junior was debriefed daily, both via telephone and in person. But it wasn't enough. It didn't suffice just to take the word of our eager informant. We had to corroborate the information he was collecting for us. Although Junior didn't give the team any reason to doubt his intentions or veracity, it was always prudent to trust but verify and authenticate, however possible. It was informant handling 101. The best way to corroborate what Junior was sharing with us was to monitor all his communications closely. However, with Junior's level of activity, it wasn't a simple task. To quote Bishop, "Junior was busier than a one-legged man in an ass-kicking contest." His assistance had us working overtime, trying to keep up with the massive flow of intelligence he was generating. He was constantly on the phone with compadre Beto and Cantu discussing dope deals. There were also recorded calls made to Junior by La Mona regarding the outstanding debt owed to the Colombian Tony. La Mona was putting pressure on Junior to pay him (La Mona) directly since La Mona was the one who had brokered the cocaine shipment in the first place. Listening to the calls, we noted that La Mona's tone sounded increasingly threatening. We hoped it was part of his UC role-playing.

"Junior's off to a good start, Pinche," Bishop said.

"I know... we've got to get him down to Mexico so that he can meet face-to-face with these guys. It's one thing to have a phone conversation; it's a whole other ballgame when you're there in person," I said in agreement.

"Let's hope that once back in Mexico in his comfort zone, he doesn't do like my dog when he knows he's off the leash," Bishop quipped.

"Yeah, Mickey had the same concern. I don't think we're gonna have that problem with Junior," I replied. "We need to get with him and discuss that debt issue with the Colombian and find out why La Mona's been trying to collect on it."

"You've told Jimmy where we're at with Junior?" Bishop asked.

"He knows," I said. "I'm waiting to hear back from him on what the Miami guys think of it all."

As we sat in Bishop's office, I admired his cool NFL swag from his days of being a Broncos' Offensive Right Guard. Drafted from Baylor University in 1980, Bishop wore number 54 and eventually blew out his knees protecting his quarterback and best friend, John Elway, as they made their way into three Super Bowls – 1986, 1987, and 1989. Hungry for another adventure, he hung up his cleats and joined the feds. I noticed he also had a photograph of himself taken during a 1981 "strongest man in the world" competition held at the Playboy Resort in Jersey. He placed sixth. Despite his displays, nobody could ever accuse Bishop of being braggadocious or arrogant over his accomplishments. He was just as accomplished in DEA as he was with the NFL, but you would never hear about it from him. The stuff he exhibited had more to do with sentimental memories than self-aggrandizement. Bishop was one of the most modest individuals I had ever met.

Just then, Trish walked by his door and Bishop yelled out, "Trish! Get that list of targets to 'Jimmy the Craig,' okay?"

"Got it!" Within minutes, we saw the list on Bishop's computer.

SAC Craig,

As you requested, these are the key targets that we are focused on in support of the Band of Brothers. We will coordinate our efforts with other offices (McAllen, Miami, New York, and others as appropriate):

(Foreign-Based High Value Targets)

Luis & Esteban Rodriguez Olivera *(Leadership of "Los Gueros"): Federated Organization*
Oscar Nava Valencia *(nephew of Armando Valencia Cornelio – head of Millennium Cartel and Member of the Federation)*

Artuto Beltran Leyva

Ignacio "Nacho" Coronel *(Federation leader who runs Guadalajara Plaza)*
"Los Bigotones" *(Mexican business partners named Ramiro and Barney, large-scale transporters)*
Beto Bravo: *Junior's criminal associate, closest friend ("Compadre")*

Note: *Beto and Bigotones will be our initial focus since they have potential as future cooperators*

Colombian Targets:

Tony Baca: *AUC source of supply who recently supplied La Mona, Junior, and Beto.*

With over a ton of cocaine, it will likely be Miami's target.

Note: this target holds Junior responsible for the drug debt. Reference debriefing report.

(Domestic-Based High Value Targets)

Gerardo ("Jerry") & brother Heriberto Cantu: *McAllen Trucking Business Owner; Guero's transportation crew (Houston is coordinating with both McAllen & New York)*
Juan Arturo Sanchez, aka "Pantera": *Houston-based mid-level distributor; Cantu subordinate who distributes Gueros cocaine in Houston and the surrounding region.*
"Vladimir": *Dominican; NY-based distributor for Los Gueros; takes deliveries from Cantu (Coordinating with New York)*

Other Domestic Targets: *to be determined as we move forward with Junior's UC activities & corresponding wire intercepts.*

While reviewing the list, I called Jimmy in Guadalajara to let him know I was sending the list.
"Jimmy…"
"Hey, Bro!" He quickly responded.

"Okay, so a lot has happened since we last spoke," I started. "I just sent you a summary of what we think this dude can do. As you can see, we've fully debriefed him, and this list represents what we all think are viable targets thus far. What do you think?"

"Wow! We hit a little jackpot with his guy…if we can pull it off… holy shit!" There was excitement in Jimmy's voice. "Do you want me to share it with the Miami guys, or do you think it would be better coming from you?" he asked.

"I take it they didn't know about La Mona's tip?" I asked.

"No, there was no need… had Junior gone to Miami, we would have sent them the lead," Jimmy responded.

"Okay, when you talk to them, give me and Bishop a shout. If you want, we can make it a conference call," I said.

Shortly after hanging up with Jimmy, Darren, Mickey, and Trish walked into Bishop's office.

Darren said, "We heard from New York and McAllen about their targets. New York is looking at Vladimir, a major cocaine distributor sourced by Guero, while McAllen is working on Jerry Cantu, the transporter who brings cocaine to New York from the border. He hides the dope in perishable goods like fruit and veggies from the valley."

"I'm working up some intel on both Cantu and Beto," Trish added. "Junior asked us again to leave Beto out there so he can continue to work."

"Any reference to La Mona?" I asked.

"Frankly," Darren said. "I think La Mona is wearing Junior out over the Tony debt. He doesn't much like taking La Mona's calls right now."

"Hmm," I said, wondering if Miami and Jimmy were aware of La Mona's involvement.

"Beto appears to be right in the middle of everything Junior has going on, and he thinks Beto is trying to ingratiate himself with La Mona while distancing himself from the debt issue with Tony," Trish related, adding, "Junior says the debt was Beto's doing, but Junior is being held solely responsible by Tony and La Mona."

"Okay, I think we need to drill down on the nature of this debt before we send Junior back to Mexico. After seeing Junior's eye, it appears he's already been threatened by Tony's guys."

"We also learned Beto has a Cuban financier he calls 'Cubas' who invests in most of the loads transported by these Bigotones guys. The Cuban has dope sent to Atlanta, and we think he's working with Arturo Beltran's guys since they control Atlanta," she continued. Pausing, she shook her head and added, "This can get quite busy for us if we don't rein Junior in. I'm not sure we can keep pace with him."

"I know, he's excited about turning things around and making shit happen. I'll talk to him and get him focused. That's one of the reasons why I'm looking forward to working with Miami. We can sort things out and direct both Junior and La Mona in a way that doesn't have us tripping over one another."

As Mickey, Darren, and Trish walked out of the office, Bishop turned to me and said, "Pinche, I've been going through the line sheets on our wire and we're finding some common numbers with those Junior gave us for Beto. I remember Junior saying that Beto's uncles were MFJP comandantes and had ties to the Gulf Cartel and the Zetas. Am I mistaken?"

"Nope, I've read the debriefing reports, and it's true. Junior informed us that his compadre Beto had access to Gulf traffickers and their Zeta associates, and that's how they were able to cross their dope into Texas, that they had to pay a tax and turn it over to a guy Beto referred to as Z-71, as in the Chevy truck."

"Yes, his name came up, as well. Keep the numbers coming our way so we can see about tying Beto into our case, as well. God, this is good shit… God Almighty, I gotta pinch myself," Bishop said. I left his office and headed back to the fourth floor.

Darren and Mickey were waiting in my office. Mickey was holding his super-sized iced tea from Whataburger, a Texas-based franchise known for its hamburgers, fancy ketchup, and its unmistakable iconic orange-and-white striped restaurant colors. I came to learn that Whataburger iced tea was Mickey's daily staple.

Mickey said, "Junior is due to meet with both Beto and Cantu over the next couple of days. We've got the hotel rooms all picked out and we're ready to install our recording equipment."

Darren added, "We also had a conversation with New York. This agent, Eddy Pieszchata, is a good guy and wants to work this case with us."

"Okay, I'm waiting to hear back from Jimmy down in Guad. He's going to chat with our agents in Miami so that we can sort out who's gonna be doing what," I informed.

Bishop looked at his watch and said, "Let's head to Champs." It was one of DEA's favorite lunch spots across the street. It also had the best happy hour within a five-mile radius.

The call came towards the end of the day, at around 5 p.m.

"Mike, it's Jimmy."

"What took you so long?" I asked, anticipating good news.

"Ahh, had to meet with La Mona, then wait till Williams was available to talk so I could kill two birds with one stone. I sent the list up to both him and Chapman right after I got it so we could discuss it during our phone call."

"And did you make contact with Williams?"

"Yeah... you're not gonna like what he had to say..."

"What?" I said, surprised.

"He gave me an earful. He and Chapman were bent out of shape over the fact that I got you guys involved."

"Did you tell him it was *me* you gave the lead to? They should have been okay with *me*, right?"

"I know, Mike, they know you, but you're in Houston now. They're in Miami and think they control Band of Brothers. They said the lead should have been sent to Miami, so they could've decided on whether to approach or not."

"That's bullshit!" I exclaimed.

"Don't kill the messenger, bro!" Jimmy responded.

"Ahh, fuck, here we go again. I'm telling you... it never ceases to amaze me on this fucking job. Don't they know that you and I started this whole Band of Brothers thing well before they ever got involved? *Jesus!*" The veins in my head began to pulsate. "So, Miami sees this more as a career opportunity rather than a DEA opportunity to take down multiple assholes... is that it?"

"I know, dude... I don't wanna be in anyone's crosshairs with all this. I'm stuck in the middle. They are running the Colombian concurrently with our office and have been coming down here regularly, as you know. They like their Guad trips… You know that." There was a brief silence, then Jimmy added, "Look, Mike… the lead went to where it needed to go. He was in your backyard. You had all the background on the case. There was no sense in letting them weigh in on that decision. They're being ridiculous. I didn't offer any apologies." After another pause, he added, "Don't be surprised if they want to come out and sign him up as *their* informant. It's all about control for them."

"Yeah, well… that's not gonna fuckin happen!" The pulsating temples turned to a straight-on headache. "Thanks, Jimmy. I didn't see this coming, or I would have called them myself. Let's see how this unfolds… *fuck!*"

"No, Mike… it was right for me to tell them about Junior's cooperation since I have been interacting regularly with them for a while now. Their reaction was bullshit, though."

The next call I made was to Bishop. "Problems with Miami," I told Bishop.

"¿Qué pasa, Pinche?"

"Our emailed list of targets made its way up to Miami," I said.

"So, we expected it would… what's the problem?"

"No problem on our end. It's their fucking response that's the problem."

"What happened?" Bishop asked, changing his tone.

"Dave Williams bit Jimmy's head off for sending the Junior tip our way. They didn't like us approaching him."

"What?"

"Seems they feel we have stolen control of *their* operation."

"What?" Bishop asked. "You're shittin' me, Pinche."

"Wish I was."

"Parochial sons-a-bitches," Bishop angrily quipped.

"Yep, they want to be in the driver's seat. I'll come on down and we'll call to see if we can't reason with these guys."

Five minutes later, the two of us were together in Bishop's office. Bishop just sat there, shaking his head. We were in disbelief that something so good could leave us feeling so angry.

"So… what does Jimmy say about all this? Whose side is he on, anyway?" Bishop questioned.

"He's trying to be neutral, just stuck in the middle, trying to do the job. Of course, he thinks their reaction is ridiculous." I paused and said, "Let's get this over with."

Bishop grabbed his phone and dialed the headquarters command center's number, waiting for the operator to answer. "Drug Enforcement Administration, how can I direct your call?"

"Keith Bishop, GS from DEA Houston, please patch me to Miami Special Agent Mark Chapman or Dave Williams's cell phone."

"Hold a minute, please."

A minute later, he answered, "Mark speaking…"

"Mark, this is Keith Bishop, and I'm sitting here with Mike Chavarria. We've got you on speaker. We wanted to chat with you regarding the Band of Brothers operation."

"Sure," he responded. "Hi Mike, how are you liking it in Houston so far?"

"Love it, Mark. Just looking for some cowboy boots," I said.

Bishop interjected, "Are you updated with the latest events regarding our recruitment of Raul Valladares?"

"Yeah, just got off the phone with Dave. He filled me in on his chat with Jimmy."

"What are your thoughts, Mark?" I asked.

"I'm gonna be honest, Mike," Chapman started.

I covered the phone and said, "Ohh, here we go…"

"I am a bit conflicted about it all. I'm glad you guys had success with Valladares, but I'm concerned that now we have two informants bumping into one another, creating confusion."

"What confusion?" Bishop asked, his head shaking in disbelief.

"Did you guys already know about Junior?" I asked.

There was a pause before Chapman said, "Well…," hesitating to answer, "La Mona related Junior wasn't as significant as Nacho and Guero, so he didn't think it important."

"Doesn't that concern you guys, Mark?" Bishop asked. We looked at one another, rolling our eyes.

"Didn't you see the target list?" I asked.

"Yeah, we did. We're interested in debriefing Junior ourselves. We want to sign him up concurrently with you and Guadalajara," Chapman replied.

"What do you mean, work him concurrently?" Bishop asked.

"Well, we thought we'd do what we did with La Mona and your office, Mike. We worked him jointly," Chapman explained. He started to speak again, "And…"

I interrupted, "That was a different situation, Mark. You were the domestic office that recruited La Mona, but you needed us in Guadalajara to help direct him in Mexico. It was procedurally required that we sign him concurrently. That's not the case here, Mark."

"Well, I don't see the difference, Mike. It's our operation, not Houston's."

"Mark, I just came from SOD. It's not uncommon for multiple offices to target the same individuals; however, it's unusual for a domestic office to direct an informant from another city. Why is this necessary?" Bishop asked. "And nobody says we can't work this operation together with you guys." Bishop sat up in his chair and cracked his neck to relieve the building tension.

"That's why we wanted to come out and sign him up, Keith," Chapman insisted.

"We're not going to have two domestic offices directing this guy, Mark… sorry. We'll need to coordinate our respective efforts to avoid stepping on one another," I added.

"Mark, have you forgotten it was Pinche, I mean Chavarria, who started this whole Band of Brothers operation from Guadalajara?" Bishop, who had the patience of a therapist, was beginning to get irritated. He started rocking in his chair, his football muscles pulsating just like the veins in my head. Both of us knew a storm was brewing.

"We're a bit disappointed with Jimmy that he didn't call us first, Mike, especially since he's been working so closely with us. We could have weighed in on this," Chapman insisted. "But I know he's loyal to you and all, so I understand that."

"Weighed in on what?" I asked, rubbing my head again.

"Well, on the approach, Mike."

"You're in Miami. I'm in Houston. Junior is in Houston. The tip was time-sensitive. We did it, it's done… he's onboard… end of story, Mark."

"Well, we can agree to disagree, Mike. I've gotta go right now, but we can discuss it all later and coordinate our travel plans over the next couple of days. The boss here is going to insist on it."

"Before you go, Mark, one more thing… you seemed to have an issue with the fact that we now have two well-placed cooperators involved in the operation. What is your problem with that?" I asked impatiently.

"Well, if Miami is controlling them both, there should be no problem, no duplication. We think it makes more sense that way." Bishop and I looked at one another, knowing he lacked either experience, common sense, *or both*. The rationale and importance of having two informants continue to operate unwittingly was a no-brainer. It was a basic informant handling strategy to have two informants independent of one another – one not knowing the other was a cooperator – targeting subjects of common interest. It was optimal to have them reporting on one another, as well. It would offer us the ability to monitor them both and hold them individually accountable. It was our obligation as agents to demand accountability from our informants. At trial, two informants corroborating one another were a prosecutor's dream.

"Don't you think it would be good to have each informant reporting independently so we can have an honest picture of what is going on?" Bishop asked.

"That can be accomplished more efficiently by having the same controlling agents involved," Chapman doubled down. Bishop and I could see it was going nowhere.

"Okay, Mark. Why don't we end it there… Just let us know when you plan to come out, okay?" We thanked Chapman and hung up.

"Hell, Pinche, there wasn't even any discussion about the content of what Junior had to offer. It was just about the control." Bishop sat there looking bewildered and disappointed. We shook our heads, and since it was happy hour, we decided to walk across the street to Champs.

"Thank God for Jimmy the Craig, Pinche," Bishop said as we clicked mugs. "He's all about doin' the right thing for the right reason. Those poor bastards must be under a ton of pressure to produce some results, and La Mona's not getting it done."

Bishop was right. In Houston's case, the tone was set by SAC Craig. DEA was focused on targeting the most significant drug traffickers worldwide. We spent three hours discussing DEA's bureaucratic issues. Although we were taught at the academy that stats weren't of primary importance, the reality was quite different. Every federal agency had to fight to secure funding from Congress to remain competitive, which improved an agency's chances of achieving annual success. It was a straightforward budget issue where SACs needed to report positive results to headquarters so the DEA's Administrator could then testify before Congress and demand more funding. DEA SACs called this the "game of metrics." Unfortunately for many agents, this game of metrics sent pressure down the chain to the field agents. The agents were then compelled to compete with one another to give the bosses their metric victories. It was bad enough when it occurred among agents of different field offices, but often the need to show results led agents—even within the same enforcement groups—to hold back relevant intelligence. Pettiness seemed to find its way into every office around the country.

"Part of me feels bad for Chapman and Williams," I said.

"Fuck em, Pinche. We all get paid well to go out and put fucking bad guys away, and that's what we're offering the mother fuckers in Miami… a chance to work with us to put the bad guys in jail. They are choosing to compete with us on this operation, at least that's how I see it… it's a bad start."

"Let's give them a chance. They may come around," I told Bishop.

We finished our last round and called it a day.

The next morning, Bishop caught Trish walking past his office, headed to the Xerox copier, and yelled out, "Hey Trish, come in here for a second."

"Miami's coming out here to take a crack at Junior. Let Darren, Mickey, and Bostick know. Pinche and I would like you and an agent to be present in the room with them while they speak with Junior. We wanna keep the train from going off track. Let's not get cross with the Miami agents. They're angry now, but it'll probably work itself out as things move forward," Bishop said.

"I'm sure they will," Trish replied sarcastically with an eyeroll. "Yep, they see Junior's recruitment as something they should have controlled. It's turning into a competition, right?" Trish stood there shaking her head. She had seen it before. "Okay, I'll pass the word to the guys upstairs. We're getting together to go over some of the wire intercepts and emails now."

"Pinche and I want to try to make it work with them, so for now, let's please put them on distribution for all of our reporting," Bishop directed. "If any games are being played, it's not gonna be from Houston."

CHAPTER 9
CALL ME BOND...
JUNIOR BOND

"Okay, I've been told the Miami guys are arriving tomorrow, and they intend to sign Beto up as an informant. I don't want to go to war with the Miami Field Division over their ridiculous ideas of directing Junior's activities. I say let the fuckers sign him up. Junior will take direction from us and us only," I instructed Mickey, Darren, Bostick, and Trish. "Don't fight with the agents, be nice, helpful, etcetera. Let's make sure we know what is being related to them, okay?"

"Got it… understood," was the response from each of them as they shook their heads displeasingly.

"Now, please brief me on all the details surrounding Junior's debt problem," I said. "We're not letting him go to Mexico until we get this clarified and remedied somehow."

Trish explained that several months ago, before the incident with Junior's daughter, there was a cocaine shipment of about 1,500 kilos sourced by the Colombian Tony Baca. La Mona introduced Tony to Junior and asked Junior and Beto to assist with the shipment. Junior involved Ramiro as the transportation expert to handle the paperwork so the coke could be shipped in a container of palm oil. "By the way," Trish said, "apparently Ramiro looks like an ape, so his nickname is 'Simio.'"

"Hah... they call him an ape?" I loved Mexico's descriptive use of nicknames.

"Yeah, I can't wait to see what he looks like. Junior says it's all in the way he walks," she related. "Hehe, we were all giggling like school kids afterwards when Junior described Ramiro to us." She went on to explain how Ramiro accompanied Junior to meet Tony in Bogota. They arranged for the first load of 1,500 kilograms to be concealed in the container of palm oil and sent from Cartagena, Colombia, to Puerto Progreso on the Yucatán Peninsula. The containers cleared customs and were sent overland to Monterrey using Beto's trucks. Junior said that once the 1,500 kilos arrived in Monterrey, the cocaine was stored by Junior and Beto for safekeeping while Tony worked on arranging for his New York clients to signal when to ship the cocaine north. "Junior and Beto were investors in a one-hundred-kilo portion of the larger shipment."

"Why the pressure from La Mona, then?" I asked.

Junior said La Mona made the initial introduction, and besides that, Junior believes he also had an investment interest in the load," Trish related, explaining that La Mona demanded *he* be paid directly because Tony refused to deal with Junior. "But that's not true. Junior has been in regular contact with Tony, reassuring him that the debt would be paid."

"So, what happened? How did things get all fucked up?" I asked.

She then recounted Junior's version of events. It was clear that Tony wanted to sell the whole load together in

New York; however, Beto convinced Junior that it would take too long to see a profit. Instead, Beto persuaded Junior to remove 100 kilos and send it to Atlanta, where Beto's financier, Cubas, could quickly unload the cocaine. This way, they could make their profits in half the time. Beto delivered the coke to his contact, Z-71, who crossed it into Texas, and Beto and Junior coordinated its delivery to Atlanta. The problem arose once it arrived in Atlanta. The coke was sold, but the promised money was not returned.

"Oh, shit," I said. "So, the money was never returned to Junior."

"Yeah, apparently Beto chalked it up to a miscommunication, telling Junior his associate, Cubas, thought they wanted to take the profit from the sale and use it to reinvest in a separate coke shipment.

"Junior is furious and holding the bag for the hundred kilos lost. Tony didn't want to hear anything about Beto… he held Junior responsible."

"Fucking Beto," I said. "And stupid fucking Junior… so how much does he owe?"

"Seven hundred grand," Trisha said.

After discussing the debacle with Junior, it was clear that he (Junior) was going to start making payments directly to Tony Baca to remove some of the pressure. When asked about La Mona's involvement, Junior insisted, "He must have had a financial interest in the load."

"What will you tell La Mona, then?" I asked Junior.

"That he can fuck off… I'm paying Tony directly," Junior said with a smile.

I decided not to bring it to Miami's attention. Bishop and I chose to let it play out to see how things unfolded with La Mona before mentioning it to them. Instead, I checked with Jimmy, who knew nothing about La Mona pressing Junior to pay him directly.

Trish added, "Also, Junior described Beto's access to overland transportation for loads entering Mexico from the seaports. He controls a small fleet of look-alike commercial trucks, I mean identical knockoffs of Mexico's nationally known bakery company, 'Bimbo.' Same truck models, paint jobs, and commercial labels — the whole bit. These perfect replicas run across the country loaded with cocaine, and nobody searches them," she explained.

I added, "That, and Beto has a multitude of corrupt Mexican police he can call on from various agencies – locals, state, and fed cops – to help escort loads when necessary."

It was mid-September when the Miami agents finally arrived in Houston. SA Mark Chapman, the senior of the two, was in his late forties, about 6 feet tall, clean-cut, with a slender but athletic build. He was well-tanned and had the look of a Secret Service agent, complete with sunglasses. He seemed like he might be an avid tennis player or golfer. Quiet, well-mannered, and seemingly soft-spoken or shy, his introverted personality was often overshadowed by that of his younger partner, Dave Williams. In contrast, Williams was in his late twenties, shorter, with a heavier and more muscular build. His hair was cut high and tight, clearly a US Marine Corps veteran, as indicated by the tattoo on his right forearm bearing the Corps' emblem, "Semper Fidelis," in red ink. Williams, also clean-shaven, wore a more serious expression as the agents entered the office building.

Waiting to check them in were Mickey and Bostick. After quick introductions, Mickey and Bostick acquired visitor badges for Chapman and Williams at the security desk. Then they escorted them up to the second floor where the rest of us were waiting. Despite the rough start the week before, Bishop and I hoped to reboot our efforts and get everyone on the same team so we could work together on our ambitious operation.

I stood outside the conference room and watched the four of them walk down the hallway. From Mickey's and Bostick's expressions and the battle-ready, game face of the younger Williams, it was clear we faced an uphill battle.

"Hey guys, good to see you!" I began.

"Hey, Mike! How've you been?" Chapman responded amiably, smiling.

"Hi Mike," Williams said, business-like.

As we all entered the conference room, I introduced everyone: "Guys, this is Mark Chapman and Dave Williams from Miami." Everyone stood up and exchanged typical handshakes, noticing the different personalities and the tense vibe. The taller, older Chapman gave a standard handshake, while his younger partner greeted everyone with a firm, almost aggressive grip, revealing his calcitrant, inflexible demeanor. Of course, Trish shook Williams's hand with the same intensity, catching him off guard. There was no unnecessary small talk as everyone took a seat around the oval-shaped conference table. Trish leaned over and whispered to Darren, "He looks like that Flintstone character, 'Barney Rubble,'" referring to Williams, prompting Darren to laugh quietly, which drew a distracted glance from the visitors.

"We just wanted to welcome you guys to Houston and let you know you'll be meeting Junior at a nearby Embassy Suites Hotel, where we've reserved a large space for this afternoon and tomorrow morning," I said, kicking things off.

Williams interrupted before Chapman could speak, saying, "Mike, I hope there's no issue with us signing him up."

"Wow, Dave... you don't waste any time, buddy. Look, this doesn't have to be a contentious situation," I said, attempting to ameliorate the tone of the discussion. "We're not gonna fight it... you do whatever you think is right."

"Well, Mike, it's just that we were broadsided with this whole thing. You were in Guadalajara, and you knew we were working this Band of Brothers operation," Williams quickly replied as his senior partner continued to smile while remaining uncomfortably silent.

"Dave, I think you're blowing things a bit out of proportion here. This guy came to Houston on his own. We didn't invite him. Jimmy called me with a tip passed by La Mona, knowing I was up here."

"Well, Jimmy should have called us instead," Williams insisted.

"And you guys would have done what?" I asked, entertained by his comment.

"Well, we probably would have flown out here and set up some kind of surveillance to find out who he was meeting with," Williams retorted.

"What are you talking about? The guy's kid is dying, Dave. He wasn't here to meet and negotiate a dope deal. Are you listening to yourself?"

"Well, it happened the way it did, and that's fine, but now we'd like to talk to him and sign him up so that we can work him concurrently with you guys."

"You guys can talk to him until you're blue in the face, Dave. And if you sign him, it'll just be an administrative exercise because Miami will not direct Houston's informant." I paused and then added, "Two of our folks will be with you in the room, by the way."

Bishop interjected in a friendly tone, "We were hoping we could get you guys on board with us so we could approach Band of Brothers as one team."

"We appreciate that, Keith," Chapman said agreeably, and we plan on doing that, but our boss wants us to get a full debriefing on Junior and sign him up so we can work this with you guys." Chapman had years of experience compared to his junior partner and attempted to explain Miami's position with greater finesse, but it fell flat.

"I think we can work on different aspects of the Band of Brothers. Like Dave, though, I'm a bit concerned about the potential for the informants complicating things rather than enhancing our abilities to infiltrate these groups." He paused, as though he wanted to continue, but stopped short, unsure of himself. Bishop and I just looked at one another, knowing whatever we tried wasn't going to work.

"Okay, guys," I said. "Why don't we let you get going with Junior, and we can talk more later?"

Bishop, unsettled by Chapman's response, asked, "Why do you think two informants working the same targets are going to complicate things, Mark?"

Before Chapman could answer, Williams interjected, "Because it'll be a potential nightmare when it comes time for our cases to go to court. Two informants working the same crooks, potentially contradicting one another…? That'll be a nightmare when it comes to discovery."

"You're jumping way ahead of yourself, Dave," Bishop said. "We don't make cases based on what informants tell us during debriefings. We rely on corroboration. The informants need to corroborate fact-based evidence. There ain't gonna be two sets of facts. If there are, then someone is lying — and we're going to need to know that, too. I don't mind us prosecuting a lying fuck of an informant," Bishop popped off. I could see his temple pulsate. I thought about what he must have looked like wearing a Broncos uniform on game day.

Four hours later, Bostick and Trish returned from their first session with the Miami guys and Junior. "Chapman and Williams left the Embassy Suites and returned to their hotel to check messages, make calls, and grab a quick bite. I think they're done," Bostick said. "Junior had to return to the hospital to join his wife, Sara. I think he's had enough, as well."

Junior had earlier informed me that his daughter's prognosis was looking bleaker by the day. He and Sara were slowly losing all hope that Xochilt would survive the fight.

Trish pointed out that Junior was incredibly patient with Williams and Chapman despite them treating him as if he were in handcuffs with one foot in jail. Trish and Bostick fought the urge to interrupt Williams and Chapman, halting the interview. They desperately wanted to remind the Miami agents that Junior was not in custody but an informant who was fully cooperating. However, they held back to avoid being accused of interfering later. Williams was challenging much of what Junior provided, as if trying to find flaws and inconsistencies. "It was more like a defendant interrogation," Trish said. "After the interview, they documented Junior as their informant and then left the hotel, looking pleased as if they got what they wanted–the credit for Junior's work."

"Pathetic," I noted.

Afterward, we all gathered in the conference room to hear about Miami's interview with Junior. Trish and Bostick began flipping through their notes as Trish started by saying that most of what was discussed was a summary of what we had already reported on an outgoing cable, with the Miami agents on distribution and in receipt of the information. Williams and Chapman were digging around, hoping to catch Junior off guard with information he had already provided us.

Bostick said, "I take my hat off to Junior, given his daughter's situation. We should have warned him that these guys were going to challenge him. He kept looking over at me and Trish, hoping we could intervene. He didn't understand what was going on."

Trish added, "Junior rehashed a seizure he previously told me about—the Panamanian seizure back in July, where 1,345 kilograms of cocaine and 15 kilos of Colombian heroin were taken from the arm of a large Caterpillar-type crane." She went on to describe Junior's account of how La Mona secretly arranged for the 15 kilos of heroin to be placed in the crane so he could avoid paying Ramiro's required transport fee. "Junior explained how it pissed Ramiro off and caused a rub between Junior and La Mona."

"The Miami agents challenged Junior on how he knew the heroin was La Mona's," Trish added, "And Bostick and I were looking at Junior to see his response."

"They were particularly concerned regarding the palm oil load and had Junior explain it all again. They didn't seem pleased hearing about La Mona's role in that," Bostick related.

"Remind me about the heroin part of that shipment," I asked.

Junior said the heroin was sourced by a North Valley leader named Leyner Valencia, who goes by the nickname 'Pirana,' like the man-eating fish of the Amazon," Trish said. "I ran his name through our database and determined Leyner Valencia is a major coke source for Sinaloa's leader Arturo Beltran." She paused and added, "La Mona coordinated this venture, separately and secretly, directly with Leyner."

Among the Federation leaders, Beltran was seen as the link between the Sinaloa traffickers and corrupt officials in the Mexican government. He allegedly made bribe payments for the Federation. He was also believed to be importing more cocaine than his peers, which caused a bit of an issue between the Beltran brothers and their cousin, Chapo Guzman.

Trish added, "This is why Junior didn't want us to go after Beto. He said Beto could get us to Arturo Beltran and even some corrupt cops."

After the meeting ended, Darren and Mickey left the building to install audio-video recording equipment in a room to capture the upcoming meeting between Junior and Cantu from McAllen. Junior was instructed to discuss past shipments and seizures, which could be researched and used for historical conspiracy charges. Cantu was a key link to the Gueros brothers, as he was the person moving their cocaine from the Texas border to New York.

"Jesus Christ… trying to keep up with this guy is like running a marathon against a Kenyan," I said, jokingly. Working with Junior was exhausting, but we had to keep pace with him. Mickey and Darren were instructed to remind Junior to ensure that his recorded conversations with Cantu included references to the Gueros sending cocaine to their guy, Vladimir, in New York.

New York prosecutors, whether from the Eastern or Southern Districts, teamed up with our New York agents and aggressively targeted cartel members. They focused on building cases around well-documented seizures that could be tracked and verified through evidence and witness testimony – often involving cooperators like Junior.

Mickey and Darren were monitoring Junior's intercepted phone conversations with Cantu, identifying various associates based in Houston. One such individual was identified as "Pantera" ("Panther"), whose nickname came from the color of his clothes, ball caps, boots, and pickup truck—all of which were black. Pantera was Cantu's top distributor in Houston and was also expected to attend the meeting.

Pantera was in the business of supplying lower-level distributors in Baton Rouge, Louisiana, and other cities in neighboring states. Junior was waiting for both Cantu and Pantera to arrive at the hotel where their conversations would be recorded. Afterward, agents planned to follow both individuals to identify other associates, as well as their residential and business locations.

On cue, around 9:15 p.m., Cantu arrived in the parking lot of the Embassy Suites, driving his brand-new, black Ford F-150. The Embassy Suites was located in the heart of Houston's Galleria Mall, the second-largest tourist attraction in the country. Just behind Cantu, driving his new-model black Dodge Dakota, was Pantera. Both men slowly circled the parking lot, cautiously watching for signs of law enforcement. Junior greeted the two outside so surveillance agents could take photographs of them meeting together.

They headed up to Junior's suite. Inside, Junior had a bottle of Chivas whiskey and a bucket of ice waiting. He knew how effective booze was in loosening the tongues of his associates. Before the meeting, Junior joked with a quick wink, saying, "Loose lips sink ships...and so do loose women!"

"Junior, I have two hundred units stored in a warehouse just south of the border," Cantu said, referring to Reynosa, the Mexican border town opposite McAllen.

"It's ready to cross as soon as I get the green light from Pantera's clients in Louisiana," Cantu advised. The three men knew how fluid the ports of entry were, especially for coke coming across in large commercial trucks equipped with hydraulically activated false compartments. The three began laughing at how "NAFTA" (North American Free Trade Agreement) did nothing but enhance their ability to cross dope into the US.

The alcohol was doing its job. It was another successful round of covert recordings. Junior should have been a DEA agent. It was clear how his charm and wit helped him rise in the drug world. He could sell a desert lot to a pineapple farmer. Watching him was incredible. He seemed to instinctively know when to talk and when to be quiet and let his drug trafficking partners reveal incriminating details. Junior was a natural.

As their meeting concluded, Pantera invited Junior and Cantu to a nearby "Gentleman's Club," where he had a connection with the manager. He boasted about having unlimited access to all the private lap dances they could handle, only needing to cover their bar tab. Junior and Cantu thanked him but declined. Junior wanted to race back to Sara, who was starting to fall apart emotionally.

Pantera left and was trailed for about forty-five minutes to an address we suspected was his home, located at the end of a cul-de-sac in the remote county of Rosenberg, near the border of Richmond, Texas. It was difficult for agents to keep their eyes on Pantera due to his deliberate, evasive, and erratic driving. He was conducting "heat runs" to make sure he wasn't being followed. Despite his efforts, Darren's surveillance team managed to place him at an address that was added to our future target list for search warrant executions. Database checks showed that other vehicles were also registered at the same location. Those vehicles led to the identification of different addresses, criminal associates, and businesses, such as car repair shops, which were believed to be used for installing "vehicle traps" (hidden compartments for hiding drugs and money). Our Houston team gathered enough information from Junior's UC recorded meeting, along with details obtained from subsequent surveillance, to support court orders for nine wire intercepts.

Over the following months, our wires provided enough actionable information that we could collaborate with our local and state partners to make multiple seizures of both drugs and bulk cash. These seizures and arrests were carried out in a way that did not reveal the larger operation, allowing us to expand our case until everything was ready for a simultaneous takedown of all targets. Our goal was to dismantle as many cells, both domestically and internationally, as possible. Domestically, we identified distribution networks in neighboring states, such as Louisiana and Arkansas, which could then be traced back and tied to Junior's first UC meeting.

Once the UC meeting concluded with Cantu and Pantera, Mickey took his surveillance team and followed

Cantu, who drove to a nearby "Westin" hotel. He checked in with only a small sports bag and ate dinner at the hotel restaurant. Cantu, a Mexican man in his thirties, was of average height, heavy-set, clean-shaven, with a pockmarked face and short hair. Like Junior, Cantu hated wearing flashy jewelry or clothes. He was photographed wearing a short-sleeved yellow shirt and blue jeans.

Mickey sought out Westin's security chief and received authorization to access Cantu's room after his check-out. The next morning, Mickey entered the room after Cantu had left the hotel and headed back toward the border. With one of the hotel managers, Mickey quickly searched the room for any valuable papers or trash Cantu might have left behind. He found a small piece of folded paper on the floor at the foot of the bed, with two numbers (with New York area codes) handwritten next to the name "Vladi." Mickey then turned and went into the bathroom, focusing on the trash can. To his embarrassment, he found what looked like a cloth napkin wrapped around a beige-colored dildo. Standing there, stunned and confused, he suddenly realized he was being watched by the hotel security official. Turning a shade of red, he blurted out, "What the hell kind of drug traffickers are these!" Despite not touching it, Mickey instinctively washed his hands twice.

Once back in the group, he walked into my office and shared the numbers he pulled from the piece of paper he found in the room. We assumed the phone numbers were related to Vladimir in New York. "I'll get with Darren and call Eddy to pass along the numbers we found." As he turned to leave my office, he couldn't help himself... he had to share the dildo story. After Mickey recounted it in his typical expressionless, monotone fashion, I looked at him and asked why he hadn't kept it as evidence.

His excited response was, "Hell no, I wasn't about to keep that thing!"

"But, Mickey," I said. "We could have used that to entice his cooperation. Can't imagine he would have wanted that brought up on the witness stand," keeping a poker face.

"I don't know what you were taught in the academy, but I wasn't told a dildo was a good piece of evidence," he said, to which I returned an amused grin.

"So, what did the hotel guy say?" I asked with a smile.

"He wasn't shocked at all. He said in his Brit accent, 'I've seen it all, mate.' And of course I replied, 'I thought I had too… then he said, 'Cheers' and proceeded to lock the room up."

"I guess maids get to see it all, as well," I exclaimed, laughing.

Several days after Junior's UC meeting with Cantu and Pantera, Junior agreed to meet us in a large hotel suite, which we secured for another lengthy debriefing. We wanted to make sure we had all the necessary information before sending him to Mexico for face-to-face meetings with our subjects of interest. We also wanted to ensure his outstanding debt issue with Tony Baca wouldn't put him in unnecessary danger. We reminded him that he would have to rely on himself once he crossed that international border. "There's no rescue team, Junior." I reminded.

"I've made arrangements to make a partial payment to Tony," Junior reassured. "Don't worry, he wants to keep doing business but just wanted to know I was willing to show some good faith at least. He and I are still good," Junior insisted. "I paid him a couple hundred thousand to get him off my back." He paused and said, "I am apparently on La Mona's shit list," Junior said with a chuckle, adding, "He'll get over it."

As we wrapped up the meeting, I slapped him on the back, congratulating him for all he had done up to that point.

He responded proudly, "I am going to be your number one undercover agent... Call me 'Bond... *Junior* Bond!'"

Everyone congratulated him with handshakes, wishing him well on his trip. I told him, "Junior, we normally just call our undercover guys 'UCs,' but I think we'll use '007' for your code name," to which he beamed a contented smile.

CHAPTER 10
SMOKE CITY

The domestic side of Band of Brothers was moving full steam ahead with multiple targets identified and labeled as either transporters, distributors, or both. Darren and Mickey were so inundated with leads that they were delegating them to other members of the group. They now needed to join Bostick as their operational focus shifted south of the border. Junior's first meeting was set to take place at a hotel in Mexico City. The capital, known as "Distrito Federal" (Federal District), mirrored our "District of Columbia." The narcos preferred to call it "Smoke City," often shortened to "Smoke" – a nod to the smog.

The meeting was arranged and scheduled by Junior's friend, Beto, in coordination with Ramiro. Several topics were to be discussed. At the top of Beto's list was his interest in recovering losses (amounting to $900,000) he and his Cuban companion sustained from the Panamanian "crane seizure" in July. Beto demanded that Ramiro pay the money he had advanced for their 100-kilo share of the total load of 1,345 kilos of cocaine. The Panamanian authorities received an anonymous tip, which led them to the Free Trade Zone, where they searched the arm of a large crane and found the hidden cocaine.

Junior explained the seizure to us and said that his friend Beto unfairly blamed Ramiro for the loss. Instead, the blame belonged to Ramiro's partner Barney (*), who decided to use the crane for temporary storage while waiting to gather more cocaine before putting it in a container and sending it to Mexico's port at Progreso. As Junior explained, Barney lied to Ramiro, Beto, and the other investors, telling them he had already put the cocaine in a container and loaded it onto the ship, which was supposed to have left Panama for Mexico. Junior said Barney's motivation was twofold. He wanted to stop Beto and the others from pressuring him, and he also wanted to wait and load more cocaine to earn a bigger commission.

I asked Junior why Beto was so insistent on blaming Ramiro, and he told me Beto knew Barney was untouchable, protected by a violent Guatemalan kingpin known as "Gordo Mario" (Jorge Mario Paredes Cordova). Gordo Mario was supplying the Gulf and Zetas. It confirmed intelligence we had that the Zetas aimed to expand into drug trafficking. There were whispers that they wanted to form their own cartel. Because of this, their relationship with Gordo Mario was key to their plans for growth, and Barney played an essential role in making that happen. Driven by self-preservation, Beto decided to hold Ramiro solely responsible, arguing that since Ramiro and Barney were partners, they were both liable for each other's mistakes. Junior chuckled, noting that his compadre would get so worked up he'd shout expletives and call Ramiro a "fucking monkey."

Junior also revealed that it was common for Bigotones partners to send large cocaine loads using a single conveyance to multiple investors representing various cartel organizations, citing Oscar Nava and Gordo Mario as examples. Oscar Nava, a representative of the Sinaloa

Federation who sold much of his cocaine to other federated members, and Gordo Mario, who served as a source for the Zetas. The fact that cocaine loads were often shared among adversaries using common conveyances was very revealing to us in the DEA. Junior pointed out that it was all about the money. The broker and transporter would take responsibility for separating the investors' cocaine once it arrived in Mexico, so it could be delivered to the respective organizations. Whether they were allies or not didn't matter. Nobody earned a dime if the product wasn't delivered to Mexico. Junior also explained that once in Mexico, each group would take responsibility for moving its own product using its organizational infrastructure.

"This is how Beto and I have been so successful," Junior said, adding, "We get paid by everyone, no matter the cartel affiliation." Junior laughed at how the DEA liked to describe cartels in a cookie-cutter way. He said, "My father told me that you all gave us that name, 'Cartel.' He said we didn't call ourselves anything, except families and clans."

In preparation for his meeting in Mexico City, we equipped Junior with recording devices so he could document incriminating conversations that we could later use as evidence. He expected the following individuals to show up: Ramiro, Beto, La Mona, a Colombian representative of the North Valley Cartel nicknamed "Matematico" (Mathematician), and "Chivo" (Goat). Matematico's nickname reflected his background as an accountant and his reputed mathematical skills. Chivo, as Junior was told, was Ramiro and Barney's employee at their import-export business. While at a party hosted by Nava, Chivo managed to impress the cartel leader and was offered a position as Nava's assistant.

The attendees were eager to hear about Ramiro's Panama-based company, "Cumepa" ("Cubiertos Mecanizados de Panama"). Cumepa was another front company used by Ramiro and Barney to send legitimate merchandise together with cocaine. In this case, Ramiro intended to offer this conveyance and its legitimate cover load of galvanized roofing tiles as a new option for moving bulk cocaine to Mexico. The company was strategically based in Panama's Free Trade Zone and was formed for the express purpose of exporting coke. The investors were told to expect their first shipment during the beginning months of 2006.

Before leaving Houston, Junior told Sara he was taking a quick business trip to Mexico City, returning in two or three days. Junior went with Mickey and Darren as they headed to George Bush Intercontinental Airport. Mickey drove while Darren gave Junior last-minute instructions on how to properly use the recording devices and explained the downloading procedures afterward. Junior needed to send them to Houston promptly.

Darren reminded Junior, "We have our undercover number programmed into your burner phone. If anyone happens to get hold of the number and wants to check on you, they'll see that it is registered at the Children's Hospital here in Houston. Everyone is now aware of your personal crisis, so we've made it appear as though it's a hospital number, but it's forwarded to our undercover line. Let it ring... it'll come to us on the third ring. We will always answer, 'Children's Hospital – Critical Care Unit.'"

An overconfident Junior was developing his UC swagger and enjoying his new identity as 007. "Don't get cocky, Junior," Darren told him. You might be back home in Mexico, but you will be under the microscope.

"I know… I know, Darren," Junior said cavalierly.

"Okay, Junior… you might even see us doing surveillance from a distance. Don't make eye contact with us… your friends will be watching you." Darren added.

As they pulled up to the airport, Darren and Mickey wished Junior well, to which he responded, "007 has this."

"Did he get off okay? Is he clear on how to download the recordings and send them up here?" I asked.

"He's got it," Darren said, adding, "He's like a little kid off to play his first baseball game."

Junior's directions included regular emails using undercover accounts set up to facilitate and document evidentiary records of all his communications. We established two separate "Hushmail" accounts: one for sending downloaded recordings, and a second for sending messages in "draft."

That evening, Mickey and Darren took a flight to Mexico to coordinate surveillance efforts with local agents. Jimmy Martinez from Guadalajara would also be there. Their goal was to observe Junior's meetings and take photographs if possible. This would complement our discreet audio recordings and provide evidence for a prosecution. Junior's testimony and authentication would be crucial.

The meeting was scheduled at the Nikko Hotel, a 38-story building in the heart of Polanco, one of Mexico City's upscale districts. This neighborhood is known for its luxury shopping, especially along Avenida Presidente Masaryk. It features numerous Michelin-star restaurants and luxury hotels, all within walking distance. Polanco is often called the "Beverly Hills" of Mexico City.

Beto chose the hotel restaurant, "El Jardin," and scheduled the meeting for that Friday at 1 p.m., two days after Junior and the agents arrived, to allow enough time for surveillance coordination. Mickey and Darren, dressed as international businessmen, took positions inside the restaurant to discreetly photograph those attending. Their seats were strategically placed near the entrance, enabling them to get close-up photos of each target as they left the meeting.

Junior arrived early and picked a large table in the back of the restaurant. Jimmy knew better than to go inside since La Mona was probably there. Instead, Jimmy watched the place from outside. He was more interested in following Ramiro.

Everyone was punctual but Beto and La Mona. Ramiro arrived first, followed by Junior, then Chivo and Matematico. Beto and La Mona arrived about half an hour late. Darren, with his discreetly disguised camera, was busy snapping away. La Mona was easily identifiable, given that Jimmy had sent up a photograph. Ramiro, as well, was unmistakable with his uncanny resemblance to an ape – sporting straight, jet-black hair, a monkey's facial features, and long, dangling arms like those of an Orangutan. Darren described Ramiro as walking without swinging his arms, even curling his fingers. We couldn't wait to see the photos.

Although Junior was not wired, he was wearing a secret recording device; however, the background noise from the restaurant was an issue, as it could likely drown out the conversation and reduce its clarity. Junior was seen happily chatting, his arms flailing like a flamenco dancer, raising his voice to charm the group. Watching 007 from across the restaurant, Darren whispered to Mickey, "I hope he shuts the fuck up and lets the crooks talk a little… we need good conversation from the bad guys."

"Junior, tell La Monita about the Italian," Beto interrupted. Junior glared at Beto, angry that he mentioned his Italian transporter. Bruno was a close family friend of the Valladares family. He was a legitimate businessman who owned a manufacturing plant that built commercial-sized ovens used mainly in Europe to make household porcelain products like sinks and toilets. Bruno's brother operated a plant in Colombia, while Bruno's was built in Monterrey. Junior kept Bruno's identity and role very secret and used his services carefully and rarely. Bruno's brother reportedly regularly supplied Colombian sources by sending 500-kilo coke loads per oven to organized crime groups operating in Europe. Although Bruno and his brother were mentioned during our debriefings, we thought it was best to share this information only with our DEA counterparts in Europe, given the risk of compromising our operation. Since the cocaine being shipped by the Italians wasn't meant for US markets, we decided it was wise to wait a bit longer before involving European host-nation partners.

Beto knew about Bruno's ovens and desperately tried to exploit them for financial gain through commissions, especially since he knew traffickers like Nava looked for ways to ship more cocaine to Europe, where it sold for twice as much per kilo while avoiding the long arm of the US justice system. Junior was furious at Beto and aware that his compadre was forming closer ties with both Chivo and Nava. Bruno's ovens could easily hide up to 500 kilos per shipment, something that appealed to Mexican drug barons eager to send coke to European markets.

"So, what about this Italian, then?" La Mona asked, suddenly intrigued.

"He's visiting his brother in Colombia right now," Junior snapped while looking over at Beto, still seething.

Chivo leaned in, nodding his head, interested to hear more about the Italian.

"We're here to discuss our Panamanian options," Ramiro interrupted, sensing Junior's frustration. Junior explained earlier that despite meeting Ramiro through Beto, Ramiro preferred dealing directly with Junior because of trust issues Ramiro had with Beto. It became a serious point of contention between the two because Beto thought of himself as Ramiro's boss.

La Mona, aggravated about the change in topic from Bruno to Cumepa, then leaned across the table and directed his comments to Junior, "More importantly, Raul, let's discuss Tony's debt." Junior was incensed by La Mona's sudden use of his given name and began to respond when La Mona interrupted him, asking, "By the way, how is your daughter?" It came across as both insensitive and insincere

"Thank you, she's hanging in there," Junior replied. "And, by the way, I have made a sizeable payment to Tony," Junior said.

"I'm aware," La Mona responded dismissively.

La Mona wouldn't back down. He grew more agitated with Junior, starting to rebuke and even berate him for not taking the overdue debt seriously enough. "Junior, I was the one who introduced you to Tony," La Mona insisted. "Tony doesn't want to deal with you directly. I am the broker, the middleman here… you need to pay him through me, Junior."

"I have wired him money already, La Mona. He doesn't seem to mind."

"You're fucking with me, making me look bad, man," La Mona whispered angrily, not paying any mind to the onlookers at the other end of the table.

"La Monita...," Junior responded, "We can talk about this later. Let's please focus on what we're here for... what we're doing with Cumepa. There's a lot of money to be made, Compadre."

Before sending Junior to Mexico, Bishop and I were confident and resolved that Junior wouldn't find himself in a precarious and dangerous situation. Junior made it clear to us that Tony was a businessman and wanted a sign and a good-faith gesture that Junior would take responsibility for the coke debt.

Junior told us, "It's how this business works. It's in nobody's interest to hurt me over one drug debt, especially given my reputation," he said proudly. "What usually happens is, if a load gets lost or stolen, the profits on the next shipment usually more than cover it. Besides, dead men can't repay debts... it's not in their best interest to kill someone useful. That's not how it works in this business," Junior reassured. "That is the game, and I'm good at playing it," Junior boasted. Junior explained it was common in the drug trade for drug lords to put transporters and their brokers to work (for free) to cover losses of merchandise, but only after carefully assessing the cause. Junior called the repayment process "working it off" and described it as a form of indentured servitude. "Yes, it can occasionally get ugly, especially if the losses pile up."

Ramiro then directed his comments to La Mona, saying, "As far as your interest in the crane seizure, I don't understand how you can demand anything for the heroin you lost. Barney arranged that shipment, and he knew nothing about your heroin you had hidden together with the coke. You can take that up directly with Leyner or whoever sourced you the heroin." That temporarily shut La

Mona up. Leyner Valencia was a well-documented North Valley Cartel leader and a significant source of supply for both cocaine and heroin. La Mona had strong ties to him and others of the North Valley.

Junior turned to Beto and said, "Compadre, Ramiro is our golden ticket… don't go to war over one little fucking seizure that wasn't even his responsibility. We stand to make a fortune from Cumepa. Be patient, Compa," he urged.

Junior, aware of his mission to gather evidence, stood up and moved to another seat near Ramiro and Matematico, or "Mate" for short. Junior knew our focus was on Ramiro because, as he said, "Ramiro was key to everyone and everything DEA needed." Besides having one-on-one conversations with Ramiro, Junior also managed to record talks with both Chivo and Matematico. Mate was in a hurry to transport the 400 kilos of cocaine he had in Panama to Mexico. After his initial buyers backed out of their commitment, he needed to find a new buyer, believing his chances were better in Mexico.

The meeting ended around 3:30 p.m. As he left the restaurant, Junior glanced over at Mickey and Darren and gave them a slick wink. "Holy shit, Mick… did you just see that?" They assumed nobody noticed because Junior led the way as everyone began leaving the restaurant. Still, it was enough to make the agents nervous that he might eventually blow their cover. "He's way too fucking cocky!" Darren said as they left. Ramiro walked out and flagged down a taxi. Jimmy and another agent from Mexico City followed Ramiro as they sped away. The other Mexico City agents followed Junior back to his hotel to ensure his safe arrival, allowing him to quickly download his recordings and send them to us in Houston.

Upon receiving the attached recording, it was obvious that background noises made some parts of their conversations hard to understand. I took the recording to DEA's forensic audio-video specialist for help. Specialized equipment was used to reduce the extraneous noises and clean the recorded conversation. Luckily, the forensic specialist was able to lessen some of the background noise, resulting in a clearer and more understandable conversation. It was fortunate, as there was valuable intelligence throughout. The improved version was copied, with the original recordings placed into evidence. While listening to the enhanced recording, I noticed that La Mona was present during the meeting and could hear him verbally assaulting Junior over the debt.

Attempts to follow Ramiro ended in frustration as his taxi driver aggressively weaved through congested traffic. Ramiro was somewhere near Mexico City's World Trade Center, located in the central part of the sprawling capital, in the affluent Colonia of Nápoles. Luckily, Junior told us he had scheduled a follow-up meeting with Ramiro the next day at the same hotel to discuss logistics for another gathering in Panama.

Later that evening, I received a phone call from Jimmy, who advised me he had been contacted by Miami Agents Williams and Chapman concerning "a trafficker meeting in Mexico City."

"Mike, not sure how they found out about the meeting, but I was asked if I knew about it and if we obtained a recording."

It dawned on me that we sent out a teletype requesting country clearance for Mickey and Darren to travel to Mexico to coordinate Junior's UC meeting with Beto, La Mona, Ramiro, and others.

"That's it, Mike. They assumed you guys would have Junior recording it, and now they want a copy."

"Did La Mona tell you or them he was there, as well?"

"We haven't heard from him yet," Jimmy replied. "What will you guys do?"

"I guess we'll eventually share the recording... we've decided we're not playing any fucking games," I said.

Junior and Ramiro met at the same restaurant the next day as planned. Although Junior had not benefited from DEA's basic undercover training, he carried himself as if he were an experienced pro, thinking quickly and positioning himself to reduce surrounding noise. Junior was acting and thinking like an agent. We agreed with Junior's evaluation of Ramiro's potential as a cooperator. Junior's goal was to do everything possible to help us facilitate a major seizure involving Ramiro, to influence his decision when the time came.

The Bigotones partners (Ramiro and Barney) set up commercial fronts across Latin America, focusing on Panama because it hosts the largest "Free Trade Zone" in the western hemisphere. Ramiro and Barney created front companies in Panama, while drug lords like Oscar Nava also set up fake businesses in Mexico to serve as legitimate destinations for cover loads shown on bills of lading. Before mixing any cocaine with legitimate goods (such as scrap metal or construction materials), they conducted numerous test runs under Ramiro and Barney's direction to gauge the risk of container searches by authorities. Junior also emphasized the importance of bribing corrupt port officials before shipping, regardless of whether the containers were loaded or not. These officials were never informed about the test runs, as they too were being evaluated.

Junior's meeting with Ramiro was brief. Their conversation focused on the use of Cumepa. Ramiro insisted he wanted to have between 3,000 and 3,500 kilos of coke stored before launching a container or two to Mexico's Port of Progreso. Ramiro told Junior he believed there would be at least five or six investors involved, naming them as Oscar Nava, Gordo Mario, Beto, and his financier Cubas, along with Mate and other Colombian associates whose identities he was not yet aware of. Ramiro assumed they were members of the North Valley Cartel. If the investors were unknown to Ramiro, he expected half the commission upfront, the amount depending on the drugs (and quantities) being shipped. The legitimate cover loads were determined by Ramiro and Barney and were heavily influenced by product demand in Mexico.

"Why wait until early next year to launch the first container?" Junior asked.

"Since Nava's portion is the majority of what we're shipping, I need to await his approval. Besides, he might want it sent closer to him. We would have to ship it to Manzanillo."

"Are you talking directly to Nava?" Junior asked.

"I'm having to go through Chivo... he's difficult," Ramiro said. "I don't mind... Nava scares the shit out of me," Ramiro explained, reminding Junior that his given nickname was "Lobo" (Wolf).

"Huh, yeah... with the nickname 'Wolf,' I understand," Junior said with a nod.

"You mentioned Gordo Mario. Are you splitting the commissions with Barney since Gordo Mario is involved?"

"Yes, every time Gordo Mario uses a Cumepa container, we'll have to split the commission since I'm the one doing the bulk of the work with Cumepa." Ramiro explained. Ramiro began recounting the history he had with Barney. Their personalities couldn't have been any more dissimilar. Ramiro was low-key and introverted in comparison to Barney's extroverted, showman's panache. Their partnership dated back to the early 1990s, when they imported clothing, toys, and electronics from Texas into Mexico. Over time, they graduated to moving stolen vehicles and alcohol, developing a taste for more risk (and returns) as business grew. Naturally, cocaine was the next commodity of interest. It was during this time that Ramiro and Barney were nicknamed Bigotones, befitting their look-alike "Burt Reynolds" style mustaches.

As their friendship grew, they formalized a business partnership and opened an office in Mexico City's "World Trade Center" (also known as "Hotel de Mexico"). Both men, thoroughly familiar with the complexities of commercial trade, applied their business skills and watched their profit margins soar. Naturally, they attracted traffickers as well as police and politicians who protected drug dealings. Both men were well-known in the business world, and corrupt politicians, law enforcement officials, and traffickers frequently sought their services. It was during the peak of the cocaine boom that Mexico became the primary destination for most of Colombia's cocaine exports.

Ramiro's introduction to the drug trade happened during the 1990s, partly fueled by his close ties to Beto's in-laws. Through the Bravo family, Ramiro met several Mexican customs and port officials who offered their services for a fee, which included everything from rubber-stamping fake paperwork to clearing imports without inspection. One thing led to another, and their reputation grew, catching the attention of dangerous narcos like Nava Valencia and others from the Sinaloa Federation. Around the same time, Barney managed to build a close relationship with the Guatemalan drug lord, Gordo Mario.

Their success relied on those key partnerships which provided access to two major seaports in Mexico: Progreso, in the Yucatan, and Manzanillo, in the State of Colima, neighboring Jalisco and Nayarit. These ports were exclusively controlled by the Sinaloa Federation.

As their second meeting came to an end, Ramiro asked a personal favor of Junior. "I cannot deal with your compadre, Junior," Ramiro said. "I want to deal directly with you from now on. Can you please take care of that for me?"

Junior, although unsurprised, knew it would cause undue friction between him and his compadre, Beto. "How can I tell him not to contact you when he's the one who introduced us?"

"I can't reason with the man. He puts too much pressure on me and then he even threatens me. Look at what he's doing regarding the crane seizure. That was Barney... not me. I will not be threatened, Junior."

"I'll do my best to back him off," Junior said to temper Ramiro's aggravation.

"He's got all these Mex Fed contacts he uses as muscle. I know he will follow through with his threats, Junior. He scares me," Ramiro said. "If you can't do anything, I'll have to appeal to 'Lobo' to shut Beto down. I don't want to get your compadre hurt, Junior."

"Don't do that, Ramiro. That'll send the wrong message because they all see Beto as my partner, too. It'll affect me, as well. Please let me handle it," Junior implored.

"Okay, Junior... just talk to him and get him to lay off." As he started to change the subject, he suddenly thought of an idea that might ease the tension with Junior's compadre. "Hey, Junior... I just thought of something. Mate is eager to move the 400 kilos he has sitting in Panama. He wants it moved in a container with scrap metal, and he wants it done soon. He needs a buyer."

"Okay, so how does that help out your situation with Beto?" asked Junior.

"Mate doesn't have a buyer yet, and since he's in a crunch to get it moved, maybe he'll drop the prices to entice Beto and his Cuban partner... just thinking..."

"Okay, let me talk to Beto. What price are we thinking?" Junior asked.

"I will drop my transportation fee if Mate is willing to unload the 400 kilos at a lower price to Beto, say $ 5,000 per unit delivered to Progreso. How does that sound?"

"Beto should jump at that since he's looking at $ 8,500.00 per brick in Monterrey."

"Maybe he will get off my back then?" Ramiro mused.

"He'll go for that. He's got his trucks to get it up to Monterrey. It'll be pure profit for him and his Cuban."

"Do you know the Cuban?" Ramiro asked.

"I've never met him. Beto says the guy doesn't want to meet anybody. I am pretty sure he works with Arturo Beltran's people because all their dope goes to Atlanta," Junior said.

Junior knew that the price per kilo delivered to the Progreso would normally fetch anywhere from $6,000 to $6,500 per kilogram. And both men knew that Matematico would serve as an excellent reference for other North Valley traffickers seeking transportation options.

Junior, embracing his UC role, convinced Ramiro to discuss previous shipments he had coordinated with Barney. After Junior's meeting ended, he went back to his hotel, downloaded the recordings, and sent them to me. Reviewing his private conversation with Ramiro, I was pleased to see that Junior cleverly discovered the names of other companies Ramiro and Barney had used in the past to send multiple containers (full of cocaine) to Mexico. One of these companies was set up to ship aluminum scrap metal as cover loads. Ramiro boasted about regularly sending between 6,000 and 7,000 kilograms of cocaine to Mexico.

Once Junior was able to call, he and I talked extensively about Gordo Mario. Junior found out that Gordo Mario wasn't just supplying cocaine to the Zetas; he was also inviting them to Guatemala to set up another base for their operations. Junior discovered that the Zetas were already connected with Guatemalan Special Forces members, known as "Kaibiles." They were using Guatemala for joint training and as a new Zeta operational base for their planned expansion. Heriberto Lazcano, also known as "Z-3," had formed close ties with Gordo Mario and other Guatemalan drug trafficking families. Junior's information came from Ramiro. He wondered, with Beto's access, why he hadn't heard any of this from him.

Junior was still confident, however, in Beto's ability to move their cocaine into Texas through the Gulf corridor without having to pay the mandatory tax ("piso") demanded of other independent traffickers.

"The rumor is the Zetas want a bigger piece of the pie and are looking to become their own drug trafficking organization because they see the money potential," Junior said.

"We've heard rumblings of that," I said.

"Ramiro says Barney talks to Gordo Mario about the Zetas all the time. He says now that Osiel has been in jail, this guy Lazcano is tired of being subordinate to the Gulf leaders and wants to slowly break away. There's a little friction with the Gulf leaders over it."

"We're hearing a little bit about this as well. Can you ask Beto what he knows?" I was gathering my information from Bishop, who was monitoring communications (using court-authorized wiretaps) between Gulf and Zeta leaders. DEA was learning that the Zetas were gradually breaking away from the organization that initially employed their services. Bishop's case agents (Dave Todd and Anthony Lewis) were also developing reliable intel that the Zetas were establishing a radio network offering rapid communication capabilities from the Texas border south to Guatemala.

Junior related Ramiro's warning to take extra precautions while operating in the Gulf's corridor, given the rumors regarding the alleged friction between the two organizations. "Yeah, Ramiro reminded me it wasn't the same cartel my father was a part of." He added, "When Osiel took over in the late 1990s, the growing violence scared the shit out of everyone. Even businessmen who could leave Mexico began moving out, relocating to places like Austin, Texas." Junior knew Osiel's cartel was different from that of his father but still felt safe given Beto's close relationships.

"Just be careful, Junior," I said. "In Osiel's absence, we are hearing the Zetas are dangerous and unpredictable."

While Junior and I were on the phone, Ramiro was being followed again by Jimmy and other agents from

Mexico City. Ramiro flagged a taxi outside the hotel restaurant and was taken back to the same neighborhood, Colonia Nápoles. He was dropped off in front of Mexico City's World Trade Center. Towering fifty stories, it is the third most prominent building in the city. Ramiro was seen walking into the lobby and entering the elevator. Since he was the only passenger, he probably got off on the twelfth floor, where it first stopped. Jimmy and the local agents returned to the embassy to meet with Mickey and Darren for their post-surveillance debrief.

Mickey and Darren walked from their hotel, Maria Isabel Sheraton, to the nearby US Embassy located on the busy Paseo De La Reforma. They approached the embassy's front gate, where two Mexican security guards greeted them immediately. The embassy was a large, four-story, rectangular building made of solid concrete. It looked capable of withstanding a strong earthquake, which sometimes occurs in the big city, the last one being in 1985. They were allowed inside after showing their credentials, then climbed a flight of stairs to a checkpoint where they passed through a metal detector. After that, they queued to be screened by a US Marine guard sitting behind thick bulletproof glass. The Marine activated a speaker and asked for their identification; they handed over their DEA credentials. The Staff Sergeant checked their credentials, confirmed the names matched the visitor list, and quickly approved their entry. Not having a diplomat's black passport, the Marine on duty called up to the fourth floor to request that the DEA send an escort to pick up the two Houston-based agents. Jimmy quickly came down and led Mickey and Darren to the DEA's fourth-floor conference room.

During their meeting, the Mexico City agents were briefed on the joint efforts of Houston and Miami in support of the Band of Brothers, with an emphasis on the newly identified organization known as Los Gueros. Their discussion then shifted to the importance of monitoring undercover meetings and the need to fully identify Ramiro and his partner, Barney. It was likely that their office was at the World Trade Center. Mickey, Darren, and Jimmy left Mexico City, hopeful that Junior had successfully opened doors that had previously been closed to the DEA. The only thing that caused some concern (albeit humorous) among the agents was Junior's overly confident attitude toward his new role as "DEA's 007."

CHAPTER 11
THE BIG APPLE

We had multiple irons in the fire on both sides of the border. Shortly after returning from Mexico City, Mickey and Darren were contacted by Eddy in New York regarding the latest developments in their Vladimir investigation. "Vladi," as he was called, was the Gueros's main distributor in New York and the DEA's opportunity to infiltrate the Mexico-based organizations from the US distribution side.

On one side of the border, we were looking to identify Ramiro and Barney, along with the kingpins who utilized their services. On the north side, we were tracking various transporters and distributors from McAllen to New York and everywhere in between. Our goal was to utilize Junior's information and collaborate with other law enforcement partners to develop independent cases against domestic-based cells. Our efforts resulted in both drug and money seizures that were documented independently and then charged and prosecuted separately at the state level, effectively walling off our federal case. We subsequently used many of the arrests and seizures as "overt acts" so that we could go back, link them all together, and charge it all as part of one federal conspiracy. Because of Junior, we seized cocaine going north and drug proceeds headed south to Mexico, none of which threatened our long-term designs for an epic culmination.

Because Band of Brothers was now a global operation, it was in our best interest to coordinate our respective investigations in a manner that would preclude adversely affecting the activities of other offices. SOD's function was paramount in this regard. Band of Brothers continued to grow globally, with coordination ongoing between US domestic and foreign offices located in Mexico, Central and South America, as well as in European countries such as Italy, Germany, Belgium, and the Netherlands. DEA targeted the tentacles of organized crime syndicates linked to Colombian sources and Mexico's Sinaloa Federation.

Eddy called us to report a crucial phone conversation recorded between Vladi and Cantu, in which Vladi complained about receiving a "damaged product" transported in Cantu's truckload of limes. Cantu was asked to make a quick trip to New York to discuss a possible solution to offset the expected loss of profit. Eddy mentioned that Junior's name came up as Cantu indicated he would invite Junior along to help calm things down before the issue was "taken up with the blondies." Eddy knew that "blondies" referred to the Gueros.

Vladimir originally came to Eddy's attention following the unrelated arrests of Dominican street-level dealers (one in Queens, the other in Staten Island) earlier that summer. Eddy worked in a Task Force Group comprising DEA agents and Task Force officers from the NYPD and the New York State Police. He was still considered a rookie agent in the group (Task Force Group T-31). Although a rookie, he managed to turn his defendants into Confidential Informants (CIs) and learned they were getting their cocaine from the same distributor, Vladi. It didn't take Eddy long to identify Vladimir as the regional wholesale supplier. From Vladimir, he discovered McAllen-based transporter Cantu.

Targeting street dealers seldom led to cocaine-sourcing kingpins. New York's lower-level distributors were too numerous to count. DEA's street-level seizures usually involved cocaine, which had already been "stepped on" with the use of an array of adulterants. Diluting pure cocaine was how local dealers increased profit margins. Eddy discovered a small gold mine in Vladimir.

Eddy laid the case out to his street-savvy boss, Group Supervisor Tim Foley, who quickly approved a long-term investigation and steered Eddy to an AUSA in the Eastern District. Within a month, a DEA UC agent was introduced to Vladimir's lower-level associates, and the case began to gain momentum. The UC traveled to McAllen and met with McAllen-based associates of Cantu. Our three offices (New York, McAllen, and Houston) were closely coordinating and collectively building our respective cases.

Learning of Junior's informant status in Houston was the icing on what was already a delicious cake for Eddy. Aside from DEA's coordination, their respective AUSAs were also in regular contact as we began to develop prosecutorial strategies. It was a textbook example of a long-term, complex criminal investigation, serving as a model for how things were supposed to work when agents and their attorneys set aside their personal interests.

A native of Spring Valley, New York, and a Magna Cum Laude graduate of the University of Albany (Rockefeller School of Criminal Justice), Eddy initially hired on with the Secret Service in 1999. While still in the Secret Service

Academy, DEA finished processing his application and offered him a job. Eddy jumped ship and became a DEA agent in the New York Field Division. The Gueros case became Eddy's first career-building opportunity, a once-in-a-lifetime chance to get involved with an international investigation traceable to both Mexican and Colombian kingpins. Eddy, Darren and Mickey hit it off from the start. They not only shared information transparently but also became close friends over time. "Thank God the guys in New York are team players," Darren said one day after a 2-hour-long conference call with Eddy.

Eddy's boss, GS Foley, was no different. He was a street agent's boss whose motto was, "Do the right thing for the case."

Mickey and I arrived in New York the day after Eddy's phone call. Junior, already aware of the damaged-kilo problem, arranged to meet us there before visiting Vladimir. We contacted Eddy and arranged to meet Junior at the New York office to strategize. The DEA office was an eight-story building located on 10th Avenue in Manhattan. It was built in 1917, retrofitted in 1930 to accommodate the tracks of the New York Central Railroad. Formerly a Merchant Refrigeration building, it was eventually transformed into both a government facility occupying the east-northeastern side and a ministorage facility utilizing the west side of the massive structure. After the refrigerated warehouse was sold in 1983, the purchasing developer reported that it took seven months for the entire building to thaw completely.

Eddy escorted us up to his wire room, located on the seventh floor. There, Eddy went over the line sheets, highlighting relevant phone calls intercepted off the wire, revealing dirty calls between Vladimir, Cantu, and Junior. Coded references were made to the Gueros, referring to them as "veggie brothers."

"Our AUSA is chomping at the bit to start a grand jury. We've got some work to do still, but we are beginning to pick up some good stuff on our wires," Eddy said confidently. "For now, we're interested in the two main brothers, correct?" Eddy asked.

"Esteban and Luis," Mickey related. "We've learned Luis runs things overall while Esteban is in charge of domestic distribution operations."

We reviewed the call summaries collected on the intercepts between Vladimir and other associates. Mickey and I chuckled while listening to calls in which Vladimir spoke with deference whenever mentioning Junior, granting him the status of a drug lord. And then it dawned on me that he did have forty-seven tons of pure cocaine under his belt. "Oh, I can never tell Junior about this... his fuckin head is big enough already. If he hears Vladi thinks he's a big-time drug lord, his head will inflate like a helium balloon," I joked.

Once Junior arrived, we had him come to the office to give Eddy some background on everything. He explained that the damaged kilos were part of a larger shipment mixed in with palm oil. He went on to describe the entire debacle involving Beto's scheme to remove 100 kilos, which could be sold quickly to clients in Atlanta.

"But Cantu transported those kilos on behalf of the Gueros," Eddy assumed.

"Miami's Colombian informant, La Mona, apparently gained access to several of Baca's kilos and flipped them to the Gueros, who in turn used Cantu to get them up to

New York. It was done behind Junior's back, all while he was in Houston dealing with his daughter."

"Why isn't La Mona up here dealing with it?" Eddy asked.

"He threw it all back on Junior," I responded.

Eddy was told that Tony Baca was Miami's target of interest and that La Mona was their snitch. It was important, given that it would likely be picked up on New York's wires.

"We rarely share an informant's identity with our monitors. But we do need to know who's who for our AUSA's benefit," Eddy pointed out. We all agreed our informants needed to be protected.

We then instructed Junior to schedule a meeting with Cantu and Vladimir at the Marriott Marquis, located in the heart of Times Square. Eddy arranged for another hotel to be used as a safe location for a post-meet debriefing.

"Junior, after meeting with these guys, take a taxi over to 'Edison' on West 47th Street. Let's make eye contact in the lobby… follow us into the elevator and to the room," Eddy directed.

Before Junior headed out, he looked at Eddy, extended his hand, smiled, and said, "It's a pleasure meeting another fellow crime fighter!"

Junior departed in a taxi and made his way to the Marriott Marquis, where Cantu and Vladimir were waiting.

"How can you not love this guy?" Eddy said, shaking his head over Junior's "crime fighter" comment.

"What's gonna happen with the damaged kilos?" Eddy asked.

"Junior was told by Cantu the kilo packages had been opened for random purity testing while still in storage in Monterrey. Once they crossed over to McAllen, the opened packages were loaded into Cantu's truck and mixed in with fresh limes. The problem arose from the use of wet boxes. The limes were already overly ripe, which I guess affected some of the kilos – I'm not sure how many. Junior will find that out during his meeting." I was anxious to have the meeting recorded.

After reviewing additional "line sheets" depicting the monitors' transcription of Vladimir's calls, Eddy could see where specific kilo numbers were mentioned. Despite the crooks' use of coded language to disguise their criminal activities, we all laughed at how often the bad guys would forget the specific codes to be used and would carelessly blurt out incriminating language, such as "kilos," "coke," "stash house," and kilogram prices. The monitors would shake their heads in amusement and congratulate us agents for "chasing and catching the dummies." Occasionally, we would even admit to ourselves, "We do mostly catch the idiots in this business."

Instead of wiring Junior up, Eddy decided to issue Junior another covert piece of recording equipment that could be downloaded but not monitored in real-time. There just wasn't sufficient time to arrange for a hotel room close enough to hardwire audio-video equipment.

Surveillance agents could see Junior and Cantu chatting in the hotel lobby of the Marriott Marquis. They stood there for about ten minutes, and then Vladimir joined them. They were photographed heading towards the elevators. "I sure hope Junior's got his recorder on," Mickey said.

Eddy had agents set up in and around the hotel to follow Vladimir after the meeting ended. Eddy, Mickey, and I left and went back to the Edison Hotel to grab a bite and wait for Junior. "Don't worry, my guys already got pics of Cantu meeting with Vladi, and of Cantu meeting with Junior. We've got it covered," Eddy reassured.

We found an Italian restaurant not far from the Edison, sat down, ordered some Calzones and iced teas, and began discussing the situation involving the Colombian informant, La Mona.

"What do you think is going on in Miami?" Eddy asked out of curiosity. "Do you think they are playing stupid, or are they naïve and in the dark about what their rat is up to?"

"We know the agents in Miami are angry that we recruited Junior in the first place. They feel like they've lost control over the operation. We wanted to work the operation together with them, but they can't seem to get past us taking control of things with Junior's assistance," I said.

Mickey added, "And it doesn't help that Junior is the one who is all of a sudden making things happen."

"Yeah," I nodded in agreement.

"It's ego, I guess," Eddy said. "Yeah, it gets in the way sometimes." He laughed and added, "You know... sometimes it's nice being the new guy where you realize *you're* the one who lacks the experience. I would welcome all the help I could get. The last thing I would want is to be manipulated by a clever snitch." The three of us spent another hour sitting there sipping iced tea before heading back up to the room to await Junior's return. Mickey asked if there were any Whataburger franchises in town. He was addicted to their iced teas.

A few hours passed before the knock on the door came. Junior's eyes were watery and bloodshot. He was distraught, with the color gone from his face. He walked into the room, handed the recording device to Eddy, sat down, placed his hands on his face, and stared at the floor. Mickey and I exchanged a glance as we realized it was likely news from home. During our last phone conversation with Junior, he shared his daughter's dire prognosis.

"Did you get a call from Houston, Junior?" I asked.

He managed to mumble his response, "Yes... my wife called me... she's gone... she's gone."

Suddenly, Eddy snapped at the fact that he had just lost his daughter.

With tears in Junior's eyes, he repeated, "She's gone. My little girl is gone." There were no words of comfort. There was no interfering with Junior's grief at that moment.

"Junior, we'll talk later... go home and be with family," I said as I placed my hand on his shoulder. "Don't worry about this... you've done a lot... go home." He managed to stand up, shake everyone's hand, and slowly make his way out the door. We just stood there, motionless and speechless. It was something no father ever wanted to experience. We had families of our own. Rehabilitated trafficker or not... the pain was the same.

We finished up in New York and headed home. Mine and Bishop's groups were reunited for a quick review of everything we had accomplished to date. Everyone knew of Junior's tragic news. We were sickened by the fact that he was in the middle of a traumatic crisis while at the same time doing our bidding – betraying those he considered close friends and business associates. The only silver lining we could see was his heartfelt commitment and earnest effort to transform his life. He was now a good guy, doing what he needed to make positive changes for himself and his family. Junior was integral to the mission and was now embraced as a member of our team. We were the ones who now felt like a "Band of Brothers" of which Junior was now a member. We developed a great affection for the man we once considered a criminal. Junior warmed our hearts in a short time as he jumped into action, putting on a smile amid his heartbreaking tragedy. *And now we felt his loss.*

Whatever initial doubts we might have had regarding Junior's commitment, they were wiped away by how forthright and forthcoming he was out of the gate. His mind was set on a positive change, whether motivated by his feelings of guilt over his family's misfortunes or perhaps by the good inside him scratching to get out. We could all see how important his family was to him. And now with his second child gone, Junior was an empty shell of a man. This was a time in our relationship where the case's importance suddenly took a backseat to our concerns for Junior.

It was the end of October 2005. Mickey and I had been back in Houston for over a week with no word from Junior. We weren't about to call him in Monterrey. He was back home with Sara and his two boys, and we knew he needed time to grieve. We were also waiting to hear from Eddy, as we were curious about the results of Junior's recorded UC meeting the week prior. Just as I asked Mickey and Darren to give Eddy a call to inquire about it, Eddy's call came in.

"Mike, it's Eddy on the line. He says he has an update on what happened last week," Mickey said as he transferred the call to my office. He and Darren joined me as I put the call on speaker.

"Yes, sir, Eddy. What's goin on? You're on speaker with us."

"Hey Mike, Mick, and Darren. So, we have quite a bit of information we gleaned now that we've transcribed the conversations," Eddy reported. "By the way, how is Junior doing?"

"He's back in Mexico with the family. We're giving him some breathing room right now," I said.

"Understood, I hope he bounces back. Junior is doing a hell of a job for all of us," Eddy said.

"That's for sure," Mickey and Darren both chimed.

"Okay, so basically, Junior just put us at a whole new level with this meeting. They not only discussed the bad kilos, but our boy Vladimir vomited all over himself with juicy details on the Gueros that I don't think even you guys were aware of. The Gueros have been sending coke up here for years now and are moving a shit ton to other cities, as well, even Los Angeles. They're good targets to go after."

"Junior told Vladi he knew nothing about the damaged kilos coming to New York, explaining that La Mona gained access to their warehouse and brokered his deal with the Gueros brothers. Cantu confirmed it all happened while Junior was in Houston dealing with his daughter." He paused to catch his breath.

"Vladi broke down the exact numbers received and damaged," Eddy said. "A total of 166 were received. Of the total, 90 were good and 76 were bad. And I don't think Junior is gonna be held responsible for the damaged ki's from the sound of things. Junior was calm and unconcerned during the meeting," Eddy explained. "Vladi also related how the brothers were sending a lot of their cocaine concealed within home construction materials and decorative items like stone pillars and columns. And, to top it off, we've got enough information to start expanding our investigation, getting other agencies like the IRS involved to start tracking assets the Gueros might have here in New York and elsewhere."

"Shit, we hit the lotto," Darren remarked.

Eddy continued, "We followed Vladi after the meeting, and I think we've identified another couple of stash houses the Gueros are using in the Bronx and New Rochelle. It sounds like they've got other wholesale distributors they're using besides Vladi. I think they're competitors of his, and it's a bit of a rub for Vladimir." Eddy knew this case was getting bigger by the day. "I think we can also start looking at some historical seizures we can pin on the Gueros, as well, which makes our AUSA happy," Eddy said, pausing. "And that's just coke," he added. "Then there are money seizures we need to look at," he said, excitedly.

Eddy referenced Vladimir's comments about sending suitcases full of cash to Mexico almost daily. Truckloads of coke were moving north while suitcases full of cash were passing them on the highway as they headed south to the Texas border towns of McAllen and Laredo. Vladimir described one money seizure of $2.1 million taken from a load vehicle as it was entering McAllen city limits. The money was divided up and stuffed into two black colored suitcases. Vladimir provided a detailed description, right down to the gold-colored key locks. According to Vladimir, an unwitting driver was paid ("no questions asked") and sent south to meet a specified point of contact using a code name to identify himself once in McAllen. The suitcases were mixed in among other household goods. Vladimir suspected the police had a tip because they pulled the vehicle over and cut the driver loose without making an arrest. It was like the police knew. Eddy also remarked how Vladimir was amused at how neither Esteban nor Luis seemed upset at the seizure. "That's how much cash these guys are sending," Eddy blurted out in astonishment.

I related, anecdotally, that when Junior was debriefed by our analyst, Trish, he told her that the main brother, Guero, had such amazing credit with certain Colombian sources that he didn't have to front a dime for a large load — multiple tons worth.

"Yeah, I'm learning just how big some of these Mexican traffickers are," Eddy replied.

"Most of what Junior passed to Trish had been related to Junior by Esteban, who runs all the domestic distribution operations. Junior is closest to *him*. Junior explained Guero can easily pull together as much as twenty-five million when he's dealing with his Colombian sources of supply... *twenty-five million dollars!*" I stressed, attempting to wrap my own mind around the figure.

"Jesus," Eddy said. "Okay... that's it from the 'Big Apple.' Now I'm late for a meeting with the AUSA on this case. Gotta run, guys!"

The second week of November arrived, and still no word from Junior. Nobody said anything, but we were all thinking it... *maybe he came to his senses and said fuck it...born an outlaw, die an outlaw*. Now our concerns had shifted back to the case. We had come too far to lose our 007 and all that he had accomplished for the "A" team. His lack of contact was worrisome. Over lunch across the street at Champs, Bishop and I put our heads together and strategized the *"what ifs..."*

I got a call as we were closing our tab. It was Darren. "007 called in on our UC line, Mike."

I looked over at Bishop with a noticeable sigh of relief. He nodded as we knew we were back in business. Once I got back to the office and got Junior on the line, it was as if nothing had happened. An upbeat Junior announced he was back in the game and "ready for another mission."

"Did you miss 007?" Junior joked. Upon asking about his family's welfare, he replied, "My wife and I are okay. It's time to get back to work, boss."

CHAPTER 12
MONKEY BOY

"I need to get down to Panama and meet with Ramiro," Junior said. "Since the whole thing happened with the crane seizure, Ramiro and I have gotten closer. He no longer likes dealing with my compadre. It's a perfect opportunity to get him ready to start working with *us*, you know, so that he can be 008," Junior said, thinking like an agent.

Junior's calendar was rapidly filling up with undercover meetings scheduled through the end of the year (2005). Investors were in a hurry to get their cocaine to market and then take off during the holiday season like everyone else. It was the one thing we were reminded of throughout our interaction with Junior. Drug lords, like agents, had family responsibilities and pressures, and were often torn between "work" obligations – albeit criminal – and their wives, children, and paramours, of course.

Within a matter of weeks, we documented incriminating conversations with both domestic and foreign priority targets: Cantu, Pantera, Vladimir, Tony Baca, Matematico, Chivo, Ramiro, compadre Beto, and La Mona. We still weren't sure which team La Mona was playing for, or whether he might be cleverly playing for both. The one thing we knew for sure was that Band of Brothers was suddenly blinking on everyone's radar, catching a lot of attention from the suits in headquarters. Our funding requests were never denied.

SAC Craig's operational direction was to run as fast and as hard as we could because time was of the essence. SAC Craig encouraged us to "think outside the box" and be creative with our ops plans. We all knew about Murphy's Law in our business – if things could go to shit, they would, and in a big way, at the most inopportune times. We were recording Junior's associates talking about drug smuggling ventures (past and present), but now what we desperately needed were identifiable drug and money seizures which could be tied to our subjects of interest – tangible corroboration for a prosecutor to present to a grand jury.

Junior's last meeting in Mexico revealed that ongoing negotiations were in progress for an upcoming cocaine shipment tentatively scheduled to leave Panama for Mexico around early 2006. We urged Junior to concentrate his UC efforts on Ramiro since Cumepa was to be used. Junior estimated that approximately 3,000 kilograms would be sent to either Progreso or Manzanillo. Progreso, located near Merida, was Ramiro's preferred choice due to his familiarity with its port authorities.

Panama served as an important staging area for Colombians. Stash houses, like dots on a map, were scattered all over the small Central American country. Ocean-going fast boats were used to shuttle multi-hundred-kilo loads into Panama, where they were hidden and safeguarded pending the next leg of northbound transit. This was where Ramiro's skill set was put to work. He coordinated directly with Colombians to take receipt of cocaine being collected on behalf of investors. The coke would then be covertly moved to warehouses associated with legitimate businesses, such as Cumepa. It would remain in a warehouse until coke could be carefully secreted within whatever legit product was used as a cover load.

Panama was ideal for so many reasons. It was like a mini-Colombia for underworld figures. Colombian presence raised no flags, given that many had already relocated to Panama over the years to escape a violent era of civil unrest. They especially loved doing business there, given the country's loosely regulated banking laws, which were conducive to a multi-billion-dollar industry where obscene amounts of cash were the norm.

Panama is a smuggler's dream spot. In the world-renowned Free Trade Zone, goods are re-exported throughout Latin America and the Caribbean. Established in 1948, it is now home to over 2,000 companies whose sole function is to import and export merchandise. There are factories and warehouses dedicated to re-packaging various products in preparation for export. It consists of a port and a transit system designed to move merchandise that has been imported, manufactured, or re-packaged. Businesses enjoy a zero tax on income derived from exporting goods, with zero tariffs and quotas on imports and exports.

What's not to like for traffickers seeking to conceal thousands of kilo-sized bricks inside thousands of maritime containers carrying legitimate cargo like scrap metal and galvanized ceiling tiles, likely never to be searched. For us in law enforcement, finding containerized cocaine was tantamount to looking for a needle in a haystack. The odds were stacked against us. Had it not been for the "Juniors" of the world, interdiction efforts would be futile.

As Panama was ideal for the traffickers, so too was it for DEA Houston. We had a close friend who happened to be DEA's Country Attaché, running operations out of the Embassy. Joe Evans was Bishop's suitemate in Quantico (1990) while Evans and I were later partnered as agents in Costa Rica (1998 – 2001).

Evans reported to Panama in September 2005 to take charge of the office after spending a couple of years in Chantilly, VA, at the DEA's Special Operations Division. Before SOD, Evans served as the Country Attaché in Caracas, Venezuela, and prior to that, he was assigned to Costa Rica. Evans made a name for himself early on in his career in Miami as a "wire guy." His true passion, however, was to represent DEA's interests in the foreign arena. He was ideally suited for it. His personality was not that of an extrovert but rather one of quiet confidence. He was strong but non-threatening to people. Those he worked for appreciated his tireless work ethic and mission-oriented self-motivation. For those who worked for him, he was dependable, unflappable, and decisive in his leadership style, with a unique ability to cultivate cohesion and loyalty. He was one of the best partners I've ever had on the job. Although a few years his senior, I often felt like the rookie, struggling to keep pace with him. It was like being paired up at "Ranger School" with a professional athlete who could operate on a no-food, no-sleep regimen. Operating on only four hours of sleep a day, he could still work circles around most agents, including me. It was no wonder Evans was a former Marine Corps "Recon" Officer before coming over to the DEA.

"Hey Pinche, let's get Smokin Joe on the phone," Bishop suggested.

"DEA Panama, how can I help you?" said a female voice.

"Hi there, calling from DEA Houston, is the boss around?" I asked.

"Mr. Evans is on the other line… who may I ask is calling?"

"It's an old friend… please tell him it's 'Gato Negro.'" It was my unlucky "black cat" nickname given to me while assigned to our office in Costa Rica. Evans and I worked closely with Gonzalo Bado, who headed a counter-narcotics unit for Costa Rica's equivalent of the FBI. Bado was known throughout the region as a tenacious, efficient, and honest cop, dismantling one cartel operation after another. He was DEA's best friend in Central America. He was also a devoted soccer fan. It seemed every time I attended a game where Bado's favorite team ("Heredia") was playing, they always lost. I was appropriately branded as the "bad luck guy" and banned from attending any further matches in which "Heredia" was playing.

"Did you say '*Gato Negro?*'" the receptionist repeated, snickering. "Okay, hold on…"

"Yes, ma'am."

"Maje…!" Evans answered using the Costa Rican colloquial term for "dude."

"You're on speaker, Smokin' Joe!" Bishop announced.

"Dude! Both of you together… it's a reunion!" Evans said.

"Hey, Joe… we know you're bored to tears down there, so we called to give you guys something to do," I joked, knowing Panama's reputation for being a workaholic's dream.

"So, what's goin on in Houston?"

"Well, besides 'dog breath' summers, we have something going on you guys might be interested in," I said.

"It's part of SOD's 'Band of Brothers,'" Bishop added.

"Okay, dude... whatever you guys need," Evans assured.

After sharing some background information, including our concerns about Miami's informant and his agent handlers, Evans responded that they were no strangers to Miami agents, as they regularly hosted visiting agents from that division office. "Which agents are they? He asked.

"The senior guy is Mark Chapman... his partner is Dave Williams," I said.

"Yeah, I don't know either one of them. Hold on, let me bring my guy in and introduce him. Lee Nash, I have Mike Chavarria and Keith Bishop from Houston on the line."

"Houston... does this have anything to do with 'Band of Brothers?'" Lee asked.

"Yeah, how'd you know?" I asked.

"Your agent, Bostick, called, and we spoke about your snitch coming down for a meeting," Lee replied.

"Good to hear... yeah, Bostick works in my group," Bishop explained.

"He broke it all down for me, including the apparent dysfunction you guys are experiencing with Miami. Join the club," Lee added. "We have Miami agents in our backyard at least once every other week wanting to do a UC money delivery or cover an informant meeting." He paused. "But I don't know either agent you guys are working with."

"So, Lee will be working on everything Band of Brothers with you guys," Evans said. "Miami hasn't called us yet. Do they know what you all are doing with Junior?"

"We keep them informed via teletype," Bishop explained.

"Okay, we'll let you know if and when they contact us," Lee chimed.

Lee Nash was the first agent Evans selected. Lee was recruited from SOD's "959 Group." The "959" group was SOD's newest weapon against international drug trafficking syndicates operating around the world. Foreign-based crime bosses have generally considered themselves out of reach and "untouchable" by US law enforcement. Title 21, US Code, Section 959 was a newly created statute that empowered the US Department of Justice to seek the extradition of traffickers whose crimes against the US were committed without setting foot on US soil. To take full advantage of the newly enacted statute, DEA set up a special "959" group at SOD in Chantilly. It was comprised of select agents with reputations for working complex international cases.

"I'll be Bostick's point of contact when he and Junior come down. I'll have a burner phone to give Junior while he's here. We have a special unit that can cover the meeting and keep tabs on him. He told us about your guy, Ramiro."

"Ramiro is just the first of many. We expect there to be several others, as well. Mexicans, Colombians, and maybe a Guatemalan or two," Bishop added. "Bostick and Junior will get with you as soon as they land so you guys can strategize."

"Yeah," Lee said. "We know about Cumepa now, so we'll put our team on developing some intel for you all."

"Lee, we're especially interested in identifying the two Mexican transportation guys who work with Junior. Besides Ramiro, there's his partner, Barney. Collectively, they're known as Los Bigotones." Bishop went on to explain their nicknames, adding, "You can't miss Ramiro... he bears a striking resemblance to a monkey... straight jet-black hair, long arms, the lips... right down to the curling fingers. It's crazy. The other partner is Barney, named after the popular kids' show, you know, the purple dinosaur," Bishop added.

"*Outstanding*... a monkey and a purple dinosaur," Lee said, amused. "I love this job."

Lee had a tenacious, case-maker reputation." He was also the DEA's poster boy for pranks. Lee grew up knowing he was gonna be a cop. He wasn't sure exactly where he would land – whether a local police officer or a fed with the FBI, DEA, or ATF – but he knew he had that "calling" to be a lawman. It wasn't a path to fame and riches, but it sure was satisfying and rewarding. Lee equated the profession to being a "fisherman of bad guys."

Thanksgiving was only five days away. Being a boss wasn't a popular position when it came to separating an agent from his family during the holidays or special events (birthdays, anniversaries, etc.). It was also one of the big reasons why so many narcotics agents' marriages ended in divorce. Chasing druggies wasn't a nine-to-five job.

Bostick and Junior arrived in Panama that holiday week, coming in on separate flights. Since the undercover phase with Ramiro was still in its early stages, it was decided that any surveillance would have to be highly discreet to minimize our risk of compromise. Lee greeted Bostick at the gate, taking him straight to the Radisson

Decapolis, located on Avenida Balboa. It was the newest addition to Panama City's list of luxury hotels, located within walking distance to a huge mall, numerous restaurants, including the gringo favorite, "Hard Rock Café." It had a fantastic view of the Pacific Harbor and its boat traffic – an amazing view, especially during that time of year, with many of the boats lit up like Christmas trees. Of course, plans were best formed over drinks. Bostick arrived while Panama's weather was at its best.

Junior arranged the meeting to take place at "Alberto's Restaurant," located at the end of Panama's Amador Causeway. Of all the eateries to choose from, it had the best view as it overlooked the picturesque "Flamenco Marina" where several boats and yachts were moored. The location was ideal for setting up covert surveillance by local Panamanian counter-drug agents using an undercover yacht, which provided a direct line of sight for taking photos and acquiring clear, receptive signals for monitoring undercover conversations, whether the targets were seated inside or outside. The causeway itself was a beautiful and scenic highway, lined with palm trees, offering tropical ocean views on either side. The Marina was one of Panama's most popular tourist spots, featuring accompanying boutiques, shops, and a lovely, picturesque, panoramic view.

Junior arrived the following day and was introduced to Lee. He was already given his marching orders via the Hush mail account. He was instructed to head straight to "Hotel Las Americas," located right down the street from the "Decapolis," where he would meet Lee and Bostick. He was told to approach the lobby and ask to be connected to "Mr. Bond's room" – Lee's idea.

"Hello… this is Junior."

"Hola, Junior… this is Mr. Bond," Lee answered, prompting Junior to chuckle. "Come on up and join the party. We're on the third floor, take a left after you step out of the elevator… third room on the right."

"Okay, be right there," he responded. He walked straight to the elevator and entered without having to wait, passing other guests as they stepped out. As instructed, he tapped second, third, fourth, fifth, and sixth-floor buttons out of habit, just in case someone was watching – clever use of tradecraft in the event he was under surveillance by bad guys.

After a melodious knock at the door, Bostick greeted Junior and ushered him into the room. After a series of welcoming handshakes, Lee introduced himself as "Bond," to which Junior let out a snort, accusing Lee of stealing his identity.

"Welcome to Panama," Lee began.

"Yes, I love it here. You can smell the money in the air," Junior said, laughing.

"So, you'll be staying at the Hotel Panama, correct?" Lee asked.

"Yessir."

"No meetings in your room because we won't have any recording equipment set up," Lee instructed.

"I think Ramiro arrives tonight, the others tomorrow, I'm guessing."

"Is Beto coming?" Bostick asked.

"No, I didn't invite Beto. Neither was La Mona invited, at Ramiro's request. Ramiro doesn't like being around either one of them. This is mainly for investors like Oscar Nava, the Guatemalan, Gordo Mario, and Matematico."

"Won't Beto get mad?" Bostick inquired.

"Yeah, he might. He'll get over it. He still stands to make money using the overland transportation we're going to offer. He always makes good commissions on the use of his trucks, you know, the 'Bimbo' bakery trucks."

"Okay then," Bostick said, adding, "but we need to have him on record as a co-conspirator, Junior."

"Don't worry… 007 will take care of it," Junior said, giving Bostick an assuring slap on the shoulder.

Bostick graduated from the University of Miami and worked there as a "Computer Programmer Analyst" until 1997, when he joined the DEA academy. His first assignment was in the Houston office. Bishop recruited him into his Strike Force team and was seeking an opportunity to involve Bostick in the first complex, long-term investigation that arose. Band of Brothers was both timely and well-matched to Bostick's skills and talents. He was an ideal fit, along with Mickey, Darren, and Trish. Now with agents in both New York and Panama, the "A" team was rapidly growing.

"We're going to hand you a couple of devices. Since you carry a 'man-purse,' we decided to swap yours out with one of our own… almost identical to the one you have. It has a device stitched into the leather. You button up this pouch where you'd place a wallet, and it turns everything on. You'll have several hours of recording and transmitting time, but be sure to unbutton after every use. It'll be important for us to get together after everyone leaves and let you identify who is who while listening to the recordings." Lee was rattling off his instructions as if talking to another agent.

"Will you guys be following everyone around?" Junior inquired.

"Probably not, since you are just kicking things off with these guys. We don't want to heat things up unnecessarily. Just do your thing and don't worry. We'll be recording everything. Once everybody is put at ease, then we'll consider keeping a closer eye on things. At some point, we're gonna need you to get with Ramiro and take a little field trip over to the Cumepa warehouse so we can take photos."

Regarding surveillance, Lee wanted to reassure Junior and prevent him from looking around for agents during his meetings—something that clever Colombians would likely notice. Lee carefully planned to send a small team of his elite, vetted counterparts from the "PTJ" (Policia Tecnica Judicial – Judicial Technical Police). The DEA's vetted team included carefully selected Panamanian police officers, screened using DEA-administered polygraphs. They became part of a "Sensitive Investigative Unit" (SIU)—one of only a few in the world.

Fortunately, the US enjoyed an extremely cooperative relationship with the host government. Moreover, Evans and the US Ambassador hit it off, which made Evans's mission much easier. The State Department realized, as did the DEA, that the FARC was expanding its footprint in Panama's Darien Province along its shared border with Colombia. It was dense jungle viewed as a dangerous "no-man's land." DEA established strategic plans to target the FARC and retard their incursion into Panama.

"While in Panama, here's the phone you should use to interact with our targets. It's prepaid, and there's no connection to us. Just don't lose it, we'll need it back," Lee instructed.

What he didn't say was that all Junior's calls would be monitored. It was just another way to keep DEA's cooperator honest. "Trust but verify" was the mantra. They spent another hour in the room discussing tradecraft-related matters — how to make contact, at what intervals, and techniques for detecting counter-surveillance, among other things. Junior was feeling like a bona fide DEA "UC" agent and enjoyed his role so much he started asking Bostick about job possibilities after "taking everyone down."

"Let me know when you can meet afterwards. Take a taxi to this hotel and come to this room. Make sure you're not being followed," Lee instructed.

"Understood, Mister Bond," Junior responded.

"What's gonna be discussed at these meetings, Junior?" Lee asked.

Junior explained their meetings were to discuss logistics surrounding an impending shipment of cocaine using Cumepa, which was to occur sometime after the new year. For investors, it was essential to know when their merchandise was scheduled to leave Panama, the tentative disembarkation date, and when they could dispatch subordinates to retrieve their respective kilos at a pre-designated warehouse. It was acceptable for them to know when the load was leaving Panama and in what conveyance – whether it was a maritime container, fishing vessel, fast boat, or by air. It was also imperative, if traveling by maritime vessel, to determine at which seaport disembarkation would occur so that corruption favors could be arranged. However, once it landed in Mexico, the logistical details were closely held secrets due to concerns about theft or seizure. It was way too risky for investors to have access to those details, especially since the broker and transporters would be held responsible if anything went wrong.

At least half of the cocaine being shipped would likely be for immediate resale to both large-scale and mid-level traffickers who would then send it to the US, with smaller portions headed to Europe, Asia, or Africa. There were no standard practices or protocols dictating decisions regarding how traffickers would break up and sell various portions of their loads. Sometimes, a large-scale cartel leader would take an entire load for himself. Traffickers like the Gueros, Armando Valencia, and Arturo Beltran were known to do just that, and they had the capital to finance it.

While the PTJ team had Junior under surveillance, Bostick was driven over to inspect the Cumepa warehouse. In doing so, Lee gave Bostick a quick tour around the Panamanian isthmus. Bostick got a good look at the sprawling city, its stunning skyscrapers, and modern architecture. It was a beautiful tropical day, prompting Bostick to lower his window and take in the fresh ocean air. He was also treated to the world-famous "Miraflores Canal Locks," considered an architectural triumph, entailing three separate chambers raising and lowering transiting vessels several feet while making their way from one ocean to the other.

After viewing Cumepa, Lee returned to the Embassy so Bostick could meet with Evans and make calls to Houston. Evans was already on the phone with PTJ's commander, who was updating Evans on their surveillance. Evans placed the call on speaker for Lee and Bostick to hear. The commander was extremely pleased and confident that they had hooked into a significant group of traffickers.

The food and booze started flowing, and the conversations were coming through clearly. Besides its aesthetic attraction, traffickers liked Flamenco Island for their meetings because of its controlled access – only one way in and one way out – via the Causeway. Located in the Gulf of Panama, the Amador Causeway is about 20 kilometers from Panama

City. Junior had the traffickers seated outside on the terrace overlooking the marina, giving PTJ agents an unobstructed line of sight for taking photographs. It was also ideal for the UC's audio transmissions.

From viewing the photographs taken, Bostick determined the same individuals (from Mexico City's meeting) were present: Ramiro, Chivo, and Matematico.

Once the meeting was underway, the conversation suddenly stopped as two men approached the group. Junior's stomach flipped upside down as he observed the look on Ramiro's face. La Mona and Beto walked up, smiling, and greeted everyone with handshakes and hugs. Junior could see the angry look etched on Beto's face as Beto gave Junior an aggravated stare.

Beto loudly asked, "How could you guys start the meeting without us?"

"Glad you could join us," Junior nervously announced, seeing Ramiro's look of disappointment turn to anger.

"We didn't know you guys were going to throw in on this one," Matematico remarked. Colombians hated surprises while transacting business.

Unbeknownst to Ramiro, his partner (Barney) had extended an invitation to another, surprise atendee—one of Gordo Mario's subordinates, his former paramour named Lorena, who arrived behind Ramiro and La Mona. She was representing her boss since he would likely be a significant investor. She was well known to Ramiro, and her presence was welcomed; however, Ramiro was perturbed that his partner had said nothing about her showing up.

As La Mona and Beto sat down at the table, they quickly summoned the waiter, ordered their drinks, and looked at one another, smiling, as if they were delighted to have crashed the party. Ramiro was visibly upset as he sat there quietly, staring awkwardly at Junior.

"Okay, let's discuss the seaport to be used, shall we?" Ramiro suggested. "Most everything I send to Mexico arrives at Progreso. I am also aware that, since most of our shipments will belong to Chivo's boss, 'El Lobo,' I believe he will recommend using the one in Manzanillo, Colima. 'El Lobo' has everything in place to receive his loads without interference."

"We are ready to go," Chivo said. "The money will be here in Panama before Christmas."

"What happened with the crane back in July?" La Mona interjected. "I heard it was poor planning on your part." He looked at Ramiro to unnerve and throw him off track. Junior could see Beto beaming a smile. "Weren't you and Barney partnered up with that load, Ramiro?" Beto sat there nodding in agreement, still angry over the fact he and his Cuban financier had sustained a financial setback of an estimated $900,000.

"First of all, that rests solely on my partner's shoulders. I wasn't responsible for what happened. I was just as confused and in the dark as everyone else. Secondly, Barney is my partner, yes. But Cumepa is under my control with this shipment. I'm fully responsible for what leaves Panama in a Cumepa container. If you don't trust me in being able to get this merchandise to Mexico safely, then don't put any of your money to work," Ramiro lectured. Junior was delighted at the juicy conversation being recorded.

Ramiro's personality was that of an introvert. He was rather demure and meek in his demeanor. He spoke in a monotone voice and appeared expressionless as he addressed La Mona's off-putting comments. As Ramiro responded to La Mona, he began to wonder what La

Mona was even doing there, showing up uninvited. Like La Mona, Ramiro was both shrewd and clever. He noticed a curious partnership forming between La Mona and Beto but said nothing to Junior.

"Naaaah, Compadre... Ramiro is okay. We're gonna be fine," Junior spoke up to calm things down. Junior looked at La Mona, knowing he intentionally poked the bear to agitate Beto and humiliate Ramiro, and could see La Mona looking over at Beto with a contented grin.

To smooth things over with Beto, Ramiro directed his attention to Matematico, who was seated next to Beto, and said, "Mate, are you still interested in getting your four hundred kilos to Mexico? Maybe Beto would be willing to take it off your hands once it arrives..., at the right price, of course." Ramiro knew Matematico still had no buyer for his product. Beto, although still angry over the "crane" seizure, begrudgingly acknowledged his interest in receiving the 400 kilos.

"Of course, we can discuss this privately, Beto," Mate replied.

Beto knew how valuable Ramiro was to many significant wholesale coke-buyers. He and Junior, together with Ramiro and Barney, had already collaborated on several large shipments out of Panama using containers filled with legitimate merchandise. Back in December 2003, using one of Ramiro's other companies ("Metales Mecanica") (*), they partnered up on a 2,000-kilo shipment of cocaine and sent it in a container full of scrap metal. Most of the coke went to Oscar Nava and Gordo Mario.

Beto ultimately calmed down and began pushing his overland transportation services once Ramiro offered, "I'll even lower the fee to three percent of the kilo's market value at whichever seaport we decide it's arriving at." Beto preferred to collect his fees in the form of cocaine, knowing he would eventually make more money selling the kilos at a higher price, whether in Atlanta or New York. Generally, coke sold for approximately $6,000 to $6,500 per kilo at either seaport, with its price increasing the further inland and north it was transported. For example, the kilogram fetched a price of $8,000 to $8,500 in Mexico City and Monterrey. Once crossed into the US, uncut coke would go for approximately $13,500 in Atlanta and as high as $18,000 to $20,000 in New York (wholesale). Beto would make money both by providing his overland service and by selling his coke to clients in the US. This suited Beto's needs since his Cuban financier had a well-established clientele in Atlanta. He was always willing to buy wholesale. Ramiro's commissions were generally around 4 percent of the value of the cocaine once it hit Mexico's shores.

The PTJ agents were thrilled with what they were hearing during the meeting. They were eager to identify the targets in attendance. They had already conducted their research on Cumepa, locating it in the San Miguelito District. They were hoping for an opportunity to follow Ramiro to the Cumepa warehouse following the meeting, so they could snap photographs of them entering the business. PTJ had worked enough cases with the DEA to know what was needed for US prosecutions.

The meeting ended at around 7 p.m. that evening. The resulting bill was over $2,000 (most of which was alcohol) and was split amongst those attending. Beto, of course, asked Junior to pay his portion.

No contact was made with Junior that evening. A loose surveillance operation resulted in a few photographs being taken of various attendees and was quickly discontinued, except for Ramiro. Ramiro was not only the key to Cumepa but also central to the Band of Brothers operation. He would lead the DEA to the cocaine sources as well as the investors. Our goal was to make Ramiro the next cooperator.

Lee's PTJ guys were able to follow Ramiro and Chivo in their dark-colored BMW, bearing a Panamanian license plate. Their vehicle was called out of the lot and was followed onto the Causeway. The mobile surveillance team was waiting to intercept the vehicle as it left Amador and crossed back into Panama City's old town area, known as Casco Viejo. Ramiro and Chivo were followed as they passed from Vista Hermosa to San Miguelito. The two men arrived at the Cumepa warehouse as was hoped. They entered and remained at the warehouse for a couple of hours, after which they were followed back into town.

The two men then drove to an upscale neighborhood of "El Cangrejo" where they pulled up alongside a condominium complex. PTJ agents managed to follow the men on foot down a winding path, arriving at a luxury condominium. Ramiro withdrew his key and unlocked the door. The two men appeared to be done for the evening. It was around 9:30 p.m. Surveillance was maintained overnight.

Upon examining the video footage taken by the PTJ unit, Lee remarked, "No shit! He really does look like an ape."

"I know he does, which is why we have nicknamed Ramiro, 'Monkey Boy,'" Bostick said, smiling.

After a brief meeting the following morning with Evans and Lee, Bostick was taken to Tocumen Airport to catch a flight back home. Lee's guys had everything under control. Over the next 48 hours, the PTJ unit developed additional intelligence by following Ramiro and Chivo.

It was determined that Cumepa's lease was under the fictitious name of "Rodrigo Lara Hernandez." (*) That was the same name used for the lease of the apartment where Ramiro and Chivo stayed. Although surveillance on Ramiro was discontinued, the PTJ unit managed to follow Chivo as he departed the apartment en route to the airport. They followed him to the gate, where he boarded a "Mexicana Airlines" flight bound for Mexico City. Immigration records revealed he traveled under the name Carlos Alberto Guzman Palazuelos (as it appeared on his passport). To everyone's surprise, it turned out to be Chivo's actual name.

On Thanksgiving Day, I received an email from Evans indicating that PTJ recognized La Mona's photograph as that of someone they had already documented as being a large-scale drug trafficker and money launderer. Although he was not tied to any seizures, their records reflected his association with the "AUC," and he was in Panama in the company of other documented North Valley Cartel members. Evans assured us that his PTJ unit would exercise extreme caution while tracking La Mona's movements in Panama, so as not to alert him that he was being watched. It became apparent after speaking with Jimmy in Guadalajara that neither he nor Miami was aware that La Mona had accompanied Beto to the Panama meeting. Evans agreed he would let us (Bishop and I) communicate that information to Miami. Jimmy was unsurprised to learn La Mona had not informed him or the Miami agents of his intention to attend the meeting.

A couple of days after receiving that email, I was at the movie theater with my family, watching the remake of Poseidon Adventure, when my phone sounded off with messages from Trish marked *"Urgent: need to pass information."* It was at a critical point in the movie where the Tsunami wave hit the ship and flipped it over. It was like the iceberg scene in the Titanic, a riveting, white-knuckled moment. I tried to ignore her messages, especially since I had promised the family an uninterrupted evening. I tried to buy time by sending a quick response: *"In the theater… will check in afterward."*

She responded: *"Important… please call… can pass quickly."*

"Ugh!" I thought.

"Please send detailed message," I responded, now standing in the hallway outside, aware the family was once again disappointed in me prioritizing work over them.

She wrote, *"I am checking immigration records and found something important that you should know about. A possible address in McAllen to check. These might be our Bigotones."*

"Hmm, the Bigotones," I thought. Although tempted, I neglected to call, and that was a mistake. I rejoined the family instead.

That was the last of the string of messages going back and forth. The remainder of the movie was a frustrating blur as I was distracted by Trish's messaging. *I should've just called her.*

The following morning, I made several attempts to contact Trish to no avail. There was no response. Several calls went unanswered. *Oh shit, now I've done it!* I thought. To make matters even worse, she had only recently given birth to her youngest of two and was likely tired as hell coming to work every day. Additionally, I discovered that she was working on her birthday while I was enjoying several days of leave. Once back at the office, I was informed that Trish had also taken a couple of days off.

Once I unlocked my office door, I found a typed note sitting on my desk.

> *GS Chavarria, sorry to have interrupted your evening out with the family. After a bit of a challenge, I was able to pull together some information to help identify two of our more important targets, the Bigotones partners. I think I've got them identified from immigration records showing past crossings. From what Bostick shared with me from his trip to Panama, I was able to review all my databases and uncover some important information. Since I operate under a lucky star, I was able to take the alias name which Ramiro used in Panama ("Rodrigo Lara Hernandez") and found that he had crossed into the US at the 'Hidalgo POE' in McAllen back in 2003, using the same name. He was in the company of another, Adrian Ramirez. They crossed again on the day I emailed you, but I couldn't get in touch with anyone. I was hoping to put them down at a business or residence, but oh well. So, I expanded my search and discovered that Adrian Ramirez had several other crossings at the same port of entry. On one of his entries going back to 2002, he was documented as being accompanied by 'Ramiro Martinez', who was identified as a passenger in his vehicle, and he was also referenced as Adrian Ramirez's business partner. They also produced a document reflecting an import/export business with an address listed at Mexico City's World Trade Center. Hope this helps. I think we've identified our 'Bitogones'.*
>
> *Regards, Trish.*

I knew I had messed up. It was the part about being a boss that I didn't like—mismanaging situations like that.

It's always a double-edged sword trying to balance home life and work. The home front, in comparison, often seemed to be a low priority. But this time, I significantly misjudged and risked offending perhaps the most important person on our team. With this realization, her persistence pushed our case to a whole new level. Now that we knew who these assholes were, we could put one or both on lookout along the border and detain them when the time was right. Thanks to Junior's efforts, I was confident that Ramiro and his business partner, Adrian, also known as Barney, would be easy to turn into informants. It was a bittersweet moment given my offense.

Upon her return to the office, I threw myself on the sword and groveled, hoping for forgiveness, to which she responded using one of her signature phrases, "For fuck's sake... do you think I'm a delicate flower or something? Get over yourself!" Trish said it all with a smile as if nothing had happened. I came to learn that despite being small in stature, she was as tough as any of the agents in the group.

After the meeting in Panama, I learned of a conversation Junior had with his compadre, Beto. Beto was angry that Junior kept the meeting a secret. Junior told him it was at Ramiro's request, given the threats Beto had repeatedly made to Ramiro over the crane seizure. Junior asked Beto how he found out about the meeting, to which Beto responded, "La Mona told me he heard about it and suggested we crash the party."

CHAPTER 13
WHAT HAPPENS IN VEGAS...

A week or so after Thanksgiving, we held another meeting in the conference room to go over the latest operational developments. Initial discussions centered on La Mona and Beto's unexpected appearance at the meeting in Panama the previous week. Junior had reaffirmed that neither of them had been invited, and it was clear that La Mona had somehow discovered the meeting was taking place.

"The question is, how did La Mona find out about the meeting?" I pondered out loud. "Do you think it's possible that Miami has been directing La Mona to show up at meetings we've announced were happening?" I directed the question to everyone in the room.

"My head doesn't even want to go there, Pinche," Bishop answered with everyone's head nodding. He and I both suspected that was the case. "I have an uneasy feeling about it," Bishop added. "The guy isn't dumb. He's been around and knows how to manipulate both crooks and cops. I don't want to believe our Miami brothers got suckered like that."

"Yeah, and they did ask us if we had recorded the meeting in Mexico City. I don't know what to think about who is directing whom over there...," I said.

"Well, if they're sharing our information with La Mona, we're gonna turn the fucking spicket off. They won't get shit from us," Bishop insisted.

"Why don't we just do that now?" I suggested. "I don't want to throw the dice now that we're so close. Let's not take any chances."

It was the holiday season, and everyone was hoping for a little reprieve from Junior's hectic schedule. We decided to take a much-needed break, shut down early, and head over to Champs. It was our favorite after-hours rendezvous location for letting off steam. It wasn't uncommon for DEA agents to work twelve-to-fifteen-hour days. It was at the end of the day, so I sent the group ahead while I walked down to grab Bishop and Bostick. Before heading out, I went to shut down my computer and noticed I had a notification on my Hush mail account. I opened it up and found several messages waiting. The first appeared as *"007 Update"*

"'M,' Compadre Beto wants to go to Vegas right away... Can I go, Daddy? 007 awaits your word."

Another message read: *"Daddy, can I go... Can I go? 007 urgently awaiting M's authority."*

Laughing out loud, I wrote: *"Call me, 007!"*

The call came in on our group's undercover line within minutes of my reply.

"Junior, how's it goin? What's this Las Vegas business? I expect you'll want a trip to Disney World next?"

"Ahhhh, jefe! Don't be that way! Come on... 007 is working hard for you guys! Beto wants to roll some dice and chase loose women!"

"Let me think on it," I said. I knew it would be another opportunity for recorded conversations and it would encourage Beto to travel to the US, which would align with our long-term plans for capturing him. "When?" I asked.

"Right away... this Friday."

"Well, today's Wednesday, let me get things moving so we can get the approval. Don't do anything until I get the authorization. We would meet you there."

"What do you mean?" Junior asked.

"We're gonna record everything," I explained.

"Everything?" Junior asked, laughing, which made me think, "What happens in Vegas…"

"Don't worry! We would wire up only your living room. We wouldn't be able to wire up his room at all."

"Thank God!" He laughed. "The fuckin guy is a pervert! Just let me know so I can get back to him. He's an impatient fucker!"

SAC Craig didn't hesitate. We had the green light to go. I then instructed Junior where to stay.

While on another call with Junior, he jokingly asked, "So what happens when the beautiful women start coming after me like they do with my gringo twin, James Bond?"

"I'll let your conscience be your guide, but I suggest you consult your beautiful wife and get her okay before exploring the 007 options."

"Hah! That will blow my cover. She still doesn't know I am a secret agent," he said, laughing.

"As long as it's not on any of our video recordings, I don't care what Junior Bond does when he's operational," I joked.

"Ahhh, jefe, you do have a sense of humor after all! And here I thought you were always so serious and boring."

Junior was instructed to pay close attention to our communications with him so we could arrange to have his room equipped with audio-video capability. "You'll have to give us enough time, maybe a couple of hours, to get access to your room, Junior." It was agreed that the hotel location would be Caesar's Palace on the strip.

"Understood, Jefe!" He sounded as giddy as a kid going on vacation.

"Keep up the good work… just don't get cocky and fuck this up, 007!"

"Don't worry, Jefe… 007 out!"

I secured approval for Mickey, Darren, Bostick, and me to travel to Vegas.

Later that day, just before leaving the office, I checked our shared Hush mail account and found Junior's response to some of my requests regarding our need for more evidence. I pressed Junior to engage with Beto regarding Beto's and others' involvement in the palm oil load, the crane seizure, and the 400-kilo shipment for Matematico. Additionally, they needed to discuss the impending 3,000-kilo shipment involving Cumepa. AUSA Sturgis was emphatic about having additional incriminating statements before arranging a grand jury.

Bishop sent Bostick to Champs to meet the others, while he and I sat down to discuss our respective operations (Dos Equis and Band of Brothers) and how they overlapped. Although most targets in Band of Brothers were of the Sinaloa type, both Junior's past and Beto's current alliances involved the Gulf Cartel and their Zeta allies. We kept one another updated on all the crossovers.

As we turned the office light out and headed for Champs, I got a surprise call from Jimmy:

"Bro, I have some news for you," Jimmy said.

"What's goin on?"

"I hope you're sittin down," he said.

"Uh oh... what happened?" I placed the call on speaker mode so Bishop could hear.

"Williams is down here TDY, and we just debriefed our boy, La Mona."

"Uh huh..."

"So, in the middle of the debriefing, La Mona says, nonchalantly, 'Now that Junior is cooperating, maybe we can start coordinating things better,' adding, 'Junior and I don't have to be present at the same meetings.'"

"*Whaaaat?*"

"Yeah, I know, Mike." He paused. Bishop and I were stunned.

"What did Williams say?"

"He turned beet-fucking-red but didn't say a word. I think it caught him by surprise that La Mona blurted it out so cavalierly."

"Ohhh, you've got to be fuckin kidding me," I said, sitting back in my chair, exhausted from the inter-office tug-o-war. But now, it was not only a nuisance, but presented an actual problem for how we might proceed with the case."

"I know... he didn't even try to explain it. La Mona just kept talking about the meeting he attended in Panama the week before, where Junior and Ramiro were talking about a cocaine shipment."

"What did you say to him?" I asked.

"Nothing... what could I say? The fuckin cat was out of the bag!" He paused and added, "Once we separated, I got with Williams and asked about it. He insisted that La Mona figured it out all on his own."

"Thanks for the heads up, Jimmy." Bishop and I have already decided to remove Miami from our cable distribution. They were clearly tracking our operational moves for their *own* purposes.

"Those mother fuckers!" Bishop muttered under his breath. We just sat there, stunned.

I looked over at Bishop and said, "Let's shut down here and head over with the others before I pop a blood vessel."

As we walked in, Bishop looked over at the bar and said, "Look, Pinche, 'Mudflaps' is working. That's at least *some* good news." "Mudflaps" was the nickname Bishop gave the bartender, as she resembled that perfectly figured nude silhouette of a woman carved in chrome, visible on the mudflaps of many big rigs. Besides looking good, she was conversational and kept us supplied with a flow of free bar food.

"Two cold ones and some pretzels for my favorite customers," she said, placing the frosty mugs on the bar. We walked over, joined the others, and caught them up on the latest from Jimmy. It's funny how therapeutic it is to hear curse words slung in unison. The news put a big damper on our exciting trip to "Sin City."

"What benefit do those idiots have in giving La Mona that information?" Bishop asked rhetorically as we settled our bill. "I lost all respect, Pinche," he added as we walked out.

We arrived in Vegas that Friday at around lunchtime. After checking in at Caesar's, the first objective was to contact Junior. Timely access to his room was critical. Junior and Beto flew into town at around 2:30 p.m. The first thing Junior did was call me.

"Honey, just wanted to let you know that Compadre and I are here. We'll probably be at our hotel in the next half-hour," Junior told me while standing next to Beto. I overheard Beto asking Junior to pass his regards to "La Señora."

"Bye-bye, Sara! Don't worry, I won't let Junior hire too many hookers!" Beto bellowed.

"Junior, once you check in, get an extra key and meet up with Darren to hand it off. He'll be in the lobby. Just look for him and follow him into the restroom. Send Beto up to his room."

Darren was hanging out in the lobby at Caesar's, waiting for Junior and Beto to arrive. People were walking all around, eager to lose their money. Vegas was a candy land for adults, with its bright lights, scantily dressed women, street performers, the sounds of laughter, and even the screams of joy coming from nearby roulette and craps tables. Overhearing the intermittent ecstatic voices coming from the floor was enough to distract even the most disciplined non-gambler. That's what we were counting on. It would make our surveillance much easier.

It wasn't long before they strolled into the lobby, joking and laughing at a decibel level matching that of the slot machines. Junior wore a red polo shirt and jeans, while Beto sported a navy blue guayabera and khaki slacks. Beto was covered in jewelry and dressed to impress. He looked like a spoiled, wealthy playboy, medium height and build, with short-cropped hair and a clean-shaven face. Darren managed to catch Junior's attention as the two men stood in line to check in at the desk. Making eye contact, Darren signaled toward the bathroom, where he would wait for Junior to hand over his room key. As planned, Junior grabbed his two keys and told Beto to go ahead and drop their luggage in Beto's room, saying, "I can't wait, compadre... I have been holding on to a much-needed bowel movement since we left the airport!" He watched Beto head for the elevator as Junior made his way toward the bathroom.

Beto unabashedly hollered, "Don't shit your pants, Compadre!"

He walked straight over to the sink where Darren was washing his hands for the third time. "Hello, partner!" Junior whispered into Darren's ear.

"I don't think we should be joking and slapping one another's backs just yet, Junior," Darren responded, again in a low tone of voice, aware the stalls might be occupied. "Let's get this done and move out. Beto may walk in on us," Darren whispered.

"Ayyy, my amigo Darren... you worry too much, but okay, here's the key and these are the recording devices daddy asked me for. I also have an extra key. And don't worry about my compadre, he's headed to his room to drop off our bags. Just let me know when my room is ready. Hey, I'm getting good at this stuff, Darren," he said, smiling. "Maybe we'll become actual partners after all this." Darren couldn't help but smile.

"We'll call you when we're done setting up," Darren said as he was handing Junior fresh recording devices. "And, please... no fucking winking or smiling at us, Junior."

"You worry too much, Darren!" Junior said. "Relax... let's have some fun... we're in Vegas!"

As Darren headed out of the bathroom, he wished Junior well and reached to open the bathroom door. As he did so, it swung open, narrowly smacking him in the face. Beto came barreling in, yelling, "Compadre!" What the fuck are you doing? Playing with yourself again? The women are waiting for us! Let's have some drinks and roll some dice!" Darren shook his head at the irony of nearly getting his nose broken by Beto while Junior stood there white as a sheet, knowing he and Darren were within seconds of being compromised.

"Fuck, Compadre… you couldn't wait for me in the room?" Junior blasted.

"I thought you were taking a shit, Junior!" Beto said, standing there, holding both carry-on bags, watching Junior as he stood near the sink.

"I did! I don't fuck around, Compadre!"

"Well, stop looking at yourself, you ugly fucker! Let's go! I wanna see some titties and have some drinks!" Beto was a force of nature, and Darren observed it up close and almost too personally.

Junior finally received the green light to enter his room after two hours had passed. Junior, although not aware where or how the audio-video equipment was installed, was sharp enough to ensure his and Beto's conversations were sufficiently loud for his DEA pals to capture clear recordings.

Anxious to head down to the craps tables, Beto came knocking on the door. "Junior…, let's get moving. No time to waste!"

Junior, a natural-born UC, convinced Beto to come into the room and chat for a while as he took the clothes out of his bag. "So, what were you asking me about, Compadre? You said something about $2 million in Atlanta…"

"Like I told you, Junior, Cubas has a bunch of his cash stacking up in Atlanta and needs to get it down to Mexico where we can put the money to work for more product." Junior convinced his compadre to relate the entire story from the beginning.

"Okay, Junior... like I already told you...," Beto said. Beto explained in more detail about Cuba's connection to the Beltran Leyva brothers and how the Cuban financier had become closely aligned with Beltran to set up a large-scale distribution center in Atlanta. Cocaine was flooding the Atlanta market so quickly that stash houses were full of drug money all over town. It became crucial to get the money back south and into the hands of the investors. Beto told Junior he needed to get the money back to Mexico quickly and into the hands of Matematico so he (Beto) could take delivery of the 400 kilos arriving from Panama.

Our quick-witted Junior suggested a creative option for his compadre to consider – the use of an armored truck security service. It was an undercover ploy, of course, to help the good guys track the bad guys' drug money.

"I'm telling you, Beto, I've done it before. It works like a charm. Nobody would ever believe that an armored truck would be transporting our fucking money! We can get the Cuban's cash from Atlanta to Houston. Then, we can move it down to McAllen or even Laredo using Cantu's guys." Junior knew it appealed to his greedy partner.

"Okay, Compadre. I'll mention it to Cubas. He has a fuck-load of cash piled up, Junior, and assured me he would invest in Matematico's four hundred kilos, but we need to do it very soon," Beto insisted. "Mate's low price is offered only if I can get him the money quickly."

"How much is Mate charging you per kilito, Compadre?"

"Fifty-five per unit... about $2.2 melons, Junior," which Junior understood Beto's total cost to be exactly $2.2 million (at a kilo price of $5,500) but wanted Beto on record, loud and clear.

Junior asked Beto about the history of his relationship with Cubas. Beto refrained from providing Junior with his background on the Cuban; however, he credited the Cuban (acting as his financier) years ago with saving a relationship Beto nearly destroyed with Arturo Beltran. Junior knew Cubas was Beto's financial gravy train but was careful not to push Beto too hard for details on their relationship. Instead, Junior wanted Beto to be recorded talking about the fallout he had with Arturo Beltran. Junior instinctively knew the more information we had about Beto's past, the easier it would be to convince him to cooperate.

Beto explained it started with "El Azul" (Juan Jose Esparragoza Moreno), a notoriously famous drug trafficker considered instrumental in the early formation of the "Guadalajara Cartel." El Azul became a full-time drug trafficker after abandoning his position as a senior official of Mexico's spy agency, "DFS" (Direccion Federal de Seguridad). Unlike the other founders of the Guadalajara Cartel, El Azul managed to escape capture, remaining a fugitive. Beto told Junior it was because he was too powerful and knew too many of Mexico's secrets and was therefore considered untouchable. Moreover, Beto reminded Junior that El Azul was like an uncle to Beto, given the relationship his father and uncles shared with the drug trafficker.

On El Azul's recommendation, Beltran allowed Beto to invest in one of his cocaine shipments, offering a chance to earn a commission for guaranteeing its safe transit to Atlanta and with the proceeds promptly returned to him in Mexico. Junior laughed as he recalled how Beto had to rely on Junior's guy (Cantu). It was also during this time that Beto introduced Cubas to Beltran, and the two became close associates from that time on.

Getting the cocaine across the border was no problem. Beto received a 50-kilo commission for moving 500 kilos from McAllen to Atlanta. Cantu was paid two kilos for successfully transporting the 500 to Atlanta. It left Beto looking like a "rockstar," since it was the most coke Beto had ever been entrusted with. Feeling ten feet tall and bulletproof, Beto told Beltran that his $10.5 million in proceeds were in safe hands and on their way to Mexico. What neither Junior nor Beto anticipated was Cantu's sudden unavailability to move the money. Since he had already told Beltran that his $10.5 million was on its way to Mexico, Beto began frantically scrambling, begging Junior to find someone to replace Cantu. Although hesitant, Junior agreed and asked Cantu to come up with an alternative plan to return the money to either Laredo or McAllen.

Cantu, after being promised a higher commission, suggested using a former associate (who was employed as a tourist bus driver). "I've never used him to move money, but I trust him," were Cantu's words. We were in the next room, listening to it all. An undercover DEA agent couldn't have done a better job.

Beto added that Cubas saved the day when he discovered the hiccup and decided to break the $10.5 million into smaller amounts to minimize their risky exposure. Cubas agreed to allow $2 million to be moved to test the replacement driver. Cubas promised Beto he wouldn't divulge Beto's little lie to Beltran.

Unbeknownst to Cantu, his bus driver friend decided to send his inexperienced 20-year-old nephew to make the run instead. Two days later, the nephew was on his way to Houston with $2 million (rubber-band-wrapped bundles of $100s and $50s) hidden underneath the back seat of his 1984 Ford Bronco. After crossing through Alabama and Mississippi, he was headed through Louisiana when the truck started to smoke. The nephew didn't panic at first as he pulled over to the side of the freeway. He lifted his hood and tried to assess the source of the smoke just as a seasoned Louisiana State Trooper pulled up behind him, lights flashing, intending to help a stranded motorist.

While contacting the young driver, the Trooper observed his nervous behavior. A few questions later, it was clear the driver's behavior was suspect, prompting the Trooper to call for a "K-9" unit to assist. Shortly into the stop, "Astro" alerted to the backseat area, which gave the officer the probable cause he needed to conduct his search. The dog received its chew toy while the officer enriched the State of Louisiana with a $2 million donation to its coffers. The nervous nephew was instantly placed in handcuffs. Fortunately for Cantu, Junior, and Beto, the young man had been properly schooled on the importance of keeping his mouth shut. He knew it was better to do a brief stint incarcerated rather than a more extended stint—*dead*.

There was no hiding the truth from Beltran. The angry trafficker summoned Beto for a face-to-face meeting in Monterrey. El Azul told Beto that Beltran planned to kill him but was warned that there would likely be retaliation from Beto's father and uncles, all MFJP comandantes. From that moment on, Beltran refused to do business with Beto. However, the disaster never affected the business relationship between Cubas and Beltran. Cubas continued to serve Beltran's needs by maintaining a network of wealthy clients in Atlanta's growing market.

Of course, Beto still benefited indirectly by hitching his wagon to Cubas.

Junior and Beto left the room to gamble and drink. We kept an eye (from a distance) on the two as they made their way through the hotel and out onto the main drag. We knew we would have to use special equipment to clean up the background noise once we got our hands on Junior's recordings. Vegas was like being at a concert with slot machines.

Junior and Beto left the room and didn't come back until well after midnight. We couldn't monitor Junior's live conversations while they were outside the room. We had to be patient and catch Junior privately to get updates on their interactions. We arranged times and specific meeting spots within the hotel, where all the gaming areas and restaurants were located. While Beto slept in, Junior agreed to meet us at 10 a.m. Nothing beats a Bloody Mary to cure a hangover.

"Okay, catch me up, Junior. I'd like to hear about the money pickup from Atlanta. That was some outstanding thinking on your feet," I said, noticing the contented grin on his face.

It was the first time since our reunion in New York that I had sat down with Junior. It was surreal how I began to see Junior as an essential part of our team. I no longer viewed him solely as an informant, although I knew he would always be one. Talking to him felt like dealing with one of my agents in the group. As we conversed, I saw him as someone I might normally be friends with, having beers or even a barbecue. We discussed his family and how losing his first child devastated him and almost ended his marriage. I asked about his relationship with his father, and he simply referred to him as his mentor and hero, despite knowing his dad was a career criminal. He admired his father and feared the day he might see disappointment in his eyes once it was revealed that his protégé son had changed paths to become the gringo's spy.

"I think that moment will kill me," Junior said as he sipped his Bloody Mary.

After we finished our drinks, the discussion turned to the details of his offer to recover the $2 million from Atlanta. While we talked, I asked Mickey, Darren, and Bostick to keep a close watch so we wouldn't be caught off guard by Beto. Darren quickly alerted me that he saw Beto approaching from a distance. Junior hurried to his feet and moved away from where we were sitting.

"Hey, Compadre!" Beto yelled out after spotting Junior on the floor near the craps tables. The two men walked over to a nearby seafood buffet and had brunch.

The trip to Las Vegas was another UC feather in Junior's cap. We were thrilled with the amount of intelligence developed and Beto's self-incrimination. The more we watched Beto in action, the clearer it became to us that we could easily turn him into a collaborator. His bravado was for show. He was a blowhard, undisciplined, and all about self-preservation. He would do anything to avoid jail. We took Junior's advice and left him alone for the time being while prioritizing Ramiro as our next objective.

Before leaving Las Vegas, I requested that Junior meet me in a separate hotel room on a different floor so we could retrieve his recording devices and send him back home with fresh equipment. I asked him about his relationship with La Mona. His response gave me pause.

"I've noticed a slight change in his attitude with me," Junior said, adding, "It also appears that he and my compadre are developing a closer relationship. It's a bit strange since La Mona always warned me about Beto telling me how much he distrusts him.

I don't understand it. Ever since I returned from Mexico City, La Mona has been different, you know, a bit stand-offish. At first, I chalked it up to the palm oil debt, but I get the feeling that there's something more. I just can't put my finger on it."

CHAPTER 14
SHOW ME THE MONEY!

Atlanta transformed into a major distribution hub for Mexican traffickers as the new millennium began. Aside from being a destination for cocaine and methamphetamine, it became a staging area for the proceeds from drug sales along the Eastern seaboard. Cities like Atlanta and Charlotte were experiencing economic growth, attracting more workers from Mexico. The inevitable result was an increase in the flow of illicit narcotics and related crimes. It became a key transshipment city for Mexican cartels. By 2004, seizures of more than 100 kilos of cocaine or cash exceeding a million dollars were common. DEA Atlanta's stats doubled from the mid-1990s figures.

And now, two million in dope profits were sitting in a stash house somewhere in Atlanta under the control of Beto's Cuban associate. We coordinated with our office in Atlanta, as they were eager to identify the drug trafficking cells working with the Cuban and Beltran's organization.

While in Vegas, Junior and Beto discussed the urgency of retrieving the money and returning it to Mexico, where it could be used to pay Matematico for his 400 kilos. Ramiro agreed to facilitate the coke's transfer to the Mexican seaport located at Progreso. The cocaine arrived at the port in mid-

December with the skids greased, allowing it to sail through without the requisite inspection. Ramiro decided to send the 400 kilos in advance of the larger load, anticipated to be closer to 3,000 kilos in total, scheduled for early 2006. The 400 were sent using a Cumepa container (with ceiling tiles) to appease Beto and get him off his back.

And now Junior was back in Houston while Beto was in Mexico City with his wife. After Xochilt's death, La Mona asked Junior why he was still spending time in Houston. Junior responded by informing La Mona and others that he was expanding his domestic distribution network with the assistance of Cantu and Pantera.

"Hey Compadre! Happy New Year! Were you serious, Compa?"

Playing dumb, Junior asked, "About what, Compadre?"

"I need those documents picked up in Atlanta, Junior," Beto said with urgency in his voice.

"Of course, my brother! When do you need it to happen?"

"Fucking yesterday, Compa! The four hundred tables were delivered, and now I gotta pay for them."

"Okay, I know you're nervous about it… what do you say we meet in Houston. How soon can you get here?"

"Tomorrow! I'm coming from the 'Smoke.'"

"Okay, I'm here now. Call when you're in town," Junior instructed.

Beto couldn't get to Houston fast enough. Everything was set up in the hotel room for another epic recording session. He knocked on the door and walked into the room where Junior was waiting with a bottle of "Buchanan's De Luxe 12" Scotch. It was the perfect beverage for a cold January evening.

"Hey Compadre!" Beto greeted, strolling into the suite.

"My esteemed colleague!" Junior responded with his arms open, welcoming Beto into the room, exchanging the traditional Mexican hug, followed by two slaps on the back.

"Ahhh, you shouldn't have!" Beto blurted, smiling while noticing the bottle of Buchanan's, two glasses, and a bucket of ice sitting on the dining room table.

"You're my compadre! I'm not gonna let you dehydrate after a long flight!" Junior said.

They sat down at the table and began plotting the bulk cash transfer from Atlanta to Mexico, as baited by Junior.

"Compadre… let's do this asap. Mate is waiting for my money. I can't lose this one."

"Beto, did you have to pay Ramiro's fees for moving the four hundred to Progreso or did Mate pick up the tab?"

"That monkey mother fucker convinced Mate to discount the kilo price for me, but I believe he charged Mate a lesser transport fee. That's his guilty conscience at work, Junior!"

"We can move the documents next week, Compa," Junior said, knowing we would need a little time to coordinate with our Atlanta office.

"How much are you gonna charge me, Junior?"

"Five percent is the going rate, Papito. I'm only charging four."

"Don't be an asshole, Compadre!" Beto demanded.

"I'm not being an asshole, Compadre… *fuck!* My people are charging me. They charge me two and a half points, and I'm trying to make some money myself! Let's be reasonable here! I'm doin' you a favor, fucker."

"How about you kick some back to your favorite compadre!" Beto suggested, grinning. "Besides, you owe me for the crane load, as well, Junior."

"What the fuck are you talking about? Enough about the damn crane load."

"Raulito, you were the one coordinating it with Ramiro and his partner, Barney."

"You're crazy… I don't owe you a damn thing. You owe me on the palm oil load."

Beto tossed ice cubes into his glass, reached for the Buchanan's, and said, "Call it even then."

Junior agreed. "Let's get this money moved."

Bostick, Mickey, and Darren sat in the adjoining room listening to them squawk about the debts owed. Darren and Mickey were ready to head to the airport and coordinate the undercover operation with the Atlanta agents. Bostick was staying in Houston and would monitor Junior and Beto as they coordinated everything from the hotel room. Beto planned to travel down to the border to oversee the transfer of the money to his associate, Z-71.

Bishop and I contacted Atlanta and managed to coordinate the operation with Group Supervisor Steve Whipple, another colleague and friend we had in common. Whipple was my classmate and, like Bishop and Evans, was considered another DEA wiretapping authority.

Whipple, a strapping West Texas native, standing about 6'4", was the youngest agent in our Basic Academy class. He grew up the son of a wealthy oilman. Regardless of his affluent environment, however, Whipple had nothing handed to him. He made his own way. After graduating, he joined the DEA, defying intense parental pressure to enter the lucrative world of big business. He just wanted to chase outlaws. He did just that early in his career, while assigned to the DEA's El Paso office. Whipple's investigation got uncomfortably close to the leader of the Juarez Cartel (Amado Carrillo, aka "Lord of the Skies"), which ultimately led to credible death threats being made against him by the vicious drug baron. DEA reacted swiftly and relocated Whipple despite his adamant pleas to remain in place.

Whipple assigned one of his experienced Task Force Officers (TFOs), TK Gordon, who was detailed to the DEA Atlanta office from the Doraville Police Department, to coordinate with Darren and Mickey.

Two days following Beto's arrival in Houston, Darren and Mickey arrived in Atlanta and met with TK. It was January 12, 2006. The plan was hatched and agreed to by Beto and the Cuban. There were two representatives headed to Atlanta representing both Beto and Junior. They were told to await direction before contacting the Cuban's people.

There was never going to be an armored truck used. It was just an undercover ploy to convince Beto and the Cuban to release the drug proceeds to Junior. Both Beto and the Cuban agreed to the plan. The idea was for Junior's representative to receive the money and hand it over to an undercover Special Agent with the US Immigration & Customs Enforcement (ICE), Department of Homeland Security (DHS). They already had the necessary approvals to receive trafficker funds to track them to foreign-based kingpins. They were part of the DEA's Strike Force. The second part of the plan was to hand over the $2 million (minus Junior's commission, which went to the government) to another ICE UC agent in McAllen, who would then deliver the money to Beto. DEA planned to maintain tight surveillance on Beto once he had possession of the drug money. After carefully studying Beto, it was determined he wouldn't pose much of a risk in terms of picking up on our surveillance. He was undisciplined and not very security conscious.

"I'll send Flaco (*) over to Atlanta to represent me. Who are you gonna send, Beto?" Flaco was Junior's cousin.

"Otto (*) can go. They work well together, Compadre," Beto replied. "They should get there tomorrow at the latest."

"Agreed," Junior acknowledged.

Later that evening, Otto and Flaco arrived in Atlanta, rented a car, and checked into the Airport Marriott. As instructed, Flaco reported in with Junior. On cue, Beto subsequently received a number from the Cuban to contact Cubas's representative.

TK advised Darren and Mickey that his team was setting up at the Marriott and would maintain surveillance on Flaco and Otto throughout their stay. Thanks to Junior, who asked Flaco for the description of his rental vehicle, as if to pass it to the Cuban's representative, TK's guys were able to locate the car, set up, and wait. Although Flaco and Otto were each using burner phones, it was impossible to consensually monitor their telephonic conversations since they were unwitting crooks working at the behest of Junior and Beto. The only discussions being monitored were those incoming and outgoing calls on Junior's cell. Surveillance would have to rely on communication from Junior.

Flaco and Otto sat in their hotel for almost two days, calling and leaving messages on the phone number they had been provided with. The call finally came. The coarse voice on the other end belonged to an older man, whose distinctive accent identified him as a native of the Mexican State of Michoacán. The meeting was set to take place the next day, and the two men were directed to drive across town to the city of Norcross, located within Gwinnett County. It was the ideal part of town, home to a diverse mix of ethnicities, including Indians, Asians, Mexicans, and other Hispanics, with an approximately equal sprinkling of Whites and Blacks. A meeting at a public venue wouldn't draw undue attention. The selected meeting location was a Mexican restaurant, "Tortas Locas," located at 6101 S. Norcross Tucker Road, a white colored building that sat on the corner of a commercial lot. It was appropriately situated next to "El Jalisco Market." It was around 1:30 p.m.

Otto and Flaco drove slowly through the commercial lot, peering into the parked cars to locate either their unidentified contact or pick out suspicious onlookers – surveilling cops. It was part of a narco's DNA to do counter-surveillance during a dope deal.

Both men missed breakfast and were starving. They decided to walk in and test out the food at Tortas Locas. Tortas were Mexican sandwiches. It was either that or their super-sized burritos. They decided on a couple of burritos and churros for dessert. It was still too early for beer, so they decided on having "horchata" (a traditional Mexican beverage of white rice soaked in water, sweetened with cinnamon and sugar).

An hour passed as they scarfed down their burritos. Rather than sitting in the car, they just ordered another couple of drinks and continued to wait. The call finally came in at around 3 p.m., and they were instructed to look for a dark-colored Ford F-150 parked at the nearby Shell Station. They hurried out and drove to the gas station as directed, looking for the F-150. It was parked on the far side near the water and air hoses. A bearded driver sat alone in the truck.

As they pulled up alongside the lone driver, the bearded man rolled his window down and asked, "Who are you guys?"

"Flaco and Otto," Flaco responded. "Who are *you*?"

"Never mind who I am," the bearded stranger replied. "You guys need to be parked outside Tortas Locas tomorrow at this time. I will be in this truck. We'll have your papers ready. You'll take the car we deliver and keep it for twenty-four hours. You'll have time to remove the papers from a hidden compartment where the spare tire goes. You'll then leave our car with the keys locked inside at a location we specify. Don't be late and don't bring any cops with you, assholes."

With that, the middle-aged stranger drove off. Flaco noticed the truck was missing its license plate as it pulled onto the street at a high rate of speed. Otto, using his phone, called Beto, who was still with Junior in Houston. Otto updated Beto on their instructions.

Per Junior's (and DEA's) directions, Flaco was told that once in possession of the loaded vehicle, he (Flaco) would then proceed to a location specified by Junior. Flaco was to leave Otto at the hotel or another area of his choice, but Otto would not accompany Flaco after receiving the money. This infuriated Beto, who accused Junior of distrusting him.

"That's bullshit, Compa. I'm just protecting your interests, you dummy," Junior quipped.

Meanwhile, Darren and Mickey were part of the moving surveillance team that followed the bearded mystery man as he left the Shell lot. Darren and I were on the phone as he gave his update. The radio was blaring in the background.

"This guy met with Flaco and Otto at a Shell Station in the Mexican part of town. I'm in the car with TK, who has his group out here following the Cuban's rep." Darren explained that the mystery man was difficult to follow, driving at high rates of speed and intentionally changing lanes as if to check to see if he was being followed. "Yeah, this asshole is doing his heat runs, going 50 in a 30 zone," Darren related. "Unfortunately, we don't have air support available," Darren added.

"Don't risk burning it," I said emphatically.

TK came over the radio, "Okay, guys, this is the second commercial strip mall this guy has entered since we left the Shell. Let's back off and let him go. We'll catch him on the flip-flop." The squelching sounds of the radios could be heard as the surveillance agents acknowledged TK's directive.

I relied heavily on Mickey and Darren. They made a good team. Although they couldn't be more different in terms of personality, their yin and yang qualities melded into what I considered an effective pairing. Darren's law enforcement career began with Prince George's County (Maryland) as a local police officer, and by 2002, the DEA hired him. He was sent to Detroit right out of the academy and was forced to roll up his sleeves and jump into action as part of a "Mobile Enforcement Team," designed to target local impact drug crimes. Ironically, the local street-quantity distributors were the most dangerous. But Darren already had the instincts of a cop, racing towards that which most people ran from.

Darren was first battle-tested during his days as a local policeman. In September 1999, while working a midnight shift, he and his partner responded to a shooting at a sprawling apartment complex located across from Andrews Air Force Base. They arrived on the scene, got out on foot, and began to walk the complex. As they quietly made their way around the building, they encountered loud noises coming from around the next corner. There were sounds of an engine revving and screeching tires. It turned out to be a drug deal with the customer speeding off into the night. Within seconds, a man appeared, armed with a semi-automatic pistol, running towards Darren and his partner from the direction of where the loud noises were coming from. The approaching man was ordered to stop and drop his weapon, but he kept charging, initiating a gun battle with rounds whistling over the heads of the officers. Taking cover, Darren, still a rookie, sent rounds back in his direction. Darren's well-placed shots found their way to the aggressor's head, dropping him like a sack of potatoes. It left the lucky drug dealer in a coma for two weeks. Fellow officers were astounded at both Darren's aim and the surviving assailant's good fortune. Darren, noticing he had remained calm throughout the event, realized he had chosen the right profession.

Mickey, on the other hand, was not one of those individuals born to be a cop. He was, however, a staunch patriot who devoted himself to government service. Mickey was a southern boy, born and raised in Charleston, South Carolina, whose family relocated to Oklahoma, where both his parents secured teaching jobs. His father, who served in the US Marine Corps during his younger years, instilled in Mickey a strong sense of patriotism. As the son of professional educators, he was raised to prioritize his academics and excelled throughout his high school years. He ultimately received an appointment to the US Air Force Academy and continued the family tradition of military service. His dad was a Marine; his grandfather and two great-uncles were veterans of World War II, one of whom flew off the Navy Carrier "Yorktown" during the Battle of Midway. After serving, he eventually left the Air Force as a Weapons Systems Program Officer and moved to Tucson, Arizona, where he was married and began to plant some roots – or at least planned to. Shortly afterward, he developed an adventurous itch and looked to become a federal agent with either the FBI or DEA. He was offered a job with both agencies but later explained his rationale for choosing the DEA, saying, "It was the way they were dressed. Whenever I went to their offices, I noticed the FBI agents always wore suits and wingtips while DEA agents wore jeans and polo shirts. It was a no-brainer," he explained. Mickey signed on with the DEA in September 1996 and was assigned to a clandestine methamphetamine lab group in the Albuquerque, New Mexico, office.

Mickey reported to DEA Houston in June 2003, worked with large-scale Asian MDMA traffickers operating between Vietnam, Canada, and the US, and eventually partnered up with Darren. As partners, they amassed some of Houston's most impressive statistics, tracking over $38 million in drug proceeds remitted through legitimate businesses. Together, the duo netted record seizures in the multi-millions. My arrival in

Houston marked their first case targeting Mexicans and Colombians.

The morning after Junior's last update, everyone gathered in Houston's conference room for a briefing on the anticipated financial operation.

Back in Atlanta, TK handed out copies of the "Ops Plan" and briefed the possible scenarios. Once the money was received, it was to be counted, photographed, and repackaged (excluding Junior's $80,000 commission). It would then have to be flown down to McAllen, TX, where it would be turned over to a second ICE UC who would then pass the money to Beto or Beto's criminal associates. According to Junior, Beto had already arranged for the money to be delivered to Z-71, who would ensure its transfer south across the border.

The call finally came the next day at around 7 p.m. Flaco was immediately directed to go back to the "Tortas" restaurant to retrieve the documents as requested. In anticipation of Flaco arriving, DEA's surveillance was already set up and waiting to see who dropped off the target vehicle loaded with the $2 million. It was impossible to have air support given the late hour. Flaco finally arrived on location, drove around the lot, and parked.

"I'm already here," Flaco replied as he answered his phone.

"The location has changed, my friend," the voice said.

"Why are you making this so damned difficult?" Flaco asked the unidentified caller.

"We don't know you, asshole… you could be police getting ready to fuck us. And we don't like getting fucked by anyone but our bitches."

"Okay," Flaco sighed, asking, "Now what?"

"Let me think about it and I'll call you back, asshole."

Fortunately, it was no surprise to TK and his surveillance team. They knew that money crews were the toughest to work. They were the most counter-surveillance conscious. Losing a few kilos here or there wouldn't set an organization back; however, losing money was a whole different scenario that usually brought a degree of heat and scrutiny to those responsible for the loss. TK's guys remained well hidden, so it would be difficult, if not impossible, for counter-surveillance to pick them out of the crowd. They were either parked off at a great distance or were on foot.

"Okay, fucker," the unidentified caller told Flaco, "the deal is down for this evening. I'll call you early and let you know what we decide…, now *fuck off* till then," the man said.

After Junior caught wind of it, he turned to Beto and gave him a ration of shit, to which Beto could only respond, "Sorry, Compadre… they're being careful. They don't want to lose the money or go to jail."

The next day rolled around, leaving Flaco awaiting another call. It came at around 1 p.m.

"Okay, asshole," he paused, then sarcastically said, "Tell your police friends to follow you to 'Lenox Square Mall.' Once you get there, we'll tell you what to do," the caller directed. Flaco, growing tired of the games, refused to reply. He just got into his car and drove to the upscale shopping mall, located in Buckhead Heights, muttering expletives the entire way. He knew the caller's comment regarding the "police friends" was in jest, given the nature of their antagonistic interaction up to that point. Flaco arrived at the mall and drove around, waiting for the next call to come. He got the call at around 3 p.m.

"Where are you, shithead?"

"Where the fuck are you, asshole?" Flaco replied tersely. He heard the man laugh over the phone.

"Drive your vehicle over to the north side entrance, mother fucker, and park."

Flaco whipped around the large commercial lot and parked as close to the entrance as he could get. The next call directed him to walk into the mall and head over to the California Pizza Kitchen. TK's guys were on foot and watching from a distance. Once at the restaurant, Flaco was approached by three Mexican males, one of whom was seen handing him an envelope. The men then departed, heading in three separate directions, leaving Flaco standing there near the restaurant entrance. He opened the envelope and withdrew a key. A handwritten note directed him to a maroon colored 2004 Jeep Liberty parked at the west end of the lot. It turned out to be a rental vehicle. Flaco got into the Jeep and was followed out of the lot.

The mystery caller advised, "The documents are all yours, limp-dick." Until they are back in Mexico, it's all on you, friend. *'Don't fuck it up!'*" The man let out a deep-throated laugh.

Whipple's team was exceptionally talented at surveillance. They knew there would be countermeasures in place to see who was watching and following. It was more than probable the Cuban's guys were following Flaco from the moment he received the key at the mall. They were monitoring things to rule out law enforcement involvement, among other things. Whipple and TK also factored in the possibility, given that there was no honor among thieves, that bad guys were already plotting to rip their own money back and blame it on Flaco. It was commonplace among rip-off crews, and in this case, they stood to double their money. What TK and Whipple didn't know, however, was that Cubas wouldn't have done that to his partner, Beto. But Atlanta was always prepared for the rip.

Junior answered the phone. "Flaco, so you have the money now? Good… okay, here's the number for my guy. Call him and arrange to drop it off."

"Okay, Junior."

The ICE agent received Flaco's call and directed Flaco on where to deliver the $2 million. There was a DEA plane up in the air following Flaco in his Jeep Liberty. TK's guys – all eight of them – were in cars following loosely behind, while attempting to pick out what appeared to be counter-surveillance, of which there were two "bad-guy" vehicles spotted trailing behind Flaco. TK's guys staged an accident scene to slow the Cuban's guys down. It gave Flaco the time he needed to evade his followers.

The ICE agent directed him to drive to a gated community and provided him with a code to enter. Flaco was instructed to ensure he was the only vehicle at the gate when using the code before entering the subdivision. Flaco was then directed to a specific home (used by ICE to facilitate the UC operation) at the end of a cul-de-sac, where he was instructed to pull into the driveway and wait. Just as Flaco pulled into the driveway, the undercover agent emerged from the side of the house. He opened the garage and motioned for Flaco to pull the car in, then closed the door afterwards. Once inside the garage, the two men retrieved two large bags from the trunk and took them into the living room, where they were opened.

Using a money counter, all $2 million was accounted for – every dollar captured on video. The ICE UC removed

$80,000.00 (calculated as the 4% commission fee for the bulk transfer service being offered). Flaco and Otto were to be paid separately for their services. It took about three hours to verify the count, during which time tech agents managed to enter the garage through a side door and affix a tracker to the vehicle's undercarriage. Flaco was then told to depart and return the Cuban's vehicle as directed. Whipple's guys were anxiously anticipating a chance to unveil the Cuban's operation there in Atlanta. They were confident they would find ties to Mexico's drug lord, Arturo Beltran.

Upon departing the gated community, Flaco dialed Junior. "It's done," Flaco informed. "Hey, Junior, you never told me your contact was such a good-looking guy. I'm not kidding… the guy looked like he was a model or something."

"What?" Junior responded to Flaco, placing the call on speaker. "You're fuckin with me, right?"

Beto was seated next to Junior, laughing his ass off. "Hey compadre, I never realized your boy Flaco played for the other team," Beto blurted, laughing so hard he blew snot out of his nose.

Hanging up the phone, a red-faced Junior kept laughing, knowing it was all being recorded. Once the story made it back to Atlanta, TK's comments prompted more laughter from us.

TK's comical response was, "Yeah, we hear that a lot, especially from our guys' wives who love seeing him at our Christmas parties. They can't keep their eyes off him. He really is a good-looking man," TK said with a chuckle.

"Well, God-damn! Dip me in shit and roll me in breadcrumbs," Bishop said as we sat there thinking about all the funny stuff we encountered over the years.

"So, the money should be on its way to McAllen. Our DEA plane will be in the air later this afternoon and is expected to arrive in a matter of hours. Junior advised Beto afterwards that he had already planned to have the money transferred to another conveyance, which would then take it to the border. Beto headed out to McAllen to prepare for its arrival.

"Do you guys have enough to run with at your end?" I asked TK and Whipple.

"We sure do, will let you guys know," Whipple responded.

Hanging up the phone, Bishop looked at me and said, "And that's how it's supposed to work, Pinche."

The bulk cash was flown down to McAllen as planned. Since working ops in McAllen was like operating in a fishbowl where the threat of compromise was constant – whether from dirty cops or too many traffickers per square mile – it was decided that a Houston-based ICE agent would be used to do the UC. As planned, Beto was given the money. Keeping him under surveillance revealed his McAllen-based associates were tied to another investigation targeting an associate of the Zetas. It was a trafficker known as "Mariano" who used the moniker Z-71 (referencing the Chevrolet Silverado 1500). The McAllen agents were thrilled as he was the key to targeting the violent Zetas.

The money was transferred on January 19 and was subsequently tracked back to Mexico, where, according to Beto, it was successfully delivered to Matematico. Beto's actions in getting those proceeds back into Mexico for purposes of acquiring the 400 kilos were the golden ticket for his eventual indictment in the Southern District of Texas.

CHAPTER 15
WE'VE BEEN HIT AGAIN!

Amid planning logistics for the Atlanta money pick-up, Junior received a call from Cantu. There was panic in his voice. "We've been hit again, Junior. It was mine and 'Peligros,'" Cantu blurted, his speech choppy, sounding both nervous and desperate. Junior knew Cantu was referring to Esteban. As we listened to their conversation, we were elated to hear Cantu cite the specific news article highlighting the drug seizure: "www.prensaescrita," accompanied by the article reference, "*Aseguran Cocaina*" ("*They Seize Cocaine*").

"What happened, Jerry?" Cantu's first name was Gerardo, but Junior preferred to use the gringo version.

"All of my savings were invested, Junior!" Cantu was frantic.

"Let's not discuss any more over this line. I'm tied up with something that will take most of this week, but get here as quickly as possible. Our team couldn't believe the gift we were given… a seizure that could be tied to Los Gueros.

"What's all that about, Junior? It sounds serious," Beto commented, still preoccupied with what was happening in Atlanta.

"*It is*, Compadre. The Gueritos lost a fuck-load of coke off the coast in Mexico."

It prompted Beto's question, "Speaking of the Gueros, when do I get to meet them? La Mona thinks I should be working with them, as well."

"They don't want to meet you, brother... sorry," Junior said, attempting to avoid a complicated explanation. The Gueros knew about Beto and his family's political hooks, but considered him untrustworthy and reckless, and therefore refused to do any business with him.

Jimmy and another Guadalajara agent contacted their Mexican Navy counterparts and arranged to collect random samples of the 5,285 kilos of cocaine seized. The agents were given access to all four of the vessels confiscated as part of their operation. Jimmy determined that the seizure was the result of a tip generated by the DEA's El Paso Intelligence Center (EPIC), which directed maritime enforcement assets to geo-coordinates off Mexico's Pacific Coast, close to Michoacán.

By mid-January, Cantu arrived in Houston and met with Junior at the J.W. Marriott on Westheimer Road, several blocks away from the Embassy Suites, located within the expansive Galleria Mall. Their meeting was audio-video recorded and became a piece of evidence our prosecutors planned to use to federally charge Cantu and the Gueros brothers, Luis and Esteban.

Junior heard the knock at the door and answered immediately. Cantu had a dejected and helpless look on his face. He rushed into the room and started spewing unintelligible words.

"Compadre, wait until the fucking door is shut," Junior scolded.

Nearly hyperventilating as he entered the room, he said, "This thing just blew up in our faces at high sea.

Esteban said he was sending the speedboats out to meet the larger fishing boat. He told me about the newspaper article that referenced the seizure. I lost a lot, Junior."

It was a typical transfer operation for cocaine arriving off the coast in a larger vessel in international waters. Fast boats were often used to greet the mother ships. The transfers were typically in international waters, approximately twenty-five miles off the coast. Once all the packages were offloaded onto smaller, ocean-going fast boats, they would make their way towards Mexico's coastline at pre-designated locations where land-based offload crews were waiting. The fast boats were ruggedly built for open-ocean navigation, powered by twin 250-horsepower outboard engines that could give the fastest Coast Guard vessel a run for its money.

Cantu continued, "Fortunately, Junior… there was another load right behind it, about twelve tons. Cantu explained the brothers were hopeful it would compensate for the loss. He went on to detail other recent jobs with Esteban, moving several hundred kilos of cocaine up to New York, New Jersey, Chicago, and Boston, and how happy he was to be working exclusively for the brothers. "I've never made so much money in my fucking life, Junior," Cantu said. "But *fuck*… this one hurt!"

Junior let him go on and on until, at one point, Cantu paused. Junior interjected, "Let's get Esteban on the phone and talk to him right now." Junior wanted it recorded for corroboration.

Unsure as to whether the DEA was monitoring Cantu's cell phone, Junior dialed Esteban from his own cellphone and put Cantu on first. After Cantu extended a quick greeting to Esteban, Junior grabbed the phone.

"*Compadre!*" Junior began, "I'm here with Jerry, and he's given me the bad news about the loss of your grandmother," Junior said in code, referring to the loss of the 5.2 tons. "I know how close you were."

"Yes, it's a shame, Junior. We are very upset. I think you should bring Gerardo down with you, and we should all be together now. The family needs to grieve this loss together, Compadre," Esteban said in response. "Gerardo knows our new address. We've moved out of our old home and are now living nearby. I can explain everything when you get here, Junior." Esteban added that he was there with his brother, Luis.

"I'm tied up with some things on this side of the border, but I will get with Jerry, and we will be down there soon. Again, I'm very sorry about your loss."

"Of course, Junior. Thank you."

Junior hung up and told Cantu, "I'm working on some things with Beto, Jerry. Are you available to go south next month?"

"Of course," Cantu responded.

"Where are the brothers now?"

Cantu responded, "They had to move out of Guadalajara because of problems with Nacho over not taking sides against the Gulf and the Zetas."

"Why... *over what?*"

Cantu went on to detail the increased strain between the Gulf and Sinaloa Cartels, explaining that it was largely due to the Zetas and the problems they were causing for everyone. "Ever since they became part of the Gulf, and especially now that Osiel is in jail, they are like rabid fucking dogs without their master to yank on their leash."

"I've heard," Junior said, referring to the rumors.

"Seems like they are even beginning to bite the hands of those Osiel left in charge, you know, Karis and Goyo," Cantu said, adding, "This Zeta leader Lazcano… they call him Z-3. The word is he doesn't respect Osiel's brother, Ezequiel. He considers him weak and doesn't much like the other leaders, either." DEA had them all fully documented thanks to Bishop's "Dos Equis" operation: Ezequiel Cardenas Guillen, aka "Tony Tormenta"; Jorge Eduardo Costilla Sanchez, aka "El Cos"; Gregorio Sauceda Gamboa aka "Goyo"; his brother Hector Manuel Sauceda Gamboa, aka "Karis"; and the top tier leaders of the Zetas starting with Heriberto Lazcano, aka Z-3. "The word is these fuckers are making a move because they want to be in control of their own cartel."

Junior relied on Beto for much of that information since Beto frequently boasted of his Gulf connections. Junior knew his compadre had a relationship because of all the cocaine they had moved through the Gulf's corridor without problems. "I'll talk to my compadre, Beto." It prompted Junior's recollection of his father's warnings about "Compadre Beto." Raul Sr. reminded Junior, "The Gulf was no longer what it used to be. Things are getting out of control," he told his son, urging caution.

"Be careful," Cantu warned. "You and Beto don't need to get caught up in all that shit."

It was common knowledge that relationships were fraying. With Osiel sitting in a Mexican jail, what had once been one organization, called "The Company," was now starting to fracture and fall apart. Bishop related his guys were picking up informative references on their wire – remarks about how the Zetas were *"tired of being the Gulf's bitches."*

Junior was unaware of just how it was all impacting the Gueros's relationship with their federated affiliates. According to Cantu's conversation with Esteban, the brothers were given an ultimatum by Nacho to either "join the war against the Gulf or leave town." Despite Nacho's close ("compadre") relationship with Esteban, the Federation allies were lining up to go to war with the Gulf leaders, blaming it all on the Gulf's inability to control their unruly Zeta partners.

With Bishop's group working on the Gulf and Zeta leaders, we were able to confirm the rift, including uncorroborated whisperings of the Federation's backing by Mexico's government. The goal was to mount more pressure against the "Company" to stem the rise of violence seen along the border. It was costing the government millions in lost tourism and international trade as the number of drug-related deaths was exponentially rising – numbers seen only in war zones. Their brutality was unmatched by any other cartel. Zeta victims were regularly beheaded, dismembered, and given "acid baths." Bodies were left dangling from bridges with notes warning the public and law enforcement that Zetas were not to be fucked with. There were even credible reports they were feeding their victims to tigers. Victims were those who represented a threat to their expansion – opposing cartel members, law enforcement, and businessmen resisting Zeta extortion demands.

"I thought Esteban and Nacho were compadres," Junior said to Cantu.

"It doesn't matter, Junior. If Nacho's associates demand he kick the Gueros out of Guadalajara… he has no choice."

"Where did they go? Are they fighting with Nacho?"

"They relocated to Leon, Guanajuato," Cantu informed. "No, I don't think they are fighting Nacho… they just can't use the 'Plaza' any longer. The fucking Zetas are responsible for the war, Junior."

"Is there anyone else who refused to fight the Gulf?" Junior asked.

"According to Esteban, the Beltran brothers and Oscar Nava are also refusing to fight the Gulf." Cantu paused and added, "The rumor is that Arturo Beltran and Chapo are also having problems of their own, independent of this war."

Junior knew from his father that alliances were fluid and constantly changing, and that he (Junior) needed to take care to avoid burning bridges.

What Cantu was telling Junior about the Gueros's refusal to go to war with the Gulf made perfect sense. Junior recalled a conversation he had with Esteban wherein Esteban recounted an interesting story about how he and Osiel met and became friends. Before Osiel was captured in Matamoros in 2003, he and Esteban lived in the same upscale neighborhood in Monterrey. Close to a quarter of a million dollars was delivered to Esteban's house, believing it to be Osiel's residence. Instead of keeping it, Esteban sought out Osiel and hand-delivered the money. From that moment on, they became close friends, and Esteban and Luis were granted authority to move their drugs through the corridor without having to pay the requisite "piso" tax being demanded of others.

"How come I didn't know?" Junior asked, feeling offended.

"Nobody wanted to bother you, bro… with Xochilt in the hospital. But you should know, 'Peligros' never stopped asking about her progress and your family."

"Thank you, Jerry. I am looking forward to seeing him," Junior said. We could hear it in his voice that he suddenly felt a little pinch of guilt, given his undercover betrayal. Both Cantu and Esteban were true friends to Junior, as much as that was possible in the underworld.

"Junior, besides us, the brothers want to see Vladimir, as well."

"Why?"

"To discuss the loss of some money that was headed down to the border," Cantu said.

"Do they distrust Vladimir now?" Junior asked.

"They just want to look him in the face... you know how it works, Junior." With that, Cantu departed the hotel room and left for McAllen.

By early February (2006), Junior and Cantu found themselves in Leon, Guanajuato. We knew it would be Junior's most important meeting of all. He would come face-to-face with both brothers, the leaders of the Gueros organization. I was especially elated at the prospect, given the work Jimmy and I had done to reveal their existence as a powerful cartel affiliate. It was our one big shot to get both brothers on record incriminating themselves with what amounted to 5.2 tons of pure cocaine, which they were about to lay claim to. Junior was given two sophisticated devices to improve our odds of securing at least one usable recording. Junior understood the importance of the meeting and realized it would be his crowning achievement with us. He also knew it would likely place him at grave risk.

"Junior, if you aren't comfortable with using recording devices during your meeting, then don't. Your safety comes first, 007. We can always build our case another way. It's up to you, Junior," I told him. That was the only time I deferred to Junior when it came to recording a UC meeting. His safety was of paramount importance to all of us in Houston.

Without hesitation, he replied, "No, sir, 007 is all in." He had his typical charming and overconfident swagger. Junior added, "I can even go in wearing a DEA ballcap and still walk out with the goods," he bragged, smiling.

They (Junior, Cantu, and Vladimir) arrived separately and were picked up by Esteban's driver. Instead of going to one of the brothers' residences, they were taken to a large suite inside a downtown hotel. Upon entering the room, the three guests were asked to remove their cell phones and hand them over. The SIM cards were removed, and their phones were temporarily confiscated. They were thoroughly searched and scanned for recording devices. Fortunately for Junior, his devices were embedded in his man purse—something they had neglected to check. Once they were satisfied that everything was clean, everyone sat down to eat and talk.

"God damnit, I'm so sorry," Junior started, expressing his concern over the loss of the 5.2 tons.

"Yeah, it was some bad luck," Esteban responded.

"How much was it again?" Junior asked for the recording.

"Five. The fucking gringos had their plane up and the Navy was out looking for it, too," Esteban explained. He discussed the load leaving Colombia, noting that the brothers had an arrangement with the Mexican Navy. He explained that by the time the gringos got involved, it was too late. "Our fucking Navy had to respond," Esteban complained.

The younger brother, Luis, calmly interjected, dismissing its significance. "Junior, we've been working for over fifteen years now. Within five days of this seizure, I already had another one underway to replace it... *it happens.*" He encouraged Junior to look to the future, suggesting, "You need to test out the Panama to Los Angeles route. It's direct, and I've been using it two to three times a year; it's extremely secure. You can move tons at a time... trust me, Raulito." Although Luis knew Junior to be working closely with Ramiro and Barney, he was reluctant to utilize them to move his cocaine out of Panama. He opted to assume the risk himself and had the capital to do so. Luis dealt directly with the Colombians.

Luis then switched the subject and turned to Vladimir to ask pointed questions regarding the money seizures. Vladimir had recently directed the transportation of over $1 million in drug proceeds on two occasions. Both times, the money was seized by Texas State Troopers, reportedly because of "routine traffic stops." But in each case, the money was seized, but the drivers were released without being arrested. Luis suspected Vladimir was either incompetent or a government rat. Either way, Luis was extremely suspicious despite Esteban's assurances that Vladimir was trustworthy. Luis wanted to read the Dominican's body language during his questioning.

Although the younger of the two, Luis, was the overall boss and managed the organization. He was clever, even brilliant, according to Junior. He routinely rotated routes and methods, preferring to operate alone and rarely sharing transportation services with other traffickers. This set the Gueros apart from their federated allies. They were meticulous about how they conducted their business and, because of that, had successfully stayed off the DEA's radar for years.

Instrumental to their meteoric rise were El Azul and Nacho, who not only mentored the brothers but also shared "Godfather" bonds. There was even a marriage tie between Joaquin "Chapo" Guzman and the Gueros's family. We knew it was a common occurrence among powerful drug traffickers to have family members intermarry to secure an extra layer of protection through loyalty assurances.

The meeting with Luis ended. At Esteban's request, Junior stayed an extra day so they could catch up, as Junior had been out of circulation given his family crisis. Cantu and Vladimir were sent home. Junior knew his recording devices were already used up, and he would have to recall everything from memory. He was disappointed because he knew Esteban spoke freely, holding nothing back.

Esteban took Junior to his home in the upscale gated community called "Campestre Residencial," where they ate, drank, and talked throughout the night. The two had become close over the years. Esteban shared his worries about Junior's family crisis. As their conversation went on for hours, Esteban poured his most expensive whiskey, Johnny Walker Blue Label. Junior loved the expensive stuff, but he knew he would need to pace himself to remember the details of their conversation. The more he drank, the more guilty Junior felt. He kept justifying his actions, knowing they would eventually lead his good friend to turn himself in. Junior believed it would change Esteban's life and maybe even save him from being killed. Junior often sought reassurance from me that he was doing the right thing. Acting as an occasional therapist was part of being an effective agent.

After several hours, Junior successfully convinced Esteban that Vladimir was not a rat and that he was still worthy of Gueros's trust.

"I knew I needed to talk to you, Compa," Esteban said. From the time they started working together in 1997, Esteban developed a strong trust and reliance on Junior. At that time, Esteban was Nacho's representative in Reynosa, Tamaulipas. Esteban was also placed in charge of the Manzanillo Seaport in Colima (neighboring Jalisco). Junior learned that Esteban had begun working for Nacho in 1986, while still in his twenties.

As their meeting came to an end, Esteban told Junior, "I bet your father is proud of you." The rest of the evening was spent discussing the Zetas and how Osiel Cárdenas lost control of them while sitting in a Mexican cell. Esteban was happy to hear Junior had Beto to run interference with the Gulf and the Zetas.

Once Junior departed Guanajuato, he let out a huge sigh of relief. *He accomplished the mission.* Upon returning to Houston, we greeted him with congratulatory handshakes and took him out for lunch at our favorite New York-style deli, "Kenny & Ziggy's." The DEA's restrictive policies precluded what we wanted to do: celebrate with Tequila. After reviewing the recordings, we were satisfied that we had finally achieved our goal. We had secured what was needed to indict the Gueros.

Our New York agent, Eddy Pieszchata, was elated at the news. We figured when the time was right, Gueros's indictment would likely be coming out of the Eastern District of New York. They were the Pitbulls of federal prosecution. The issue of prosecutorial venue was never a source of concern for us in Houston. We decided to let the AUSAs sort out the venue decision. Our focus was to indict and arrest the bad guys and let the rest unfold naturally.

CHAPTER 16
EL LOBO

On March 27, 2006, at about 1 a.m., Evans's phone rang. He kept late hours, spending a lot of time with his Panamanian counterparts. He was working with prosecutors and breaking ground on the country's first judicialized wiretapping platform. They were ironing out final details on how to change the country's constitution to permit the legal use of what is widely accepted as the most intrusive but productive investigative tool used by law enforcement.

"Dude," Evans answered.

"Joe, I'm out with PTJ... we're over here at Cumepa," Lee advised. "There was an attempted burglary. They're still counting, but they're up to about a ton of coke so far. They have three security guards in custody who say they were part of a plan to rip the load. I'm sifting through the information to see what I can find linking the coke to our targets. So far, all I have is some correspondence with Ramiro's alias."

"Okay, dude. Keep me posted. I'm just finishing up with the Fiscalia. I'll be on my phone. I'll notify Bishop and Chavarria once you get a final count. Make sure PTJ gets samples for the Houston prosecution."

"Got it." The PTJ team successfully prevented the attempted break-in while keeping up their sporadic surveillance of the Cumepa warehouse. PTJ named their part of the operation "Alamo." The Panamanians were careful to maintain a low-key approach, avoiding mention of the DEA's involvement.

Lee called Evans and gave him the total number of kilos seized—2,080 brick-sized packages bearing assorted markings, including images of "scissors." According to statements obtained from one of the defendant guards, his burglar cohorts made off with over a thousand kilograms the night before, during a short window when PTJ had no surveillance coverage. Lee reported that a total of 3,100 kilograms were stored before the theft occurred. The kilos were hidden inside galvanized ceiling tiles, as Ramiro explained during Junior's UC meetings.

Evans sent Bishop and me an email with the good news. We had just celebrated the Gueros seizure of 5.2 tons. Now we had an additional 2,080 kilos to present to our grand jury. All we needed was to secure recordings of the traffickers talking about "their dope being seized." We were anxious to file charges on Ramiro, Oscar Nava, Gordo Mario, and everyone else who had an investor's interest in the 3,100 kilos being stored at Cumepa. Bishop and I conveyed the news to our AUSA, James Sturgis, who had already selected a grand jury.

What we learned from Junior was that Ramiro was immediately summoned to Guadalajara to meet with cartel boss Oscar Nava following the seizure in Panama. Chivo directed Ramiro to report to the "Hotel El Camino Real" in Guadalajara and was given a fictitious name to use at the desk. Although fearful and prepared for the worst, Ramiro knew he had no choice but to face the music, hoping he would be granted another chance to make up for the huge loss.

Their brief but tense interaction was later described to us as follows:

"Come in, compadre Ramiro," Chivo said as he opened the door on the first knock. Ramiro couldn't help but notice his former employee's satisfying grin. Ramiro was as white as a ghost.

There he sat, sipping his scotch, holding an unlit cigar, looking as though he didn't have a care in the world. Ramiro knew better than to let his guard down with El Lobo. He wasn't called "The Wolf" because he was tender and forgiving. Nava lacked patience and was decisive about how to handle losses through carelessness. Although losses were expected, Ramiro did the math and knew 3,100 kilos was well into the millions. Ramiro knew that between Nava and Gordo Mario, he was indebted to a tune of around $9.6 million, calculating their collective portion (1,600 kilos) at Progreso's price of $6,000 per kilo. Ramiro was praying he could work it off.

"Take a seat, Señor... we have a lot to discuss," Nava said, while lighting his cigar. He was wearing dark slacks with a white colored Guayabera. He sat there, stoic and expressionless.

"Yes, sir, thank you." Chivo closed the door but did not take a seat in the living room. Instead, he hung back in the kitchen outside of Ramiro's direct view, fixing himself a cocktail, taking pleasure in seeing Ramiro nervously squirm.

Nava picked up two Panamanian newspapers (dated March 28 and 30, 2006) and showed Ramiro a headline of the one dated March 28. It read, "They Seize 2 Tons of Drugs in 'Ojo de Agua.'" Nava selected portions to read aloud. The article contained details about the seizure and the apparent theft of cocaine packages from the Cumepa warehouse. It described how the cocaine was embedded and pressed between 127 laminated sheets of zinc, industrially manufactured to serve as roofing tiles. The article clearly stated it was headed to Mexico. Luckily for Ramiro, there was no mention of Nava or Gordo Mario. The second article, titled "They Take 6 Tons of Drugs from Narcos," provided more details, covering law enforcement actions as part of a long-term Panamanian operation called "Alamo." Ramiro felt anxious, with butterflies in his stomach and his knees wobbling as Nava read the articles. Fortunately for us, there was no mention of DEA in the reporting, and the three letters never came up, according to Ramiro's account of the conversation.

"Please tell me how you feel about this little seizure of ours," Nava said calmly. "They seem to have a lot of information about this and other seizures they believe are all tied together on this so-called 'Operation Alamo,'" Nava said, finally making eye contact with Ramiro. "The seizures date back to December 2005… I'm a little concerned, Ramiro."

"Sir, as reported, there was a burglary in the early morning hours of March 27 or 28, I believe. They were burglarizing the warehouse. I have no idea how they knew about the product. Perhaps the security guards suspected something… I don't know, sir."

"I see here in the second article that they say the investigation began in October 2005. Isn't that when you all started to discuss plans to put this load together? You see where I'm going with this, don't you?" Nava said as he took another sip of his Johnny Walker. Nava suspected a *"rat"* and wanted Ramiro to dispel his fears of having a snitch in the woodpile.

As Nava spoke, Ramiro looked over his shoulder to see Chivo still grinning in delight. Ramiro started to talk when Nava interrupted him, "So, how are you gonna make it up to me?"

Ramiro began to sweat, wondering what the hell he was going to say next. Then the idea bubble popped up. "I know that you are interested in sending more merchandise to Europe. I have access to a company that manufactures ceramic ovens. They're used to make porcelain toilets and other items. He's an Italian named 'Bruno.' I don't know his last name, but he and his brother operate in Colombia and now in Mexico, and they build these commercial-sized ovens that can be used to conceal merchandise… up to five hundred packages."

"Yes, I have heard mention of Bruno from Chivo, who in turn heard it from Beto," Nava said. "Have you used Bruno before?"

Ramiro lied, "Yes, sir." Ramiro knew Bruno was Junior's man but realized that desperate times called for desperate measures. "Yes, I have," he repeated.

"Can he send ovens to Amsterdam, Germany, and Italy?"

"Yes, certainly."

As Ramiro predicted, both Nava and Chivo perked up with the mention of the Italian. Chivo told Nava that Beto had brought him up during their meeting in Mexico City in October. Nava poured Ramiro a glass of his Blue Label and toasted the new prospect. It would allow Ramiro to start paying off his sizeable debt. Ramiro wasted no time in getting to Monterrey to apologize and beg Junior for the favor of using Bruno.

When the subject of Bruno was broached, Junior's protective instincts kicked in, and he became outraged at

Ramiro's audacity. He initially rejected the plan but then reconsidered after thinking of the advantages of putting Ramiro and Bruno together to build the case against Nava. Junior knew he would need to be careful to weigh the advantages against Bruno's safety. Junior also realized the utility in keeping Ramiro safe.

Neither Ramiro nor Junior expected what would happen next. Once Nava gained access to Bruno, he convinced the naïve but greedy Italian to sign an exclusivity agreement, which would permanently tie Bruno to Nava. After a couple of successful shipments, the inevitable occurred. In July 2006, Bruno's third oven (loaded with 424 kilos of cocaine) was intercepted in Milan, Italy, on its way to Nava's organized crime clients. Ramiro was held responsible once again, effectively increasing Ramiro's indebtedness from $9.6 million to $13 million.

CHAPTER 17
THE CALL NEVER MADE

It was early May 2006 when Junior kissed his wife, Sara, and walked out of the house at around nine o'clock in the morning after a light breakfast of fruit and coffee. Their lives were slowly getting back to normal. His wife knew something was different about Junior but couldn't quite put her finger on it. Junior was turning his life around, one undercover recording at a time, and he felt good about it. Although back home in Mexico, he had his routine of checking in with us, making collect calls every other day, for updates and direction.

It was relatively cool, in the mid-sixties, and a pleasant walk through his gated community. In this wealthy suburb, his millionaire neighbors were businessmen, many of whom working in the textile, steel, and auto industries. Although friendly, Junior and his family kept to themselves. As he walked, Junior looked off into the distance and could see the recognizable "Cerro de la Silla," a notable, mountainous landmark seen on a clear day from almost anywhere within Monterrey's metropolitan area. Junior was relaxed and even optimistic about his future, despite the tragic, premature passing of his second child. He strolled through the neighborhood, wearing blue jeans, a beige, short-sleeved shirt, and brown leather Gucci shoes. His mind wandered, thinking of things he wanted to accomplish during the coming week. He fidgeted with his favorite gold necklace, rubbing its unique, minted Mexican coin, which he considered his good-luck charm. Junior had not yet shaved as he was in a hurry to return home after making his phone call. He wanted to accompany Sara to help her conduct an inventory at their jewelry store. As usual, he carried two cellular phones – one burner phone and the other a Nextel push-to-talk radio. He walked for exercise and was slowly making his way over to the nearby "Oxxo" convenience store, where he would use the public phone.

There wasn't much to report, but he was disciplined about sticking to the established schedule with us in Houston. Junior, walking along, carefree, was oblivious to the marked police car slowly following behind. He hadn't noticed the fact that there were three occupants in the vehicle, with only the driver wearing a uniform. The marked unit rolled in just ahead of Junior as he entered the Oxxo parking lot. When the car came to a stop, the uniformed driver quickly got out and intercepted Junior as he approached. The officer called him by name, "Raulito, where are you off to?" Caught off guard for a moment, Junior paused, surprised by the unexpected encounter, and replied, "I'm just, uh, you know, picking up a few things," giving the officer a puzzled look, struggling to remember him from the past. He didn't recognize the man. He glanced over the officer's shoulder into his patrol car and saw two men still seated inside. They were dressed as civilians and seemed to be looking straight ahead, unconcerned about whatever was going on with Junior.

"Hey Raul, I have some friends here who would like a few words with you… If you don't mind," the officer insisted.

Junior hesitated momentarily and responded, "Ahh, sure... okay," while slowly approaching the passenger side of the police car. As he got closer, Junior glanced inside to see if he recognized the man seated in the rear but couldn't place the face. Making his way to the right front passenger side of the car, he glanced down at an older man seated up front. Junior didn't know him, either. The window slowly rolled down, and the stranger looked up at Junior, grinning.

"So, how are things, my friend?" Not giving Junior a chance to respond, he said, "El Comandante would like to have a few words with you. Why don't you hop in, and we'll take you to see him."

"Which Comandante, if you don't mind?" Junior asked, assuming it was either a state or federal police commander. Junior's head was spinning as he thought of ways to avoid getting into the car. *Neither one of these guys is my friend...what do they want with me?*" He wondered as the man gave a daunting stare. Junior couldn't help but notice his rough look. Junior placed him somewhere in his mid-to-late forties. He had an oily, pockmarked face, with long, black, greasy hair down to his shoulders. Raul also noted how his neck was weighed down with gold chains, one of which had a large medallion bearing the familiar, narco-saint, "Jesus Malverde."

Within seconds of this unplanned encounter, Junior's good mood suddenly turned sour, knowing he wasn't going to make his scheduled call, nor would he likely get home in time to help Sara at her jewelry shop. The greasy-faced man smiled, awaiting Junior's response.

"Señor, if it's no problem, I have a couple of appointments this morning... can we arrange for this meeting at a later time?"

"No problem, Raulito. We'll take you back to the house and wait for you to get all your business taken care of," he replied. He sarcastically added, "We'll have some coffee, chat with your wife… *Sara, right?* We'll hang out till you're ready." By now, the man's body language and demeanor revealed his impatience as evidenced by his menacing leer, sending a chilling jolt down Junior's spine.

Junior didn't want these guys in his home, nor did he want them anywhere near his family. He would have to go along as requested and deal with this comandante, whoever he was. As he got into the back seat of the car, the younger man moved over to make room. He didn't even acknowledge Junior. Junior placed him somewhere in his early twenties. He was wearing blue jeans and a white, short-sleeved polo shirt. He was lean, clean-shaven, with an indigenous dark complexion. He sported a short, military-style haircut. Junior, now inside the car, became increasingly unnerved as the man seated to his left completely ignored him, staring straight forward, expressionless.

Being the consummate optimist with a gift for gab, he thought, *"I'll just go along with this charade, bullshit my way through, promise whatever I have to, and be on my way."* After all, he had done it so many times before. *"Maybe it's just another favor I need to do for the 'Mex Feds,'"* he thought. Junior figured it might be the Federales who were likely trying to extort more money from him to ensure continued protection. It was probably another case of corruption, Junior assumed, involving money for services rendered. Given Junior's career choice, it was an evil necessity to keep the money flowing for police favors. *"But Beto was supposed to have taken care of all that,"* Junior thought. Local, state, and federal palms needed greasing to keep things running smoothly, and it was Beto's job, given his family's connections.

He looked down at his Rolex and noted it was 9:40 a.m. as the car began to back out of the lot. All was quiet in the car as they left the lot, pulling out onto the main boulevard. As they headed out of Junior's Colonia (San Pedro Garza Garcia), the greasy, pockmarked narco said, "Raul, what are you thinking, compadre? Did you think you could get away with working in our area without paying us? That we would forgive and forget?" The long-haired man spoke in a coarse and alarming tone. As they merged onto the highway, the older man turned and faced his younger backseat partner, gesturing for him to place a hood over Junior's head.

"Please, Senores..., that's not necessary..., you won't have any problems with me... I promise... please...," Junior implored.

"Take it easy, Raul..., it's just a security measure, that's all... you know how comandantes can be...," the uniformed officer replied. Now blinded and feeling helpless, Junior began to pray, something he had not done since his daughter had fallen ill.

Junior licked his lips, swallowed hard, and asked, "Can I at least call my wife and let her know that I'll be running a bit late?" Junior needed to alert her to his predicament so that she could contact Beto. *He would be able to straighten things out.* The men just laughed. His stomach knotted, and his eyes began to well up with tears. Panic set in and grew with every mile driven. Now in the dark, he strained to hear familiar street noises that might give a clue as to the direction of travel, or some idea as to the part of town he was headed. He struggled to find any hint as to where he was being taken.

"Gentlemen, can you please tell me what this meeting is about?" Junior asked in a pleading tone. Instead of a response, he felt a sharp slap to the back of his head. It rattled him, leaving his ears ringing.

Another few seconds passed when Junior felt his fellow passenger lean into him and whisper, "Keep your fucking mouth shut, asshole!" The younger man pressed in even closer to where Junior could feel the man's breath as he whispered, "Chinga tu madre, puto!" ("You mother fucker!") Junior dropped his head, feeling utterly helpless, anticipating something much more serious, his mind searching for possibilities.

Junior's mind swirled with fear. *Have I finally gotten myself into something I can't talk my way out of?"*

"You're going to die, asshole," was the next thing the man whispered into Junior's ear. An overpowering, sickening feeling came over him, causing him to nearly pass out. Junior was fighting the urge to vomit.

The police car continued weaving through town. Thirty minutes later, Junior realized he was no longer in the city as the car entered a hilly, off-road area, hitting occasional potholes. There were no more familiar street sounds. The police car eventually slowed down and came to a stop. Junior heard the car doors open, and all three men got out. The car was left idling, and the doors were closed, leaving Junior alone inside. He strained to hear an exchange of greetings and muffled conversation.

Seated alone in the back seat with only his thoughts for company, he heard what sounded like a garage door opening. More people were gathering outside the car. *What the heck was going on? Who was the comandante? And what was he supposed to answer for?* He began to sweat profusely, unable to control his emotions, his erratic thoughts bouncing around his head like a pinball. A man jumped into the driver's seat, started the car, and slowly drove up a slight incline, inside what Junior assumed was a warehouse based on the echoed sound tires made as the brakes were suddenly applied.

"Get out of the car!" Junior slowly got out and stood there, still hooded, feeling helpless and vulnerable. He heard the large door slide shut. He realized he was in a warehouse. The hood came off, and Junior struggled to focus his eyes, only to become even more alarmed. Several armed men, mostly in their mid to late twenties, each of them with a clean-cut, well-groomed "soldierly" appearance, standing in formation, peering at Junior. He knew who they were... *Zetas*. There were about ten of them, all in a semi-circle, holding their AK-47s. The armed men abruptly snapped to attention. Junior instinctively followed suit, slapping his hands to his sides as if he were a private at boot camp. He stood there, shaking uncontrollably. Then he heard the familiar sound of boots smacking the concrete behind him, growing louder, closer. He knew better than to turn around. Junior stood there, eyes nervously blurred, fighting to remain calm.

From his peripheral vision, he caught sight of a well-dressed man approaching from his right side. The man came into view, sharply turned and faced Junior, looking him square in the eyes. He stood about three feet away, locking eyes with Junior like a drill sergeant inspecting a trainee. Junior immediately recognized him as Gregorio Sauceda Gamboa, also known as "Goyo." He and his brother, Hector Manuel, also known as "Karis," were Gulf Cartel lieutenants and considered upper echelon leaders of the cartel.

Goyo was dressed in a starched, white, button-down western shirt, pressed blue jeans, and wore a black Stetson and black Lucchese boots. What immediately stood out to Junior was Goyo's appearance; he looked sickly, as if suffering from an illness. Rumors had it that Goyo was gravely ill due to long-term addiction to both cocaine and alcohol. He was also considered the more ruthless of the Sauceda brothers.

Junior recalled his conversations with Ramiro and Esteban about the rising tensions between the Gulf Cartel leaders and the Zetas, especially since Osiel had been imprisoned. Junior remembered Esteban's comments about the impending war with the Gulf and their Zeta partners. With Osiel out of the picture, the Zetas were becoming overly defiant with their Gulf Cartel partners, giving rise to a growing number of violent encounters between the two groups.

"Who do we have here… the son of Raul Valladares del Angel… hmm," Goyo spoke in a low, monotone voice. "I would have thought your father explained the rules to you." Junior started to ask a question but was immediately interrupted as Goyo raised his right index finger to his lips, signaling for Junior to stay silent. "It is my understanding that you have been quite busy." Again, he kept his finger to his lips. "The rules are there to keep order. People need to respect the rules, Raulito. It's like coming to someone's house for the first time and helping yourself to an expensive bottle of tequila or a cigar without being invited. That's just not done. What am I saying here? If you wanted to work in our area, you should have asked permission and offered to pay for the privilege. We call it 'piso.' It's the polite thing to do, wouldn't you agree? Just nod if you agree, Raulito." Junior nodded while eager to clarify that his friend Beto had already secured that permission. Junior's eyes started to water again.

"Comandante, please let me have a chance to explain… everything that I have done has been in partnership with my compadre, Beto Bravo. He informed me that everything was already taken care of and that we had your authority to move our merchandise through the corridor. Also, I work for Esteban Rodriguez, who has Osiel's authorization."

"Hmm, interesting," he responded, nodding his head but showing disinterest in whatever Junior had to say. "Well, Osiel isn't here now, is he…" After a brief pause and a big smile, Goyo added, "You certainly have a lot of confidence in your friends, don't you?" At that moment, Goyo glanced over Junior's shoulder and watched as someone else approached from behind Junior. "Well, it's never too late to make amends, my fine friend," he said, keeping his gaze fixed on whoever had stopped behind Junior, a mystery person to whom Goyo shot a smile.

Upon hearing that, Junior exhaled a sigh of relief and said, "Anything, sir! How can I be of service? What can we do to fix this problem? Please tell me!" Feeling a bit more relaxed, Junior let his eyes quickly scan beyond Goyo and his gunmen and found the warehouse empty except for what appeared to be several large, black-colored 200-liter barrels, stacked in the far corner next to what looked like power tools, axes, saws, and assorted chemicals.

"Thank you, Raulito… *that's the attitude!*" He looked up to the ceiling as if to ponder. "We simply need to settle the tax situation and get past all this unpleasantness. Then, we can go on with our lives," he explained, smiling, continuing to make eye contact with whomever was standing behind Junior. It was unnerving to Junior.

"What can I do, sir?"

"Well, you can start by donating everything you have currently stashed away. It's my understanding you have a little Italian friend who currently has some kilitos he's sitting on for you?"

Junior was mystified. *How does he know about Bruno?* He stuttered and replied, "Sir, that is merchandise which belongs to Mr. Oscar Nava," hoping Goyo would reconsider.

"Ohhh, I see," he said, smiling. "Maybe we should leave a note for Señor Nava, apologizing for your irresponsibility. I'm sure he'll understand." Junior felt that sickening feeling again.

"Please don't hurt him, Comandante… it's not his fault," Junior begged.

"Well, like you, Señor Valladares… maybe he needs a lesson in choosing better friends," Goyo replied with a smile. "Raulito, we're gonna start with whatever merchandise you have and maybe take a couple of your properties, if that is okay with you?"

"I'm sorry?"

"*I'm sorry?* Is that what you just said?" His smile instantly vanished, replaced by a grimace. "Please don't make me repeat myself. If you know anything about me, well…, you should know that I have little patience."

"Yes, sir," Junior replied. His mind was racing. Bruno was storing 200 kilos, which he was preparing to send off to Holland for Nava's clients. This would put him in a bind with both Ramiro and Nava, he thought, but then quickly realized that all he wanted was to survive the ordeal and go home to his family. Everything else suddenly became inconsequential.

"I will leave you now in good hands with my friends here." He paused and added, "I hope to never meet you again," to which Junior assumed was his way of admonishing and warning about future infractions. Goyo then turned and walked towards the warehouse door. The man who was standing behind him suddenly came into view. Although Junior had never laid eyes on him, he presumed from his short stature and the way the Zetas greeted him as he walked past that it must have been Heriberto Lazcano, otherwise known as "Z-3." Both men got into a black Chevrolet Suburban, which was idling outside the warehouse. They were joined by four bodyguards, two of whom jumped into the back seat of the Suburban, while the other two got into a separate armored Suburban.

After their departure, Junior was taken to an office where he was expected to provide all the requested information. He prayed he would make it back to Sara and his boys. Junior likely reflected on the irony — the son of a high-ranking Gulf Cartel capo now losing everything he and his family owned to the very cartel that raised him. As the door closed behind him, I could only imagine what Junior must have been thinking. Did he flash back to his childhood, wondering what might have been? *Was there a fork in the road, an opportunity to choose another path? Did he realize the end was near?*

CHAPTER 18
THE SEARCH FOR JUNIOR

It had been about nine months since his recruitment during the summer of 2005. On May 8, 2006, Mickey and Darren monitored the UC line waiting for their morning call. Neither Mickey nor Darren had cause for alarm, though, because it wasn't the first time Junior had missed his scheduled check-in. They figured Junior was just busy juggling a million things. They weren't concerned enough to call me while I was on leave in San Diego.

There was no downtime with Junior. He was bouncing between Mexico, Panama, and Houston, recording meetings with traffickers and gathering evidence. We felt dizzy trying to keep up with him. There was no slowing him down. Junior was on a mission to clean his karma and start fresh. Unlike many cooperators, Junior was fully committed to his 007 role. It was a complete flip from crook to cop. He even inquired about job opportunities after helping to bring all the bad guys to justice. Had we not met Junior (the drug trafficker), he might have been exactly the kind of guy we would have recruited as a DEA agent.

Despite the conflict with Miami's agents, our case was progressing nicely. We knew Junior would be an outstanding witness during the trial phase. We had AUSAs working on aspects of the Band of Brothers in multiple venues, including Washington, D.C., New York, Miami, Philadelphia, and Texas. We knew we would have a complete list of indictable targets, both domestic and foreign, as we were already presenting our evidence to grand juries. The operational momentum was underway, with things proceeding smoothly. I had given in to a request and headed to San Diego for a family visit. I made Mickey my backup supervisor, so he coordinated with Bishop on my behalf.

"Mike, sorry to bother you, but I wanted you to know that Junior has not checked in with us. It's been a couple of days already. Bishop and I are concerned and thought you should know... maybe reach out to him online to find out what's going on?"

I called immediately, "Mickey, I received your message... I've checked online and have found no messages from Junior. Let's give it another couple of days before we alert the cavalry. He may have traveled down to Panama or elsewhere and didn't have time to notify us... I'm spitballing here," I said, hoping there was a logical explanation.

On May 12, 2006, a female source named "Lupita" walked into the Laredo office of the FBI. She claimed to be the girlfriend of Heriberto Lazcano, a leader of the Zetas. The FBI knew all about the Zetas and how Osiel Cardenas recruited them as the Gulf Cartel's hit squad.

The Bureau spent a couple of hours debriefing the 17-year-old. She described the Gulf's corridor as a region of growing violence. She said innocent people were being tormented. "Nobody is safe from the Zetas," were her exact words.

Lupita described the Zetas as "being on the warpath," looking to grab any trafficker who was moving drugs in the region without authorization. It was intel that DEA and FBI already had, but she provided corroborating details as to their vicious and brutal tactics. For instance, she described them feeding their victims to large predatory animals, such as starving Tigers. She also described the Zetas' use of sulfuric acid to dissolve the remains of their victims, placing whatever was left into 200-liter barrels to avoid their victims from being discovered. Several lifeless victims (believed to be cooperating with adversarial cartel groups or informants) were left hanging from bridges with bold messages warning the public. She described the shock and awe tactic as the Zetas' calling card, noting that it served to strike fear in the hearts of the public, warning, "violent consequences for anyone helping the enemy." Lupita explained the enemy was anyone who refused to bend to the Zetas' will. She sought out the FBI because she had heard stories from Lazcano and his subordinates about DEA agents being corrupt. When the FBI asked to take her photograph and fingerprints, Lupita suddenly became nervous and changed her mind about cooperating.

Before leaving the FBI office, however, the young woman shared several stories told to her by Lazcano – one of which made its way to our DEA counterparts in Laredo and immediately caught our attention. It involved a recent kidnapping of a son of a high-level Gulf Cartel capo; however, she didn't know the name of either the son or the father.

On May 13, we were finally notified of Lupita's information and sought additional details to corroborate her statements. Bishop and I asked Trish to inquire with all other analysts working along the border to see if there were any clues available to aid in our search for Junior.

A few days after Lupita's interview, I heard from ICE agents based in the Brownsville office. They had a source in Matamoros who provided information that matched what Lupita said and confirmed our worst fears about Junior's disappearance. The source was a private investigator in Mexico who confirmed that the Valladares family reported Junior's kidnapping on May 8th. Additionally, there was an unidentified witness who saw someone matching Junior's description entering a marked police car in the "Oxxo" parking lot. When we heard this news, our hearts dropped, leaving us feeling helpless, scared, and angry. We feared the worst, given the terrible stories we had heard.

Bishop had his guys dig through intercepted calls to find any possible leads that could help us ascertain Junior's whereabouts and fate.

The ICE office provided us with the details they obtained from their investigative source. We knew the unidentified kidnappers picked up Junior shortly after he left his residence that morning. Junior's wife, Sara, was called that same day at approximately 5 p.m. from Junior's cell phone. She was instructed to "gather $300,000 to cover Junior's outstanding drug debts in exchange for Junior's life."

After contacting the private security firm, Sara informed their closest friends, Beto and his wife, Clara (*). Beto was in Mexico City but offered to drop everything and return home on the first available flight. Later that same evening, there was an unidentified kid on a motorcycle who dropped off a Nextel radio (with a kidnapper's note attached) and disappeared.

Beto arrived that evening and, along with his wife, joined Sara and her family. Sara asked him about the drug debt, but Beto denied knowing anything about it.

The following day, Beto and Clara reportedly returned to the Valladares's residence to comfort her as she was distraught and confused about what to do. According to the private investigators, there were no assurances that Junior would survive the ordeal even with the money demands being met. The investigators suspected the Zetas were behind the kidnapping and were of the candid and realistic assumption that Junior's survival was speculative at best, but more unlikely.

It was also reported that Sara encountered Beto on a private telephone conversation he was having with someone identified as "La Mona." Sara told the investigators she suspected something suspicious, noting Beto's surprise and sudden awkwardness. He changed both the tone and nature of his conversation, raising his voice and commenting about the kidnapper's demands for payment. Sara heard La Mona respond loudly for her benefit. The investigator interpreted Sara's description of Beto's and La Mona's conversation to be somewhat stilted and rehearsed. La Mona was overheard telling Beto they should not pay the kidnappers.

Two days passed without a call. Finally, Sara's Nextel radio chirped up at around noon. On the other end of the radio was a new but equally threatening voice directing Sara to gather all the jewelry from her store and deliver it, in addition to the $300,000. The store was a business jointly owned and managed by both Sara and Beto's wife, Clara. Clara reassured Sara that it was okay and even insisted that Sara do whatever was being asked to secure Junior's safe return.

Sara responded as directed and emptied the store, managing to collect $100,000 to be delivered as instructed.

Per subsequent instructions, all was loaded into a large suitcase and was on its way out the door (in the hands of the private investigator) when Beto intervened and demanded that he make the delivery. He became emphatic about delivering it, arguing that half of the jewelry belonged to his wife, and he wanted to make sure nothing went awry.

Before anything was delivered, however, Sara was directed by the private investigators to demand proof of life. In response, the kidnappers played a recording of Junior pleading for his life and demanding his wife do whatever the kidnappers requested. The other demand made was that Sara not get the police involved. Although the request was for real-time proof of life, like a photograph alongside a currently dated newspaper, all that was received was a recording of Junior's pleading voice, which was likely taken on the first day of his abduction.

Beto, unaccompanied, took the suitcase to a nearby hotel, retrieved an envelope in Sara's name, and removed a key for a specified room. Beto reportedly left the suitcase in the room. The investigators were unable to establish surveillance without compromising their position. Once they complied with the kidnappers' demands, they waited and prayed for Junior's safe return. Hours turned to days, but there was no contact or any indication that the kidnappers would reciprocate as promised. Days turned to weeks, leaving the family devastated.

Mickey, Darren, and Trish were sent to Miami to coordinate a detailed interview of La Mona regarding his knowledge of Junior's disappearance. I also called Jimmy and asked him to put me in contact with one of our closest federal comandantes, who happened to be a former State Police investigator in Nuevo León, hoping he still had contacts at Monterrey's police department. We were desperate for anything we could find, if only for closure's sake.

While in Miami, our team faced what they perceived was a ten-foot wall of obstruction. Upon arriving at Miami's office, they were greeted by Williams, Chapman, and two supervisors, who began with a scolding lecture, accompanied by an admonishment about the offensive and accusatory nature of the interview request for La Mona.

Williams and Chapman even dismissed the likelihood of a kidnapping, instead suggesting it was Junior's elaborate scheme to evade his debt collectors. They insisted there was no proof he was even kidnapped. To add insult, Williams related that they were moving to indict Junior behind his role in the palm oil load. It left our Houston team seething yet unsurprised. We figured their goal of indicting Junior was their twisted idea of adding a stat to their case.

Our Houston team finally got access to La Mona on May 16, 2006. It was 11 a.m. when Darren, Mickey, and Trish were escorted to the agents' office area. Upon walking in, they could see La Mona seated at an agent's desk, his feet propped up while relaxed, talking on the phone. Later, Darren described the scene as shocking. They witnessed La Mona having free rein of the group's bay area, talking on the phone as if he were one of the agents. Another of DEA's strict policies was to have informants interviewed in a private room, where they were unable to view the faces of other agents, thereby avoiding the potential for compromising future undercover operations.

Williams and Chapman held up the meeting while waiting for La Mona to finish his call, and then all moved to a conference room where the interview would take place. Two hours into the debriefing, it was time for a lunch break, according to Williams. After another hour and a half, they resumed the meeting and concluded it at around 5 p.m. On top of La Mona's evasive answers, the Miami agents continuously interjected with objections and insisted on providing their own answers to the questions posed to La Mona. "It was an act of pure fucking obstruction," as described by Trish. It was akin to a syndrome of overbearing and protective parenting.

CHAPTER 19
WHAT NOW…?

Although livid, SAC Craig made it clear that the Houston office would not engage in a skirmish with another DEA office to prove a point. His position was that we needed to win the war by capturing as many of our targets as possible. We needed to stay focused on the big-picture objective: everything else was secondary and inconsequential as far as the Special Agent in Charge was concerned. He reminded us that he had encountered more than his share of challenges throughout his career but refused to allow inter-office squabbles to interfere with the mission, stating, "I won't have it in this case." SAC Craig heard our complaints about the despicable treatment in Miami and empathized with us, but he stood firm. We left his office and made our way back to the fourth floor. We knew he sought to diffuse a bad situation.

"So, what now…?" Darren asked, catching us as we emerged from the elevator.

"We keep pushing to locate Junior, no matter what… for no other reason than closure," I said. We knew that with every passing day, the likelihood of finding Junior alive became increasingly dismal.

Bishop said, "Now we start dropping the hammer on these mother fuckers."

"Monkey Boy and Beto... let's have them both put on silent lookouts," I suggested. "It's time to pounce."

Bishop agreed, "Yeah... like a duck on a fuckin June bug!" We knew AUSA Sturgis was prepared to indict both Ramiro and Beto based on all the evidence we had gathered. With his agreement, we put both men on lookout so we could detain them at any US port of entry they tried to cross. They would be entered into a system monitored by US immigration officials, accessible to inspectors at all ports. An inspector would query individuals, flagging them for temporary detention. The Customs & Border Protection (CBP) inspector would then contact the designated agent for further instructions – whether to question, arrest, or merely detain. Regarding Ramiro and Beto, we needed a discreet, face-to-face opportunity to interrogate and recruit them, as we had done with Junior.

Upon our team's return from Miami, we had another group meeting to review our operational status and objectives. Bishop and I reiterated the SAC's direction and suggested we continue our search for Junior while moving forward operationally.

"We're also indicting Oscar Nava and the Gueros," I said. "They'll likely be indicted in different jurisdictions. We can sort all that out with Sturgis and the guys in New York."

"What are we going to do about the Miami agents?" Darren asked. "Now that Junior is missing, how are we gonna know what La Mona is up to?"

"We know what he's doing," I responded. "He's moving coke and money just like he's always done. It's just a matter of time before he gets caught. It's inevitable, regardless of what the Miami agents think or do."

Just as the Houston team was beginning to believe operational momentum was coming to a screeching halt, Darren received a call during the first week of June 2006 from the McAllen agent working their part of the Cantu investigation. It was the bombshell everyone was waiting for. Darren was given several conversations to review (from McAllen's wire intercepts) occurring between May 29 and 30. The calls were between La Mona and Cantu, wherein La Mona, using coded language, warned Cantu that he was being watched by law enforcement. Unaware of the DEA's wire on Cantu, he finally slipped up and exposed himself. He was undermining the US government's mission. I was convinced, *"Now we have that asshole!"* It was irrefutable proof of La Mona's betrayal. *The Miami agents would have to acknowledge the obvious.*

Within seconds of receiving that news, I got on the phone with Williams and Chapman and explained what we had on La Mona, certain they would finally come around and open their eyes to his deception. Shortly into my diatribe, Williams interrupted and insisted La Mona was simply "staying in character, acting in his role as a drug trafficker."

"What?" I couldn't believe my ears. I threw my hands in the air and realized it was unbelievably futile. "Okay, glad we had this chat, Dave," I informed Bishop and the rest of the team of Miami's position. "We can't rely on them. Let's push ahead, stick to our plan, and go after these bastards."

The grand jury was already hearing testimony on evidence relating to the crane seizure, the Cumepa seizure of 2,080 kilos, and the 400-kilo coke shipment involving Matematico, Beto, and Ramiro. We were also giving the jury members details surrounding the related controlled delivery of $2 million in trafficker monies from Atlanta to the border, intended to purchase Mate's coke.

It was mid-August 2006. Junior's disappearance and presumed death were all but inevitable. We at least wanted to recover his body or his remains. Sadly, our agents in Monterrey, Nuevo Laredo, and Matamoros were receiving regular local police reports of dismembered bodies and liquified remains being recovered from 200-liter barrels (dissolved from caustic acid solutions). It was horrific news and disheartening to think our teammate might be among them. Those reported incidents were attributed to the Zetas' ongoing brutal rampage plaguing the entire region.

Out of desperation, I called Jimmy in Guadalajara and asked him to check with our Mexican federal commander to see if there were any updates about Junior. We nicknamed the comandante, "El Indio" ("The Indian"). Dark-skinned, he stood about 6'3" and was all muscle. He looked like a giant Comanche, fiercely intimidating. But he was one of our closest federal counterparts in Guadalajara. He had no information for us as of yet.

In response to McAllen's invitation to have a group meeting regarding our combined efforts on the Cantu brothers, I accompanied Darren, Mickey, Bostick, and Trish on a five-hour drive to McAllen. We arrived and stood in line to check in at the Embassy Suites' desk, anxious to get dinner.

Darren received a call shortly after getting his room key. "Special Agent Butler speaking."

"CBP Officer Mike Mason (*) from the Hidalgo POE. We have Ramiro Martinez Montes detained with a notice to call you."

"You're kidding!" Darren covered the phone as he shared the exciting news.

"He came through as a pedestrian about ten minutes ago," the CBP official added.

"What have you guys told him, if anything?"

"We followed your instructions. Nothing has been asked."

"Great, we'll have someone from our office come over and grab him. Thank you so much!" Darren placed an immediate call to our local agents and arranged for them to retrieve Ramiro and transport him to McAllen's office.

Within minutes, I found myself sitting in front of Ramiro. He sat there looking smug and confident as he sipped on a can of Sprite. Before getting to the point, I marveled at just how much he did resemble an ape.

"Good afternoon, Ramiro. Since we know a good deal about you already, we'll come straight to the point. You seem to be an intelligent man." Ramiro's eyes squinted. "Where do I start…? Oh, let's begin with Cumepa." His smug expression was replaced by one of nervous curiosity. "Of course, 2,080 kilos are nothing to sneeze at… granted, it's not 3,100 kilos, but it'll do nicely all the same. The jury will love it, don't you think?" Ramiro's hands were clasped together, resting squarely on the table, his eyes laser-focused.

"Are you arresting me?"

"Depends," I replied.

"What do you mean?" He asked.

"If we hear anything that sounds like a denial, you're headed to jail, and my friends and I will go have dinner." Before Ramiro opened his mouth, I added, "You're in luck, though… we have authorization from our prosecutor to grant you a little leeway here, as long as you do the right thing." I noticed a slow nod of acknowledgement. I could see he was already thinking.

"The right thing?"

"We know everything, Ramiro. We know about Barney, Junior, Beto, Chivo, his boss Oscar Nava, and Gordo Mario. We are also familiar with the Colombians, such as La Mona and Matematico. You are going to cooperate, or we're gonna fuck you, my friend." His eyes were blinking like windshield wipers. He was going to be our new running back. We were going to play quarterback and send him out to catch one pass after another, scoring touchdowns. There was no time to waste. We were going to make them all pay for Junior's sacrifice.

Unlike Junior, Ramiro had no internal conflict, no struggle with loyalty, and no need for soul-searching. It was easy math for the unscrupulous businessman. He would avoid jail at all costs. A quick telephone call from AUSA Sturgis reassured Ramiro he would receive compensatory credit for his cooperation.

Although Ramiro knew about Junior's kidnapping, he was uncertain as to the circumstances, hearing only rumors from Beto that Junior was up to his eyeballs in debt and presumably ran out of luck. When asked about Beto's demeanor while relating that theory, Ramiro described Beto as devoid of any emotion and how Beto recounted it all matter-of-factly. He found it out of character for a person considered like a brother and compadre.

Like Junior, Ramiro upped his baggage of indebtedness. However, unlike Junior's, Ramiro's baggage was valued at over $13 million. He not only confirmed the issue he had with Cumepa's loss but also related the details surrounding the 424 kilos of cocaine seized in Italy during July 2006, as well. "But I am still valuable to Nava," Ramiro insisted. "I'm his slave right now, and he's got me working it off." Ramiro knew he needed to convince us he could still be of use, desperate to avoid landing in jail.

We wasted no time putting Monkey Boy to work. It was the first week of September 2006 when we sent Ramiro to Panama. His task was to arrange meetings with as many investors as possible. We relied on Ramiro to confirm everything we had already documented about the seizures. Ramiro knew we needed to connect investors to the crane seizure (July 2005), the 400-kilo shipment for Beto and Matematico (December 2005), and the Cumepa seizure (March 2006).

Before sending Ramiro south to Panama, Bishop and I took Ramiro out to dinner to learn more about him and further assess his undercover potential.

"What do you think, Pinche?"

"Let's go to the Brazilian steakhouse, 'Fogo de Chao,'" I suggested. It was only a ten-minute drive from the office and was an all-you-can-eat place. We thought it would appeal to Ramiro as he looked like he hadn't missed any meals. Bishop and I picked him up from his apartment, and we made our way to the nearby restaurant.

"Are you hungry, Ramiro?" Bishop asked.

"Yes, I am," he answered. "Where are we going?"

"It's a steakhouse," I said. "All you can eat… is that good with you?"

"Okay, sounds good," he said.

"Fogo de Chao" wasn't cheap, but it was well worth the visit, especially for hungry meat-eating patrons. They had a nice salad bar, but most were interested in the exquisite meat options.

"You sure you're hungry?" I asked.

"Oh, yes... I'm starving," Ramiro reiterated.

The waiter broke down the meaning of the colored markers – one side green, the other red – working like traffic lights. When green was showing, the waiter knew it was time to bring the next cut of meat – a plethora of choices.

As Bishop and I rolled up our sleeves, ready for the feast, we flipped our respective markers to green and prompted Ramiro to do the same, which he did. The waiter quickly arrived and offered the first cut displayed on a heavy metal skewer. It was a juicy sirloin called the "Picanha Prime." Mine and Bishop's mouths watered as it slid onto our plates. You could cut it with a butter knife. As Ramiro was being served, he waved the waiter off and was asked why his marker was showing green if he didn't want to be served. To this, he responded that he required a salad instead. The waiter told him the salad bar was self-serve. Although curious, Bishop and I didn't pay much attention to it at first.

"Ramiro, are you okay?" I asked as I forked a juicy slice into my mouth.

"I'm fine... I think I'll have a salad, though," he said. We presumed it meant he would *start* with a salad.

"Well, okay... just turn your little marker over to the red side so they know to wait on the meat," Bishop suggested. Ramiro shrugged and turned his disc to the red side. He then got up and headed to the salad bar. The Brazilians called it the "Feijoada Bar," which had everything a vegetarian might crave. When he returned to the table, he carried a mountain of food with no meat in sight. Bishop and I exchanged glances, our eyes narrowing.

"Wow, Ramiro... for a minute, I thought you weren't hungry," Bishop said sarcastically.

On our fourth round of mouth-watering options, we had Filet Mignon while noticing Ramiro was on his second round at the salad bar.

"Okay, I'm dying to know what the hell is going on," I said to Bishop. When he finally returned to the table with his plate heaping with rabbit food, I asked, "Ramiro, you do know this is an upscale *steak* house, right?"

"Yes," he responded, expressionless. We couldn't help but notice his fingers curled as he walked.

"Well, then why are you filling up on everything *our* food actually eats?" Bishop questioned.

"I recently decided to become a vegetarian," he answered matter-of-factly. I just looked over at Bishop as we both set our forks down. We were stuffed. We had to sit there and watch Ramiro stuff himself on vegetables and salad. Bishop had the "what the fuck" look on his face, which prompted me to laugh.

When dinner was over, Bishop and I split the bill and were in a hurry to drop him off at his hotel. Although Ramiro wasn't aware of it, we had placed him under constant surveillance to avoid losing our new ace in the hole come time for trial. Without Junior, we needed a testifier to authenticate our evidentiary recordings.

Before sending Ramiro to Panama, I asked our administrative assistant to send a teletype to Panama requesting authorization and country clearance from our Panama office. When I received my return copy, I noticed that our assistant had mistakenly used an earlier formatted teletype (with its original addresses, including Miami). There was nothing I could do; it had already been sent and would undoubtedly be read by Williams and Chapman.

Ramiro arrived in Panama in mid-September and immediately began setting up meetings. To say Lee had a lot on his plate was an understatement. He was a one-man band, covering three different offices and their respective operations. Miami alone had two of its groups seeking logistical support with their cases. Lee was wrapping up his conversation with the TDY agents of the New Orleans office when he received a call from Miami SA Williams.

"Hey, Dave... what can we do for you guys?"

"Hey, Lee... just callin to give you guys a courtesy heads up that our CI is passing through your town on his way to Venezuela." Lee knew which "CI" it was but decided to have Williams spell it out.

"Okay... who are we talking about?"

"Well, I can't say his name cause we're on an unsecure line... you know, but it's our guy workin the Band of Brothers."

"Ohhh, yeah, the Colombian dude... so what can we do?"

"Just wanted to let you know he'd be passing through. He's going to Venezuela."

"Is there a reason he has to stop in Panama?" Lee's radar was up.

"Believe it or not, our guy can't get a direct flight out of either Miami or Mexico City. Besides, I think he's gonna have someone stop by the airport when he touches down. He's gonna pick up a document that we need."

"A document...? Huh..., wait, did you say your guy can't get a direct flight out of either Miami or Mexico City? You're kidding, right?"

"Yeah, I know... we were surprised, too. But, anyway, the trip needs to happen quickly, so we have no choice, and he needs to pick up that document, anyway."

"Well, okay... why don't you guys send down a country clearance teletype just to be safe," Lee suggested.

"Uh, well... he's already in the air, dude. This is just a courtesy call." DEA's protocol required a cable to be sent out by the informant's handlers whenever the source traveled through other countries in an operational mode. It was for the CI's safety.

"Ohh, I see." Lee put the call on speaker and called Evans over. "Okay, so what flight is he on?"

"Not sure," he answered nervously, "but it's no big deal, you know... he's just passing through." Beginning to stammer, he added, "He's headed directly to Venezuela after a brief layover there in Panama. We didn't have any heads up on it, sorry."

"Okay, it's all good... what's his flight number?"

There was another pause. Williams then answered, "Uhhh, I don't have that, either. But you guys don't have to bother... we don't need anything from you guys. Our guy will just be hanging out at the airport, probably...," he paused and then started talking again, "So we're just..."

Lee cut him off, saying, "Don't worry... we'll keep an eye and make sure he's safe!" And then hung up as Williams began to raise his voice, "Really! It's not..."

It seemed to be more than just a coincidence to Lee and Evans. Ramiro was busy meeting with the various investors, picking up where Junior left off. La Mona was conveniently arriving while Ramiro was in town.

Evans placed a call to us in Houston, and the first thing out of his mouth was, "These Miami dudes are out of control." He related La Mona's coincidental arrival in Panama.

"I'll be darned," Bishop responded, explaining he had gotten a call from Miami's supervisor shortly after our teletype went out, confirming Ramiro was now working at our direction. He specifically asked what Ramiro was doing in Panama. We were a bit shocked at how blatant it was. After we stopped chuckling about it, Bishop said his response was, "We have no clue what Ramiro is doing… we just send him down and let him do whatever he wants." Bishop said he then hung up, leaving the Miami supervisor stuttering. We kept laughing. "Honesty, you can't make this shit up," Bishop liked to say.

La Mona's layover lasted about eight hours. Evans asked his colleagues to "bumper-lock" La Mona if he dared to leave the airport. As expected, he got off the plane and promptly walked out of the airport, flagging a taxi as if in a hurry to catch a meeting. Evans wanted the surveillance on La Mona to be blatantly obvious to him. Evans said that early in the surveillance, Lee received a call from Williams asking why La Mona was being followed. Evans chuckled as he quoted Lee's response, "We didn't want anything to happen to your CI." After Williams hung up, Lee's team saw La Mona's taxi make a U-turn and return to the airport, dropping him off again.

"We just can't make this shit up, Pinche," Bishop repeated.

CHAPTER 20
COMPADRE BETO

Bostick and Trish were debriefing Ramiro in Houston after his third trip to Panama. As they were about to have a late lunch, Bostick received a call from a CBP Inspector, who informed him that Beto Bravo had been detained and was being held at San Antonio International Airport in response to their silent lookout. Bostick notified Bishop and me, and we dropped everything, called our airwing, and jumped aboard a DEA Cessna. We arrived in San Antonio within two hours of hearing the news. Our San Antonio agents had already brought Beto back to the DEA office, and he was told to "wait for a couple of Houston agents who wanted to chat." It was November 9, 2006.

It must have been divine intervention that Beto was dropped right into our laps. We landed, were driven to the office, and there he was. We stood in the presence of the man we had heard so much about. He was just as we imagined: a product of Mexico's aristocratic wealth and privilege. Despite a half-hearted attempt at sporting a tough-guy image, his soft features revealed his cushy upbringing. His eyes darted back and forth between Bishop and me as we entered the interview room. We stood there, peering at him for an uncomfortable few seconds without speaking. The fact that we hadn't introduced ourselves yet made him nervously tap his fingers on the desk. We needed Beto to incriminate himself. We had one shot to nail it.

"Hello Beto, we are from DEA's Houston office," I said as we remained standing there looking down at him.

"I'm Keith Bishop, Beto. I feel like we're practically family." Beto's expression was priceless. He was struggling to make sense of it all.

"I'm Mike Chavarria. By the look on your face, I can see that all this mystifies you. What my partner meant was that we've been tracking you so long, we pretty much know everything about you." Bishop and I took a seat and smiled at him. We could see his confidence waning.

I began, "Since we have a lot of ground to cover, let's get to the point. We know there are always two sides to every story. We only have one side, unfortunately, and it's the one we're basing our decision to arrest you on." His eyes grew wide. "You realize you are under arrest and you're not going home anytime soon."

"You're being charged with violating federal narcotics laws," Bishop advised. Beto's finger tapping suddenly stopped.

"*What?*" Beto blurted, starting to rise from his chair, demanding an explanation. Bishop stood up as well, towering over him, motioning for him to sit back down. "But I haven't done anything. I was coming up to San Antonio to visit my girlfriend. Can I at least call her and let her know that I won't be there?"

"You'll have plenty of time to call her *and* your wife, Clara," I said. He looked mortified. "Well, like we said, we just want to hear your side of the story, Beto," I reiterated.

"Am I gonna need a lawyer?" Beto asked nervously.

"Of course, we insist on it, but it'll take time for us to make all that happen. But if you'd like to clear things up now, we can chat for a bit before you meet your lawyer. It's up to you, but we know you're anxious to get your version of the story told," Bishop explained.

"Just keep in mind that once you ask for your lawyer, we won't be able to hear your side of the story today, Beto," I added.

Beto sat there, anxious, shaking his head, acknowledging his interest in sharing "his side of the story." Beto figured the sooner he did so, the quicker he could clear things up and be on his way. Beto's arrogance betrayed him. He was precisely as Junior described him, both in personality and physical appearance: about medium height and weight, clean-cut, clean-shaven, with short-cropped brown hair. It was clear he had spent his life deflecting punches, never struck, never humbled.

After hearing his rights read from the DEA's yellow colored 3 x 5-inch laminated card, Beto quickly waived them and signed a rights waiver, anxious to "clear his name." Bishop and I were hiding our excitement at the fact that we had the man who was about to reveal everything.

As predicted, he initially minimized his involvement in the drug trade, claiming he had partnered with Junior to assist *him* in the business. He described Junior as the ringleader who masterminded everything. Then we played several recordings wherein he (Beto) came off sounding like a wannabe kingpin. Once we hit the play button, he recognized his distinctive voice, blabbering away to Junior during the Atlanta money operation, talking about his urgent need to purchase 400 kilos from Matematico. It was suddenly apparent to him that we were not falling for his minor role in the drug trade. It was at that moment that he lowered his head in a capitulating fashion and decided to confess his sins.

He acknowledged his participation in the palm oil load with Tony Baca (*), the transfer of $2 million from Atlanta to be used for the cocaine purchase from Matematico. Beto even admitted to his role in the 2005 crane seizure in Panama. He also described his close partnership with the Cuban, identifying him only as both "Cubas" and "Montecinos."

Anxious to return to Houston, Bishop and I borrowed one of the DEA San Antonio cars and made the two-and-a-half-hour road trip, recording our ongoing conversation with Beto. To our shock and amazement, he acknowledged his trip to San Antonio was to meet his wife's sister-in-law, as they were having an ongoing affair. Infidelity was the least of Beto's problems, Bishop told him. And then it happened. I felt the timing was right to bring up his compadre (Junior). It was now or never, and I thought we had developed sufficient rapport to break the ice.

"Okay, Beto, we knew there was some tension between the three of you. I'm referring to you, La Mona, and Junior. We learned of Junior's abduction and your involvement. It was difficult for you, no doubt, but tell us what prompted it all."

Beto was momentarily stunned, but to our astonishment, he revealed his role in setting the kidnapping event in motion. "It wasn't my intention to have him killed," he explained, knowing that the Zetas had permission from the Gulf Cartel to grab Junior. Beto related it was all about the debts and how they were piling up. The debt issue was weighing heavily and becoming an impediment to ongoing business. Beto acknowledged that Junior's indebtedness had become an issue for both him (Beto) and La Mona, and the two were distressed at how it was affecting their credit with Colombian sources such as Tony. Beto even admitted wanting to take Junior's place and become La Mona's new broker associate.

Although appearing hesitant to disclose La Mona's role in the kidnapping plot, he at least made it clear that La Mona was aware of Beto's tentative plans to arrange for Junior's abduction. He kept saying that neither of them thought Junior would be killed, just stripped of his assets. It was clear from Beto's statements that he was not aware, nor did he ever suspect that Junior might be a DEA informant.

Beto, although pressured, held back from giving specific details about his conversations with Gulf members. He indicated that all his dealings with Gulf leaders were mediated through intermediaries, such as his contacts in the Mexican police. Beto refused to incriminate either his father or his uncles, all of whom were federal police commanders. Beto had conveyed information relating to Junior's smuggling of cocaine through the Gulf-controlled corridor without paying the requisite tax of $300 per kilo, a tax which the Zetas demanded on behalf of their Gulf Cartel partners. Beto also expected Junior to offer up whatever cocaine he was safeguarding, as well as other assets, such as properties, to settle his debts. Beto explained that the Sauceda Gamboa brothers, "Karis" and "Goyo," had negotiated a deal with Zeta boss Lazcano (Z-3), agreeing to the Zetas taking Junior's assets—including cash, hidden cocaine, properties, and jewelry. According to Beto, it was the Gulf Cartel's gesture to appease their frustrated and angry Zeta partners, describing how the two partnered organizations were becoming adversarial over dope trafficking rights and earnings. Beto was asked about the jewelry store that was jointly owned by Junior and his wife, Clara. Beto ultimately confessed that one of his conditions with the Gulf Cartel was that he and his wife would be permitted to keep all the jewelry as part of the negotiated deal involving Junior's abduction. After all, the jewelry store belonged to Beto and Clara, as well.

"I never thought they would actually kill him, though," Beto repeated.

As we pulled into Houston, Beto was asked about how he felt regarding his betrayal of Junior but was unable to answer. Instead, he looked down, his eyes watered, and he remained silent throughout the remainder of the drive.

Once Beto was paired up with a high-dollar Houston-based defense attorney, he quickly recanted his statement, asserting it was made under duress. Although retracted, Bishop and I were confident that he had given us an honest account.

There was no interest in recruiting Beto as an informant or seeking his proactive undercover assistance. He would be compelled to be a witness, however. All the doors opened to Junior in September 2005 were now slammed shut to his compadre. Ramiro was the key to putting the finishing touches on everything Junior started.

After briefing AUSA Sturgis regarding Beto's post-arrest statements, he considered filing charges against Miami's informant; however, Sturgis quickly realized it was pointless, given what would become an internal, bureaucratic battle. And then there was Beto's recanted statement, posing another courtroom challenge.

Shortly after Beto's arrest, a meeting took place at the DEA office in Houston. Williams, Chapman, and their supervisor were present, along with their Washington D.C. NDDS Prosecutor Jacob Olstein (*). Jimmy arrived from

Guadalajara. Houston's entire team—Bishop, Bostick, Mickey, Darren, Trish, and I—was there. AUSA Sturgis also attended. After initial greetings and introductions, the SAC thanked everyone for coming. We (DEA Houston) started by sharing our perspective on everything that had happened, both positive and negative.

By the end of the meeting, it was clear that once again, our federal bureaucracy had victimized us. No one was blamed or held accountable. It was all dismissed as "miscommunication." La Mona was too valuable to risk damaging the overall success of the operation and the related investigations. The meeting concluded, and we still hadn't received our justice.

Following the meeting, Bishop and I invited the Miami supervisor (Charles Goodwin) (*) across the street to grab a bite. Mudflaps tended bar.

We ordered up and sat there quietly for a bit. Out of character and breaking from routine, it was Bishop who started with a tongue-lashing directed at Goodwin over letting his two ambitious agents (Williams and Chapman) run amok with La Mona. The supervisor attempted to defend his agents by insisting their hearts were in the right place. Bishop's paraphrased words were, "Williams and Chapman were way the fuck over their heads and were completely manipulated by that piece of shit Colombian informant." The supervisor had little to say in their defense. Instead, he accounted for his lack of oversight by citing personal issues that greatly distracted him during much of the time his two agents were working with us.

"That's the problem... they *weren't* working with us," Bishop sharply pointed out.

CHAPTER 21
LUCKY COIN

It was a late afternoon on January 19, 2007, when SAC Craig announced there were three planeloads of extradited prisoners inbound from Mexico – kingpins our government had long since requested. Among them was Osiel Cardenas Guillen, aka "Friend Killer." We had two hours to gather the troops and head out to Houston's Joint Air Reserve Base, "Ellington Field," to receive the incoming prisoners. Bishop and I were told we would be handling Osiel. Osiel was on the first airplane to arrive. A Mexican Federal Police Boeing 727 bearing its agency, "Policia Federal Preventiva" ("PFP"), landed at 7:40 p.m. and taxied up the runway to where our cars were strategically parked. Given that we expected three planeloads of prisoners, there were at least twenty of us agents on the tarmac wearing our marked "DEA" jackets. Osiel was on the first plane and was taken off in handcuffs, escorted by PFP agents wearing all black with face masks to conceal their identities. They turned Osiel over to us with an acknowledging salute. As was typical in Mexico when prisoners were transported, Osiel walked with his head down – a practice employed in Mexico to prevent kingpins from seeing police officials' faces.

It was no secret that despite Osiel's incarceration in Mexico, he was still very much in control of the Gulf

Cartel and was making decisions from behind bars. Besides finally getting our hands on a ruthless drug lord who threatened to kill two of our US agents in 1999, Bishop and I were hopeful he might shed some light regarding Junior's abduction. There was a presumption that kidnappings and killings required his authority.

After processing him into the US with the assistance of Homeland Security officials, I read him his rights. To everyone's amazement, he agreed to talk and even swelled at the thought of being considered one of the most wanted men in America, a reputation he seemed very proud of.

Osiel inherited the Gulf Cartel after a brief struggle over who would take the place of the Gulf's former leader (Juan Garcia Abrego). Garcia Abrego was arrested in 1996 and quickly extradited to face US federal drug charges. In his absence, the Gulf experienced a brief period of disarray, marked by uncertainty over the Godfather's replacement. By the late 1990s, however, Osiel wrested control over Gulf's operations and began to shape its new direction with an iron fist. Unlike Junior, it wasn't a birthright that offered Osiel his opportunity. An auto mechanic by trade, Osiel's skillset was used to help him mastermind a car-theft ring, which he then parlayed into the world of narcotics trafficking.

Osiel's genius was his charming talent for manipulation. He skillfully gained favor with Mexico's federal police and was assigned an unofficial "madrina" role, which involved a range of duties—from courier to gunslinger. One of his responsibilities was to carry out ritualistic, torturous beatings of defendants before their official interrogation, believed to be a useful tactic to encourage cooperation.

Osiel had a knack for sniffing out dope deals, helping his Mex Fed cohorts interdict drug shipments, which they stole and resold back to traffickers. It earned Osiel commissions. Over time, Osiel graduated from "madrina" to "capo" and began subordinating the police and directing them to commit crimes at his behest. Using wit and entrepreneurial skills, he quickly rose within the Gulf Cartel. By the late 1990s, he scaled the ladder and joined the Gulf's leadership ranks. He found himself partnered with another rising star (Salvador Gomez Herrera, aka "El Chava"), and they began forming close bonds. Their budding friendship, however, didn't last very long as Chava's growing popularity threatened Osiel. Osiel proceeded to orchestrate Chava's execution, thereafter earning himself the nickname "Friend Killer." Osiel then assumed sole control of the cartel by July 1999. His infamous notoriety, however, had more to do with recruiting active and former Mexican special forces soldiers, turning them into his private army – an enforcement wing of the cartel. They became known as the "Zetas" (taking their name from their military call signs).

And now it was our opportunity to pick his brain about everything he knew, which of course included Junior's whereabouts and possible fate.

"Do you know who Raul Valladares del Angel is?" I asked.

"Of course," he responded.

"Did you authorize the Zetas to pick his son up last year, 2006?"

"No," he answered. "I don't even know his son."

"Don't you have to give approval before the Gulf and the Zetas go out and kidnap or even kill people, especially those affiliated with your cartel?"

"Since I was picked up in 2003, things have fallen apart. I was the one keeping it all together." Osiel spoke proudly of his ability to control his vicious army of Zetas. "Why was he picked up?"

"Supposedly, for moving coke north without paying the tax," I replied.

"Ohh, well…, stands to reason," Osiel said, cavalierly. His ego and blunt disregard for human life were coldly apparent.

Out of curiosity, Bishop and I asked him how he managed to convince so many soldiers to betray their military oath and abandon their posts to join the Gulf Cartel. He proudly responded, "Besides a lot of money, I convinced them they could still serve their country honorably by sending the drugs north to your country while keeping Mexico drug-free." It was as if the devil were talking. Fitting a psychopath's profile, he spoke stoically and without remorse. It was unnerving and made our skin crawl.

Our attempts to find the truth surrounding Junior's fate failed once again. The diabolical murderer either refused to acknowledge or didn't know about Junior. A month went by after our chat with Osiel. He was our last hope to learn something of Junior's fate. It was bleak, and we were left feeling as though we had failed Junior.

By late 2007, our undercover operation was nearing its conclusion. Provisional arrest warrants were prepared and submitted, resulting in extradition orders being issued for most of our foreign-based targets. We also secured domestic search, arrest, and seizure warrants.

I was given orders to report to Mexico City as SOD's Liaison Agent. Bishop's transfer followed as he was recruited to take over SOD's new office in Afghanistan's war zone. In keeping with tradition, we decided one more Champs reunion was in order. At the workday's end, everyone headed over to Champs. As I shut my office door, I heard my desk phone ring. Anxious to leave, I reluctantly answered.

"Chavarria!" I quickly recognized his voice. It was the "Indian."

Comandante! What a surprise! I exclaimed.

"Yes, Chavarria…! I hope you don't mind… Jimmy passed me your number!"

"Of course not, Comandante… so good to hear your voice, Señor!"

"Chavarria, I wanted to get this information to you as soon as possible. My contact in Monterrey called me last night. They have something. Do you recall the jewelry that was described…? The necklace?"

"Yes…," I said hesitantly, suddenly nauseous. I knew he was referring to the Mexican minted coin Junior considered his good-luck charm. I slowly sat down to hear the rest.

"Well, Chavarria… I think we have found your guy." He mentioned the coin and indicated it was recovered from an abandoned 200-liter barrel left half-buried off the highway in a remote area outside Monterrey. "Inside were human remains… not enough for an identification, Chavarria."

"Thank you, Comandante," was all that I could get out. As soon as we hung up, Bishop called.

"Where the hell are you, Pinche?"

"Oh, sorry… I'll be right over." I sat there in the dark for another ten minutes with images of Junior racing around my head. It felt like a nightmarish dream, but it was real. Junior was gone. Despite his life's mistakes, he didn't deserve that ending. I wondered what his last thoughts were, his regrets, and realized instinctively his images must have been of his family.

Once I reunited with Bishop and the others, I shared the horrible news. What started as a celebratory occasion turned sullen and somber. There was no sweetness, only bitterness. We shared an uncharacteristic affection for our informant. It was not something commonly experienced in one's DEA career. Ultimately, we raised a glass to his memory and were at least comforted in knowing his death was not in vain. "God Almighty," Bishop said again as we gave our final toast to Junior.

EPILOGUE

All of us felt his loss. We were fortunate enough to get to know him and experience the person hidden beneath the drug trafficker's veil. What struck me about the man was that he wasn't much different from me, except that our beginnings were uniquely different. Whereas I was fortunate enough to grow up in San Diego, the son of a blue-collar commercial fisherman, Junior wasn't as lucky. My father's guidance was, "Get a good education and be whatever you want." Junior's choices were heavily influenced by his environment and circumstances beyond his control. Of course, he had the love of his father, but the guidance he received led Junior down a destructive path. Junior's future was predictable, given Raul Sr.'s view of the world and how to best survive in it. I thought about how many other Juniors are out there – men feeling trapped in a life they would willingly change given the opportunity.

Ironically, this operation was initially dubbed, in a "tongue-in-cheek" fashion, the "Band of Brothers," because it focused on a band of outlaw siblings ("Los Gueros"). Once Junior entered the picture, however, an unexpected phenomenon occurred. Our Houston-based team morphed into an *actual* Band of Brothers, of which Junior was an integral part. He was transformed from informant to teammate and ultimately became part of what felt like a family. News of his abduction and then of what was a horrific, torturous death left us all grief-stricken. Then, it triggered a ferocious need for vengeance and a passion to bring those responsible to justice. Our efforts were bittersweet.

The takedown phase of Band of Brothers commenced in April 2007 and entailed the arrests of most of our primary targets. Things kicked off in Panama once we received the green light from the US Attorney's Offices in the Southern District of Texas, Eastern District of New York, and the DOJ's Narcotics and Dangerous Drugs Section.

What almost cost the entire operation, however, was an unexpected event in Mexico City involving Ramiro's family. On April 16, 2007, while in Panama with Bostick and Lee, Ramiro received word from his wife, Alicia (*), that her twin sister, "Elvia" (*), was kidnapped during the early morning hours as she was closing their business (Discotheque "El Astro") (*). Elvia, mistaken for Ramiro's wife, was forced into a van by armed strangers, gagged, blindfolded, and driven off. El Lobo's orders were to kidnap Ramiro's wife to force Ramiro to settle his $13 million debt. Elvia happened to take her sister's place as Alicia had another business obligation to attend.

Lee and Bostick stood there in shock as they overheard the telephone conversation Ramiro had with his irate wife, screaming and blaming him for the kidnapping. Ramiro remained stoic, devoid of emotion throughout the entire phone conversation, and even afterward as he related the incident to Bostick and Lee. Ramiro reassured the agents he would finish helping set things in motion for the big takedown before returning to Mexico to help resolve the family crisis. Ramiro knew Nava (El Lobo) was not to be trifled with and fully intended to pool monies together to show Nava his good faith intention to repay the debt.

After weighing the options, we decided it was best to inform the DEA in Mexico City but to hold off on notifying the Mexican counterparts for fear of provoking a violent reaction from Nava that could have led to Elvia's death. Ramiro believed she was safe, especially since they knew they had mistakenly taken the twin sister.

Elvia was held captive for close to nine months before being released, but only after two payments were made totaling $2.5 million. She suffered unmentionable abuses, including rape and being forced to witness the barbaric torture of other captives. Upon gaining her freedom, we brought her to Houston circa January 2008, where she underwent psychotherapy and professional trauma counseling. She courageously detailed her horrifying experiences while held captive, recalling her captors referring to their boss using two nicknames: "El Señor" and "Lobo." She also recognized the voice of Ramiro's former associate, Chivo, who was acting as Nava's right-hand man. She overheard messages being passed to the captors.

While still in Houston, Elvia agreed to meet with members of Mexico's PGR prosecutors and bravely signed a sworn statement wherein she provided valuable descriptive details surrounding her nightmarish experiences. Shortly afterward, the PGR tasked a specialized unit of "GAFES" (Army Special Forces) to raid a house believed to be used by narco gunmen working for Nava. The GAFES operation occurred in the town of "Tlajomulco de Zuniga" (an area historically controlled by Oscar Nava and his uncle Armando Valencia). It resulted in the arrests of several gunmen and the rescue of various hostages. Photos of the gunmen were later shown to Elvia, and she was forced to re-live her trauma while emotionally confirming their identities as the same men who held her captive.

As DEA operations go, Band of Brothers was one for the record books. It was unique in that its reach went far beyond a single cartel. Junior's access to suppliers, investors, and other facilitators between Colombia and Mexico opened windows of opportunity that were rarely available to us in DEA.

Takedown operations commenced in 2007 and ensued for over a decade, entailing law enforcement actions across the globe, including countries in Latin America and Europe. European counterparts successfully dismantled organized crime rings, working with both Colombians and Mexicans. Initial stages alone accounted for over thirty-three major drug traffickers, including cartel kingpins, being arrested, prosecuted, and sent to prison. Both foreign and domestic cartel cells were disrupted and dismantled. A total of twenty-five metric tons of cocaine were seized, while millions worth of assets were stripped from traffickers. The successes were attributed to what Junior had started in 2005.

Junior's story is one of irony. Those who helped launch Junior's successful drug trafficking career were his closest friends and trusted confidants, yet they were the very ones who betrayed him in the end. Likewise, although the protege son was born of the Gulf Cartel, his horrible fate rested in their hands.

Acknowledgements

WHERE TO BEGIN. My brother Carlos, a fellow lawman, told me twenty years ago to keep a detailed diary and record my DEA adventures. He said, "People will want to read about it someday." Thank you, Carlos. For those of you (my named colleagues) who helped make both the Band of Brothers and this story possible, you have my undying gratitude and respect. To make Junior's story easier to read, I have narrowed the list of characters and omitted the names of many other essential colleagues who contributed significantly to the operation's success: Associate SAC Arnold Moorin, ASACs Nadine Moorin (RIP) and Elizabeth Kempshall; also, Agents Darrell Sobin (UC), Donaciano Garcia, Moises Ambriz, Eric Barnard, Prentice Coleman, Anthony Lewis, and Dave Todd. I also want to acknowledge the close, supportive coordination received from our SOD Staff Coordinators, Mike Franklin, John McCabe, Dan Stitt, and Intelligence Analyst Derek Whitlock. This wouldn't have been a success without your respective support. I was humbled throughout this investigation and consider myself fortunate to have served with all of you. Band of Brothers was an incredible group effort.

The transition from investigative reporting to storytelling was admittedly challenging, and I am grateful to the following distinguished authors, mentors, and friends for their patience in coaching me along the way: Elaine Shannon, Damien G. Lewis, and Benjamin Smith. It was an arduous journey, and now my skin is thicker. I want to thank my Literary Agent, Linda Langton, and Operational Director Rachel Swyer (of Langton's International Agency), and professional editor and renowned author, Jason O'Toole. I would also like to acknowledge the editing services of my former DEA colleagues: Cesar Avila, Jimmy Martinez, and Mike Messier. Your edits and insights were invaluable!

Finally, I am forever grateful for the support and patience of my beautiful, blended family, and, of course, my lovely wife and best friend, Trisha.

About the Author

MIKE BEGAN his federal law enforcement career with the Naval Criminal Investigative Service (NCIS) in 1984, laterally transferring to the Drug Enforcement Administration (DEA) in 1985, where he spent 32 years fighting the war on drugs. More than half of his career was spent working in Latin America. Early in his career (1987-1993), he participated in paramilitary operations targeting cocaine source countries (Peru, Bolivia, and Colombia), working with host nation counterparts and US Special Forces to locate and dismantle remote jungle-based cocaine laboratories. His career was marked by commendations, awards, and accolades over the years, including the coveted Administrator's Award. On May 10, 2007, he was honored to receive the prestigious title of "Super Cop," awarded by a Texas-based organization known as "The 100 Club." It was specifically for his role in bringing the Band of Brothers to a successful culmination.

A recognized subject-matter expert, Mike works as a consultant and has given interviews to news networks and has also appeared in two documentaries: a National Geographic documentary, "Narco Wars," featuring the

Gulf and Zetas episode, "Rise of the Narco Army"; and is featured in various episodes of the French-produced docuseries "Narco Circus," which explores corruption issues related to drug trafficking in Mexico. Mike has also appeared on Podcasts and has been sought out by journalists for his expertise on Latin America's drug trade.

Photo Gallery

PANAMA "CRANE SEIZURE" (JULY 2005):
1,345 kilos of Cocaine Removed from a Crane's Arm

PANAMA "CUMEPA SEIZURE" (MARCH 2006): 2,080 Kilos Removed from Roofing Tiles

Panamanian Front Company Warehouse "CUMEPA"

"CUMEPA" Roofing Tiles used to Conceal Cocaine

"CUMEPA" Tiles Being Deconstructed

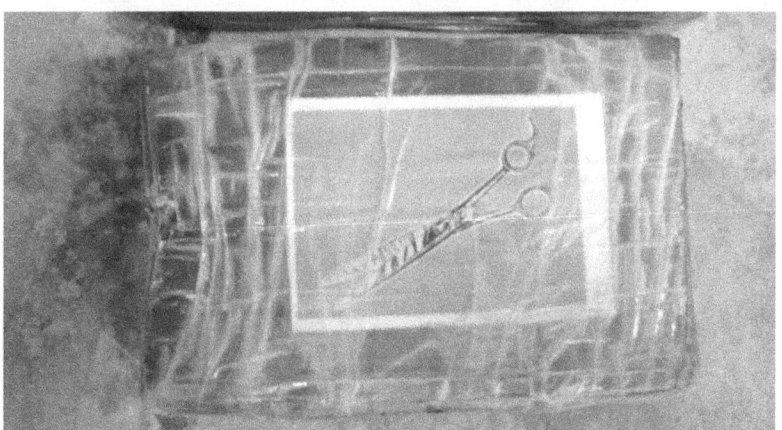

Kilo Packages of Cocaine Bearing Scissor Markings removed from Tiles

CUMEPA Cocaine (2,080 kilos) Presented for Inspection

PANAMANIAN RELATED OPERATION ("OPERATION ALAMO"): Cocaine Seizures

Kilos of Cocaine Seized (December 2005)

Kilos of Cocaine Seized (February 2006)

BAND OF BROTHERS TEAM MEMBERS

Houston

Mike in Guadalajara

Keith Bishop

Mickey Teague

Darren Butler

Mike Bostick Escorts Oscar Nava Valencia aka "El Lobo"

Trish Skidmore

Guadalajara, Mexico

Mike & JimmyMartinez

Panama

Joe Evans, Country Attache,
DEA Panama Office

Lee Nash, DEA Panama Office

New York

SA Eddy Pieszchata, DEA New York

SA Eddy Pieszchata Escorting Esteban Rodriguez – Extradition

BAND OF BROTHERS TARGETS

Luis Rodriguez

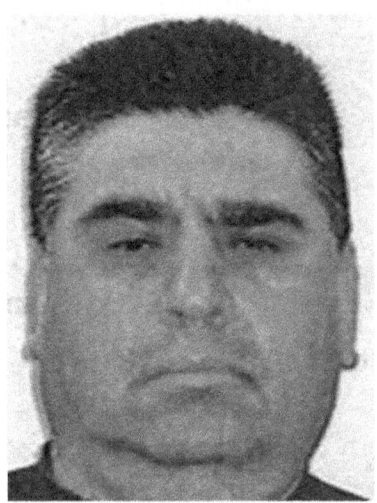

Esteban Rodriguez

Oscar Nava Valencia aka "El Lobo"

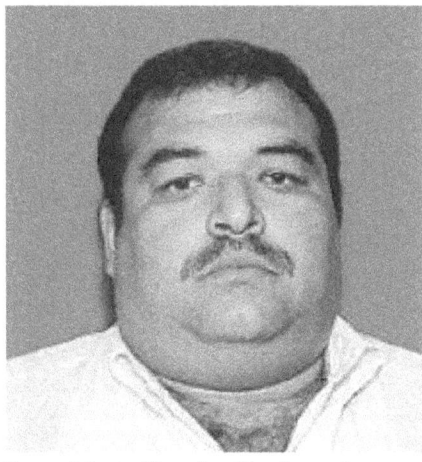

Jorge Mario Paredes Cordova aka "Gordo Mario"

www.ingramcontent.com/pod-product-compliance
Lightning Source LLC
Chambersburg PA
CBHW020532030426
42337CB00013B/818